INFORMATION WARFARE

BATTLEGROUND OF THE DIGITAL AGE

RAHUL PANDIT

To the Indian Army and its Bravehearts,

Who stand resolute at the borders, defending our sovereignty with unwavering courage, and who, in the face of both visible and invisible threats, continue to protect the nation with unparalleled valor.

This book is a tribute to your sacrifice, your resilience, and your unwavering commitment to safeguarding India—not just on the battlefield, but also in the digital realm where new-age wars are being fought.

Jai Hind!

Contents

About Author

Rahul Pandit is an accomplished IT Consultant and Technology Specialist with extensive expertise in leading innovative projects, particularly in E-Governance and Smart City initiatives. As the CEO and Lead Consultant at Ideogram Technology Solutions Pvt Limited, Rahul has spearheaded transformative technology projects for government organizations, driving advancements in urban management, public services, and citizen engagement.

In addition to his leadership in IT, Rahul is a passionate Cyber Security Enthusiast. He has been a sought-after resource person, imparting training and providing consultancy on Cyber Security and Cyber Crime for various government organizations and law enforcement agencies. His dedication to fostering secure digital ecosystems and his impactful contributions to technology-driven governance have established him as a visionary leader in his field.

Preface

In an era where wars are no longer confined to battlefields and borders, information has emerged as the most potent weapon of the 21st century. From political narratives shaped by artificial intelligence to psychological operations executed through social media, the battlefield has shifted into cyberspace, where perception is power and misinformation is a strategic tool. **Information Warfare: Battleground of the Digital Age** delves into this evolving domain, where nations, corporations, and individuals must defend against an invisible yet omnipresent adversary—disinformation.

India, as a rising global power, finds itself at the crossroads of geopolitical cyber conflicts, state-sponsored propaganda, and digital influence operations. The revocation of Article 370, the Pulwama attack, the Balakot airstrike, and ongoing tensions with China and Pakistan have all witnessed sophisticated information warfare campaigns designed to manipulate public perception, create unrest, and weaken national security. From deepfake technology to AI-driven misinformation campaigns, from cyber espionage to state-sponsored troll armies, India has faced an unprecedented digital onslaught. This book seeks to analyze these threats, decode their methodologies, and chart a course for strategic preparedness.

The rise of cyber troops, fake news ecosystems, and automated bot networks has fundamentally altered how societies consume and respond to information. Social media, once a tool for global connectivity, has now become a battleground where narratives are shaped, elections are influenced, and entire communities are radicalized. The proliferation of deepfake videos, AI-generated disinformation, and encrypted dark web operations has made it increasingly difficult to distinguish reality from manipulation. As adversaries weaponize the internet, India must proactively strengthen its cyber defenses, counter digital propaganda, and educate its citizens on media literacy.

This book is not merely an analysis of information warfare but also a call to action. It explores the need for a dedicated Information Warfare Command, the integration of AI in cyber defense, the role of ethical hackers, and the importance of national cybersecurity policies. The private sector, startups, and think tanks must collaborate with the government and military to create a comprehensive digital security framework that can withstand the evolving challenges of cyber warfare.

As India navigates this new era of digital conflict, it must move beyond reactive responses and develop proactive strategies to counter disinformation, mitigate cyber threats, and uphold national sovereignty in the information age. With a blend of real-world case studies, expert insights, and strategic recommendations, Information Warfare: Navigating the Digital Battlefield provides a blueprint for defending India's digital frontiers.

This book is an attempt to bring clarity to the murky waters of cyber conflicts, where perception is often manipulated, and truth is a casualty. It is a wake-up call for policymakers, security professionals, media experts, and the common citizen to recognize that the war of the future will not only be fought with guns and missiles but also with algorithms, narratives, and data. Understanding information warfare is no longer an option—it is a necessity.

Understanding Information Warfare

CHAPTER I

The Evolution of Information Warfare

Defining Information Warfare

Information Warfare (IW) is a multi-dimensional strategy that involves the manipulation, disruption, corruption, or exploitation of information to achieve strategic, political, or military objectives. It encompasses a range of tactics, including cyber warfare, psychological operations (PSYOPS), disinformation campaigns, propaganda dissemination, and the use of artificial intelligence (AI) to influence public perception. Unlike traditional warfare, which relies on physical confrontation, Information Warfare operates within the digital and cognitive domains, making it an invisible yet potent tool of modern conflicts.

Information Warfare can take many forms, including cyberattacks on critical infrastructure, mass disinformation through fake news, social media influence operations, and even economic warfare through data breaches and financial disruptions. The advent of digital technology has amplified its reach, allowing adversaries to manipulate societies at an unprecedented scale.

One of the defining aspects of Information Warfare is its ability to shape narratives in real-time. With the proliferation of social media platforms, information campaigns can target specific demographics, spreading misinformation, polarizing public opinion, and undermining trust in institutions. This makes it a powerful tool for state and non-state actors who wish to destabilize governments, manipulate elections, or incite conflicts without engaging in open warfare.

The increasing sophistication of AI and machine learning has further enhanced the effectiveness of Information Warfare. Automated bot armies, deepfake videos, and AI-driven content manipulation are now being deployed to create realistic yet completely false narratives. Such techniques have been used to influence elections, defame political opponents, and incite violence in various regions across the world.

India, being a large democracy with an ever-growing digital population, is particularly vulnerable to Information Warfare tactics. The country has already faced numerous cyberattacks, misinformation campaigns, and coordinated attempts to manipulate its political and social environment.

Given these emerging threats, India must develop a robust Information Warfare strategy that includes cybersecurity enhancements, media literacy initiatives, and active counter-disinformation measures.

In the modern era, wars are no longer just fought on battlefields but in the cognitive domain—where perceptions, beliefs, and ideologies become the new frontlines. Understanding and countering Information Warfare is essential for national security, political stability, and the protection of democratic institutions.

The Historical Evolution of Information Warfare

From Psychological Operations to Cyber Wars

The roots of Information Warfare can be traced back to ancient civilizations where deception, misinformation, and perception management played critical roles in warfare. Chanakya's *Arthashastra* (4th Century BCE) detailed the use of spies, covert intelligence gathering, and strategic misinformation to weaken enemy states from within. His teachings advocated the use of deception not just in direct confrontations but also in diplomatic negotiations and economic affairs, emphasizing a holistic approach to statecraft and warfare.

Similarly, Sun Tzu's *The Art of War* (China, 5th Century BCE) laid the groundwork for modern psychological warfare by asserting that "all warfare is based on deception." His strategies encouraged misleading the enemy through false intelligence, misdirection, and the careful manipulation of information. Sun Tzu's emphasis on winning battles without fighting has directly influenced modern information operations, where perception control is as vital as military strength.

During the Persian Empire (6th Century BCE), rulers used psychological tactics to maintain control over vast territories, leveraging rumors and controlled narratives to prevent rebellions. The Roman Empire further advanced the use of propaganda by erecting statues, engraving achievements on coins, and using public speeches to reinforce the emperor's legitimacy. The Roman Senate and military leaders carefully crafted state-sanctioned messages to shape public perception, setting a precedent for state-controlled narratives in the modern world.

As societies evolved, the role of information in warfare expanded. The Byzantine Empire (4th-15th Century CE) was known for its sophisticated use of espionage, counterintelligence, and rumor-spreading to destabilize enemies before military campaigns. In medieval Europe, religious institutions often served as centers of information control, influencing political and social discourse through carefully curated doctrines. The Catholic Church, for example, exercised immense power over knowledge dissemination, ensuring that only state-approved narratives reached the masses.

By the Renaissance and Enlightenment eras, information warfare began to take on new dimensions with the advent of the printing press. Governments could now distribute mass propaganda, influencing political movements and public opinion more efficiently than ever before. The Napoleonic Wars (19th Century) saw the French military employing propaganda to boost morale and demonize opponents, while the British Empire mastered the art of colonial psychological control through controlled education and information suppression.

The **20th century marked the industrialization of propaganda.** In World War I, British and German propaganda played a crucial role in shaping global opinion. Governments leveraged posters, newspapers, and controlled media to influence public perception, encourage enlistment, and demonize the enemy. Britain's use of the War Propaganda Bureau (WPB) systematically disseminated emotionally charged content to maintain domestic support and rally allies, while Germany's propaganda efforts painted the war as a defensive struggle against external aggressors.

By World War II, Nazi Germany had perfected the art of mass propaganda through Joseph Goebbels' Ministry of Propaganda, which controlled media, literature, and cinema to maintain the Nazi ideology. Nazi propaganda infiltrated every aspect of German life, from educational institutions to entertainment, reinforcing messages of nationalism and anti-Semitism. The use of radio broadcasts, cinematic propaganda like *Triumph of the Will,* and newspapers such as *Der Stürmer* ensured that the Nazi Party's narrative remained dominant.

Meanwhile, the Allies engaged in counter-propaganda, broadcasting messages to occupied territories to undermine enemy morale. The British Broadcasting Corporation (BBC) played a significant role in countering Nazi disinformation, providing factual news and rallying occupied Europe against Axis forces. The United States, through its Office of War Information (OWI), produced films, pamphlets, and radio broadcasts to sustain domestic morale and present the war as a battle between freedom and tyranny. Leaflet drops, radio transmissions, and strategic messaging campaigns were utilized to turn the tide of public opinion in favor of the Allies.

The effectiveness of propaganda in World War II demonstrated that controlling the flow of information could determine the outcome of wars, influencing military strategy and shaping international alliances. The post-war era saw the emergence of propaganda as a permanent fixture in geopolitical conflicts, setting the stage for the Cold War's information battles.

The Cold War further demonstrated how information could be weaponized on a scale never seen before. The United States and the Soviet Union engaged in extensive ideological warfare through radio broadcasts (Voice of America, Radio Free Europe, Radio Moscow), psychological operations, and misinformation campaigns to influence populations behind enemy lines. This battle of narratives extended beyond military and political spheres, infiltrating cultural, educational, and economic domains.

The United States utilized Voice of America and Radio Free Europe to broadcast Western ideals of democracy and capitalism to Soviet-controlled regions, countering communist propaganda. Simultaneously, the Soviet Union leveraged Radio Moscow and other state-run media to paint the West as imperialistic oppressors, fueling anti-American sentiment in the developing world.

Psychological operations (PSYOPS) played a crucial role in this conflict. The CIA and KGB both engaged in disinformation campaigns, planting false narratives in newspapers, manipulating political movements, and even fabricating scandals to discredit opponents. The Soviet Union, for example, propagated the false story that the U.S. invented HIV/AIDS as a biological weapon, a claim that gained traction in parts of the Global South.

The Vietnam War provided another lesson in the power of information—while U.S. forces achieved significant military victories, the failure to control the narrative at home led to widespread protests and declining public support. The Tet Offensive (1968) was a turning point; despite being a tactical loss for the North Vietnamese, it was presented in Western media as a U.S. failure, leading to a shift in public opinion. The role of journalists, live war footage, and increasing anti-war sentiment demonstrated that controlling public perception was just as critical as battlefield success.

As technology advanced, television and print media became major battlegrounds. Propaganda was no longer confined to radio waves; it now included visual storytelling, emotional appeals, and curated imagery to influence hearts and minds. The Cold War effectively transformed warfare from a primarily physical confrontation into an information-driven conflict, a legacy that continues to shape global geopolitical strategies today.

By the late 20th century, the Gulf War (1991) became the first war where media played a decisive role. CNN's 24-hour news cycle brought real-time war coverage to the world, carefully curated by the US military to project an image of technological superiority and a "clean" war. This was the first conflict where live broadcasts, embedded journalism, and military press briefings shaped public perception on a global scale.

Operation Desert Storm was marketed as a precise and high-tech military operation, leveraging advanced weapons systems, smart bombs, and strategic airstrikes. The Pentagon controlled the information flow through daily press conferences, ensuring that the dominant narrative focused on military precision and minimal civilian casualties.

However, critics argued that this conflict marked the emergence of perception management as a warfare strategy. The US military's control over information meant that certain aspects, such as the devastating impact of airstrikes on civilian infrastructure, were underreported. The infamous bombing of the Amiriyah shelter, which killed hundreds of civilians, was only briefly covered compared to other high-tech military feats.

This war also highlighted the **power of psychological operations (PSYOPS)** in modern warfare. Leaflet drops, radio broadcasts, and televised messages targeted Iraqi troops, urging them to surrender. Many Iraqi soldiers, overwhelmed by the relentless media portrayal of American dominance, surrendered without engaging in combat.

The Gulf War set a precedent for future conflicts, where controlling the media narrative became as crucial as battlefield success. This marked the beginning of media-driven conflicts, where information control was as important as military strategy. The lessons learned in this war were later applied extensively in conflicts such as the Iraq War (2003), where media narratives were carefully crafted to shape public support and influence global opinion.

The Digital Age and the Rise of Cyber Warfare

As the world entered the 21st century, Information Warfare expanded beyond traditional propaganda into cyber warfare, AI-driven disinformation, and real-time social media manipulation. Nations began to recognize the power of hacking, cyberattacks, and online propaganda as effective tools to disrupt adversaries without engaging in direct military conflict. The rapid digitization of economies, governance, and communication platforms has created new vulnerabilities that state and non-state actors are actively exploiting.

Cyber warfare is now an integral component of military strategy, employed for espionage, economic disruption, and infrastructure sabotage. The 2007 cyberattack on Estonia, allegedly launched by Russia, was one of the first large-scale instances of a state-directed cyber offensive. In response to a political dispute over the relocation of a Soviet-era monument, Estonian government websites, banks, and news organizations were crippled by Distributed Denial-of-Service (DDoS) attacks. This incident showcased how cyberattacks could be used as instruments of geopolitical coercion without traditional military engagement.

The 2010 Stuxnet attack, reportedly carried out by the US and Israel, marked another milestone in cyber warfare. The sophisticated malware targeted Iran's nuclear enrichment facilities, causing physical damage to its centrifuges. Stuxnet demonstrated the ability of cyber weapons to inflict tangible harm on critical infrastructure, setting a precedent for future cyber conflicts.

The rise of social media has further amplified the scope of Information Warfare. Platforms such as Facebook, X (formerly Twitter), Instagram, and YouTube have become digital battlegrounds where states engage in influence operations. The Arab Spring (2011) illustrated both the power and the risks of social media in political movements. Initially, social media was used to mobilize protests and organize civil resistance against authoritarian regimes. However, governments quickly adapted, using the same platforms for counter-propaganda, surveillance, and information control. Countries like China and Russia have since perfected techniques for manipulating social media to suppress dissent, spread misinformation, and create artificial consensus.

The 2016 US Presidential Election brought global attention to state-sponsored disinformation campaigns. Russian influence operations, conducted through troll farms, fake social media accounts, and targeted advertising, sought to manipulate public opinion and exacerbate societal divisions. AI-driven bots were deployed to amplify specific narratives, while hacked emails and strategically leaked documents influenced voter perception. This event underscored how cyber-based information operations could shape democratic processes and erode public trust in institutions.

Artificial Intelligence (AI) has taken Information Warfare to unprecedented levels. Deepfake technology, AI-generated text, and automated bot networks can flood digital spaces with misleading content, manipulate elections, and incite social unrest. Deepfake videos have been used to impersonate political figures, spread false statements, and fabricate scandals. AI-powered analytics tools can micro-target populations, delivering tailored misinformation to different demographic groups based on their psychological profiles. This level of precision makes it increasingly difficult for individuals to differentiate between real and artificial narratives.

Cyber espionage has also become a critical aspect of modern geopolitical competition. Countries engage in cyber intrusions to steal sensitive data, military intelligence, and trade secrets. Chinese-backed hacking groups, for instance, have been accused of targeting governments, tech firms, and critical infrastructure worldwide. Similarly, North Korea has utilized cyber operations to fund its nuclear program by hacking financial institutions and cryptocurrency exchanges.

The threats posed by cyber warfare extend beyond national security and into the economic sphere. Cyberattacks on financial institutions, power grids, and supply chains can have devastating ripple effects on global markets. The 2017 NotPetya ransomware attack, attributed to Russian actors, initially targeted Ukrainian businesses but quickly spread worldwide, causing billions of dollars in damages to multinational corporations.

India, as a rapidly digitizing economy, faces a growing number of cyber threats. State-sponsored hackers have targeted Indian defense agencies, financial institutions, and election systems. During the Doklam Standoff (2017) and Galwan Valley Clash (2020), Chinese cyber units allegedly attempted to infiltrate Indian government networks and disrupt power grids. The increasing reliance on digital infrastructure makes it imperative for India to develop robust cyber defenses, invest in AI-driven threat detection, and enhance cybersecurity education across sectors.

The Role of Technology in Modern Conflicts

The modern battlefield is no longer defined by physical frontiers but by digital ecosystems, where social media platforms, AI-driven algorithms, and cyberattacks dictate the course of geopolitical events. Disinformation, fake news, and manipulated media have become key instruments for destabilizing societies, influencing elections, and shaping public discourse.

In the digital age, technology plays a pivotal role in enhancing the capabilities of both state and non-state actors in conducting information warfare at an unprecedented scale.

Social Media as a Weapon

Platforms like Facebook, X (Twitter), Instagram, and YouTube have emerged as the new battlegrounds for influence operations. Governments, intelligence agencies, and adversaries deploy digital campaigns, viral trends, and selective censorship to shape narratives. State-sponsored troll farms, AI-powered propaganda, and coordinated bot networks can amplify false narratives, creating alternate realities that millions of users perceive as truth. Social media algorithms, designed to prioritize engagement, inadvertently fuel misinformation by favoring sensational and divisive content.

Deep Fakes and AI in Disinformation Warfare

Deepfake technology and synthetic media have revolutionized disinformation campaigns. AI-driven tools can fabricate hyper-realistic videos of political leaders delivering false statements, sparking misinformation crises. AI-generated text, manipulated imagery, and voice synthesis further blur the lines between fact and fiction. The ability to spread and amplify false narratives in real-time has made fact-checking and digital literacy critical defense mechanisms in modern conflicts.

Cyber Attacks as a Warfare Tool

Cyberattacks have evolved into a strategic weapon, replacing missile strikes in some conflicts. Governments engage in cyber espionage to steal secrets, disrupt financial institutions, and weaken infrastructure. Critical infrastructure, such as power grids, banking systems, and defense networks, is now a prime target in cyber conflicts. Malicious actors deploy ransomware, denial-of-service attacks, and malware to disrupt national security apparatus and create economic instability.

The Rise of Autonomous Warfare and AI-Powered Decision Making

Advancements in autonomous weapons, AI-driven military analytics, and algorithmic warfare are transforming modern combat. Nations are investing in AI-powered decision-making tools to analyze vast datasets, predict enemy movements, and optimize military strategies. Autonomous drones and robotic warfare systems can execute missions with minimal human intervention, changing the very nature of engagement in conflicts.

Blockchain and Quantum Computing in Security and Misinformation Prevention

Blockchain technology is increasingly being explored for its potential in securing information integrity. Governments and organizations are leveraging decentralized ledgers to prevent data manipulation and ensure transparency. Meanwhile, quantum computing presents both an opportunity and a threat—while it can revolutionize encryption, adversarial quantum capabilities could render current cybersecurity protocols obsolete, prompting the need for post-quantum cryptographic defenses.

Implications for India and the Global Security Landscape

India, as a rapidly digitizing economy, faces a growing number of cyber threats. State-sponsored hackers have targeted Indian defense agencies, financial institutions, and election systems. During the Doklam Standoff (2017) and Galwan Valley Clash (2020), Chinese cyber units allegedly attempted to infiltrate Indian government networks and disrupt power grids. The increasing reliance on digital infrastructure makes it imperative for India to develop robust cyber defenses, AI-driven threat detection, and enhanced cybersecurity education across sectors.

The fusion of technology with modern conflicts has redefined warfare strategies. Nations that invest in digital resilience, artificial intelligence, and cyber defense capabilities will emerge as the dominant forces of the future. As warfare continues to shift from conventional battles to digital battlegrounds, understanding and leveraging technology will be essential for national security and global stability.

The modern battlefield is no longer defined by physical frontiers but by digital ecosystems, where social media platforms, AI-driven algorithms, and cyberattacks dictate the course of geopolitical events. Disinformation, fake news, and manipulated media have become key instruments for destabilizing societies, influencing elections, and shaping public discourse.

Case Studies: How Information Warfare Shapes Modern Conflicts

The Gulf War (1991) – The First Media War

The Gulf War was the first modern conflict where media played a central role in shaping public perception. The US military and its allies controlled the flow of information, ensuring that CNN and other global news networks broadcast a carefully curated version of the war. Daily Pentagon briefings emphasized high-tech warfare, precision bombings, and minimal civilian casualties. However, certain key events, such as the bombing of the Amiriyah shelter, where over 400 civilians were killed, received minimal coverage compared to footage of smart bombs hitting military targets.

Psychological operations (PSYOPS) were heavily employed to demoralize Iraqi forces. Leaflets were dropped over Baghdad, radio broadcasts encouraged desertion, and manipulated imagery was used to create an illusion of overwhelming US superiority. The "shock and awe" strategy, as described later in military circles, was not just about military power but also about projecting an image of invincibility through media coverage. Many Iraqi soldiers surrendered without engaging in battle, influenced by the perception that resistance was futile.

The Russia-Ukraine War (2022-Present) – Cyber and Disinformation Warfare

Russia's invasion of Ukraine in 2022 marked the most significant use of hybrid warfare, combining cyberattacks, misinformation campaigns, and military aggression. In the weeks leading up to the invasion, Russia launched coordinated cyberattacks against Ukraine's power grids, banking systems, and government websites, creating confusion and economic disruption.

Disinformation was a key component of Russia's strategy. Russian state media, Telegram channels, and coordinated bot networks flooded social media with narratives justifying the invasion, claiming Ukraine was controlled by neo-Nazis and that Russian-speaking citizens were under threat. Deepfake videos and AI-generated propaganda were used to create false narratives, including fabricated speeches from Ukrainian President Volodymyr Zelensky calling for surrender.

Ukraine, however, countered Russia's information warfare with a highly effective digital resistance strategy. Using social media, Ukrainian leaders, including Zelensky, engaged in real-time communication, broadcasting messages of defiance that resonated globally. Viral videos of Ukrainian civilians confronting Russian troops, images of destroyed Russian tanks, and memes mocking the invaders helped rally both domestic and international support.

Additionally, Ukraine leveraged **open-source intelligence (OSINT)**, using satellite imagery, drone footage, and citizen reports to expose Russian troop movements, which were then shared widely on social media. The role of **Elon Musk's Starlink satellite internet**, which provided Ukraine with uninterrupted connectivity despite cyberattacks, further strengthened its information warfare capabilities.

China's Information Warfare Against India

China has long employed a comprehensive strategy of information warfare against India, combining cyber espionage, social media disinformation, and psychological operations. During the Doklam Standoff (2017) and Galwan Valley Clash (2020), Chinese cyber units reportedly launched cyberattacks on Indian government websites, military networks, and power grids to create instability.

China's disinformation campaigns have also targeted India's domestic politics. State-backed media outlets, coordinated Twitter bot networks, and fake social media accounts have been used to spread anti-India propaganda, often exaggerating internal divisions and promoting narratives that question India's global standing.

One key tactic is the use of WeChat and TikTok for influence operations. Before its ban in India, TikTok was identified as a major tool for spreading misleading narratives. Coordinated campaigns sought to promote anti-government sentiment, fuel communal tensions, and disrupt national unity. Similarly, WeChat, which is popular among Chinese-speaking communities, has been used to influence political discourse in border regions.

China's cyber espionage efforts have also been relentless. Indian defense establishments, major corporate firms, and even India's power grids have been targeted by Chinese-backed hacker groups such as APT41. In 2020, a massive power outage in Mumbai was reportedly linked to Chinese cyberattacks, highlighting the vulnerabilities of India's critical infrastructure.

To counter these threats, India has increasingly focused on building digital resilience, strengthening cybersecurity frameworks, and countering misinformation through fact-checking initiatives. However, the asymmetric nature of China's information warfare tactics poses a continuous challenge, requiring a multi-layered response combining cyber defense, strategic communication, and public awareness initiatives.

These case studies illustrate how modern conflicts are no longer confined to battlefields but extend into the digital and cognitive domains. Information dominance is now as crucial as military strength, and nations that fail to control narratives risk losing wars before they even begin.

CHAPTER II

The Pillars of Information Warfare

Modern Information Warfare is built on multiple interconnected pillars that shape the geopolitical and military landscape. These pillars include **Psychological Operations (PSYOPS), Cyber Warfare, Media Manipulation, Social Media Disinformation, and Economic & Technological Information Warfare.** Each of these elements serves a distinct function in influencing perceptions, disrupting adversaries, and gaining strategic advantages. These tactics are employed by governments, military agencies, intelligence organizations, and non-state actors alike, often operating covertly and without direct confrontation.

Psychological Operations (PSYOPS) aim to manipulate the psychological state of adversaries, whether by targeting civilians, influencing military decisions, or shaping public opinion. Cyber Warfare enables nation-states to cripple an opponent's infrastructure remotely, disrupting communications, finances, and even national security mechanisms. Media Manipulation is a long-standing tool used to control narratives, suppress opposition, and reinforce state propaganda, while Social Media Disinformation campaigns leverage digital platforms to influence democratic processes, incite unrest, and polarize societies. Finally, Economic & Technological Information Warfare plays a crucial role in leveraging financial markets, trade dependencies, and technological advancements to exert control over adversaries.

As the world becomes increasingly interconnected, mastering these pillars of Information Warfare has become as critical as conventional military power. Countries that excel in these tactics can shape global events, secure economic advantages, and undermine adversaries without engaging in traditional warfare. Understanding and countering these threats is imperative for maintaining national security in the modern era.

Psychological Operations (PSYOPS)

Psychological Operations (PSYOPS) involve the strategic use of information to influence emotions, motivations, and perceptions on an individual or mass scale. Governments, intelligence agencies, and military organizations employ PSYOPS to weaken enemy morale, manipulate public opinion, and exert control over the cognitive battlefield. Unlike traditional warfare, which relies on physical force, PSYOPS operates on psychological and emotional levels, often shaping conflicts before any bullets are fired.

PSYOPS strategies can be categorized into **white, gray, and black propaganda**, each serving different objectives and varying in the level of transparency and deception involved.

White propaganda is openly attributed to its source and aims to reinforce national identity, boost morale, and rally public support for government policies or military operations. This form of propaganda relies on factual information but presents it selectively to emphasize favorable aspects while downplaying negative ones. White propaganda is often disseminated through state-owned media outlets, official government statements, and patriotic messaging during times of crisis or war.

Historically, World War II saw the extensive use of white propaganda by Allied and Axis powers alike. The U.S. Office of War Information (OWI) produced films, posters, and radio broadcasts emphasizing the heroism of American soldiers, the importance of war bonds, and the evil of the Axis powers. The British Ministry of Information played a similar role, promoting narratives that strengthened public morale and encouraged resistance against the Nazis.

During the Cold War, white propaganda was instrumental in ideological battles between the United States and the Soviet Union. The U.S. established Radio Free Europe (RFE) and Voice of America (VOA) to broadcast pro-democracy messages to Eastern Bloc countries, countering Soviet-controlled media narratives. Meanwhile, the Soviet Union used state-run newspapers like Pravda and radio broadcasts to promote communist ideology and discredit Western capitalism.

Modern examples include China's CCTV and Global Times, which promote state-approved perspectives on international affairs while countering criticism of the Chinese government. Similarly, Russia's RT (Russia Today) operates as a government-funded international broadcaster that presents Russian perspectives on global events while countering Western narratives. In the United States, government-backed media outlets such as Voice of America and Radio Liberty continue to function as instruments of white propaganda, promoting democratic values in authoritarian regions.

The rise of digital media has further expanded the reach of white propaganda. Government-sponsored social media campaigns, official YouTube channels, and fact-checked information portals now serve as modern platforms for disseminating state-approved narratives. The challenge remains in distinguishing white propaganda from biased reporting, as even openly attributed information can still shape public perception in strategically beneficial ways.

Gray propaganda exists in an ambiguous space, blending truth and misinformation while keeping its origins obscure. Unlike white propaganda, which is openly acknowledged, gray propaganda is designed to appear as independent or neutral while covertly serving a strategic interest. Governments and intelligence agencies use gray propaganda to subtly shape international narratives, manipulate public opinion, and sow confusion among adversaries.

A classic example of gray propaganda was the U.S. government's support of Radio Free Europe (RFE) during the Cold War. While RFE presented itself as an independent news source providing accurate information to Eastern Europe, it was secretly funded by the CIA to counter Soviet narratives. The public was not aware of the U.S. government's involvement, making it an effective tool for psychological influence.

Another well-documented case is Operation Mockingbird, a covert CIA initiative in the 1950s and 60s that recruited journalists and media outlets to disseminate pro-American and anti-communist content. The stories published under this operation blended factual reporting with strategic misinformation to align global public opinion with U.S. foreign policy interests.

In recent times, gray propaganda has evolved into covert sponsorship of think tanks, anonymous leaks of selective intelligence, and the manipulation of news through social media influencers. For instance, leaked documents revealing corruption or human rights abuses may contain genuine information but be strategically released at a time and manner that serves a political agenda. Similarly, certain online influencers, bloggers, and journalists may receive undisclosed funding from governments or lobbying groups to promote specific viewpoints while appearing to be independent voices.

Modern gray propaganda also takes the form of fabricated social media accounts posing as grassroots movements, promoting divisive narratives that blend truth with speculation. Russia's Internet Research Agency (IRA) has been linked to numerous influence campaigns where real news stories are mixed with misleading interpretations to stir unrest and manipulate political events.

The challenge with gray propaganda is that it operates in the gray zone between fact and fiction, making it difficult for the public to distinguish between genuine information and strategically placed narratives. Governments and intelligence agencies continue to refine these methods, making the detection and countering of gray propaganda a crucial aspect of modern information warfare.

Black propaganda is the most deceptive form, fabricating narratives that are falsely attributed to an adversary to sow discord, manipulate perceptions, and justify countermeasures. Black propaganda is typically used to create divisions within enemy ranks, discredit political figures, or incite unrest. It differs from other types of propaganda because it disguises its true source, making it appear as if the disinformation originates from an opponent or neutral entity.

One of the most infamous historical examples is the Gleiwitz Incident (1939), where Nazi Germany staged an attack on its own radio station, making it seem like a Polish assault to justify their invasion of Poland. Similarly, during Operation Himmler, Germany executed several false flag operations to provide a pretext for launching World War II.

During the Cold War, intelligence agencies on both sides engaged in black propaganda. The CIA's Operation CHAOS aimed to spread disinformation about civil rights leaders and anti-war activists, portraying them as communist sympathizers. In the Soviet Union, the KGB's Operation INFEKTION falsely spread the narrative that the U.S. had created the HIV/AIDS virus as a biological weapon, an idea that gained traction in parts of the developing world and influenced global perceptions.

In more recent times, black propaganda has become even more effective with digital technology. Deepfake videos, AI-generated content, and bot-driven disinformation campaigns have enabled state and non-state actors to fabricate incidents, impersonate political figures, and manipulate elections. In 2016, Russian-backed operatives used social media platforms to spread misleading stories disguised as grassroots movements, aiming to influence the U.S. presidential election.

Governments and intelligence agencies continue to refine black propaganda techniques, exploiting anonymous online forums, leaked documents with forged elements, and fake whistleblower reports to undermine political adversaries and international institutions. The ability to detect and counteract black propaganda is now a critical aspect of modern information warfare, requiring advanced AI-driven forensic analysis and international cooperation to identify and expose deceptive narratives.

In the digital age, propaganda tactics have evolved, incorporating AI-generated content, deepfake videos, and social media influence campaigns to amplify false narratives more effectively than ever before. The rapid spread of information and the difficulty of verifying sources have made distinguishing between white, gray, and black propaganda increasingly complex, requiring sophisticated countermeasures to detect and neutralize disinformation campaigns.

Throughout history, PSYOPS has played a critical role in conflicts. During World War II, Allied forces dropped millions of leaflets over enemy territories, persuading soldiers to surrender by spreading misinformation about military defeats and the humane treatment of POWs. Similar strategies were employed in the Korean War and the Gulf War (1991), where psychological campaigns weakened enemy morale before direct military engagement.

Modern PSYOPS has expanded into the digital realm, utilizing AI-driven behavioral manipulation, deepfake videos, and disinformation campaigns to shape public opinion. Russia's Internet Research Agency (IRA) has been implicated in using AI-powered bots and social media campaigns to manipulate global discourse, highlighting the growing sophistication of psychological warfare in the digital age.

Cyber Warfare and Digital Espionage

Cyber Warfare has become a key instrument of modern conflicts, allowing nation-states and cybercriminal organizations to conduct attacks without direct military confrontation. Cyberattacks can cripple critical infrastructure, disrupt financial systems, steal sensitive data, manipulate political processes, paralyze national security frameworks, and even influence global diplomatic relations. The evolution of cyber warfare has introduced AI-driven cyber offensives, ransomware-as-a-service (RaaS), deepfake-enabled social engineering attacks, quantum computing threats, autonomous hacking systems, and cyber-psychological warfare techniques, making this domain increasingly complex and dangerous.

In addition to traditional hacking attempts, modern cyber warfare now includes cyber-kinetic attacks, where digital intrusions result in real-world consequences. Attacks on power grids, water supply systems, and defense infrastructure can cause catastrophic failures, disrupting essential services and even triggering cascading economic collapses. Cyber weapons like Stuxnet have demonstrated how digital sabotage can be as impactful as physical warfare.

Furthermore, cyber deterrence and preemptive cyber strikes have become key strategies for nations looking to gain an advantage in digital warfare. Countries are investing in cyber intelligence networks, AI-powered cybersecurity tools, quantum cryptography, and offensive cyber units to mitigate threats and launch countermeasures when necessary. The race for cyber supremacy is no longer limited to traditional military superpowers; emerging nations and non-state actors, including hacktivist groups and cyber-mercenaries, are also becoming significant players in the cyber warfare landscape.

As the threat landscape continues to evolve, multi-domain operations (MDO)—where cyber warfare is integrated with electronic, space, and traditional military operations—are shaping the future of global conflicts. Governments and private organizations must rapidly develop adaptive cybersecurity frameworks, international cyber coalitions, and next-generation threat intelligence systems to counteract these growing threats and ensure digital resilience in an increasingly hostile cyber environment.

In recent years, cyber warfare has taken on a more strategic role in geopolitical conflicts. Russia's cyber operations against Ukraine have included sophisticated attacks on power grids, financial institutions, and government agencies, demonstrating how cyber warfare can be used alongside traditional military aggression. These cyberattacks have not only disrupted essential services but also inflicted economic damage and psychological distress on Ukrainian citizens. The NotPetya cyberattack (2017), widely attributed to Russian state-sponsored hackers, initially targeted Ukrainian systems by infiltrating widely used accounting software, but quickly spread beyond its intended scope, affecting multinational corporations such as Maersk, FedEx, and Merck, causing an estimated $10 billion in global damages. This attack underscored the borderless nature of cyber warfare, showing how a nation-state's cyber offensive can inadvertently spiral into a global economic crisis. Additionally, Russian-backed cyber groups have been implicated in disinformation campaigns, hacking government databases, and launching malware attacks against Ukrainian military infrastructure, reinforcing cyber warfare as a fundamental element of hybrid warfare strategies.

State-backed cyber units are now integrating machine learning and AI algorithms to automate cyber intrusions, adapt to security defenses in real time, and deploy increasingly sophisticated malware. These AI-driven techniques allow adversaries to conduct autonomous cyber reconnaissance, real-time vulnerability exploitation, and adaptive malware deployment, significantly increasing the efficiency and impact of cyberattacks.

China's APT41 and Russia's APT29 (Cozy Bear) have been linked to extensive cyber espionage campaigns aimed at stealing military intelligence, vaccine research, and trade secrets from Western nations. APT41, a notorious Chinese state-backed hacking group, has been implicated in supply chain attacks, intellectual property theft, and global cybercrime operations, often using novel zero-day exploits to infiltrate corporate and government networks. Russia's APT29, linked to the SolarWinds cyberattack (2020), has demonstrated an advanced ability to infiltrate highly secure U.S. government agencies and major technology firms, underscoring the persistent nature of nation-state cyber threats.

Meanwhile, the rise of hacktivist groups, cyber mercenaries, and deepfake-enabled misinformation campaigns has added further layers of complexity to modern cyber warfare. Hacktivist groups like Anonymous have targeted both governments and corporations, engaging in cyber disruptions that blur the lines between activism and digital sabotage. Additionally, cyber mercenaries—private hacking groups that offer offensive cyber capabilities for hire— are becoming key players in cyber conflicts, conducting espionage, ransomware attacks, and state-sponsored digital warfare for financial or political gain.

Deepfake technology has further complicated the cyber warfare landscape, enabling threat actors to fabricate convincing video and audio impersonations of political leaders, military officials, and corporate executives to spread disinformation, manipulate markets, and incite unrest. The increasing sophistication of these tools makes it harder to distinguish between authentic and manipulated content, intensifying the challenges faced by cybersecurity experts and intelligence agencies.

The use of deepfakes and AI-powered disinformation campaigns has blurred the lines between traditional hacking and psychological warfare. State-sponsored social engineering attacks now leverage deepfake videos to impersonate political leaders, spread fake news, and manipulate public opinion on an unprecedented scale. The ability to create hyper-realistic but entirely false content has made detecting and countering cyber threats more difficult than ever before.

As cyber warfare evolves, governments and private organizations must invest in quantum-resistant encryption, zero-trust cybersecurity architectures, AI-driven threat intelligence, real-time anomaly detection systems, and cyber-resilient infrastructures to counter evolving threats. Public-private partnerships must be strengthened to enable intelligence sharing and coordinated cyber defense strategies across sectors. Additionally, cyber deterrence frameworks—including offensive cybersecurity capabilities—are essential to dissuade adversaries from launching cyberattacks.

Without proactive measures, cyber warfare could become one of the most destabilizing forces in global security, affecting economies, democracies, and military capabilities alike. The rise of cyber-mercenaries, state-sponsored hacking groups, and ransomware-as-a-service (RaaS) has made cyber threats more sophisticated and persistent, demanding continuous innovation in cybersecurity solutions. Nations must also focus on developing cyber education programs, training cybersecurity professionals, and enforcing stricter cyber regulations to create a resilient defense against the increasing complexity of cyber warfare.

One of the most infamous cyberattacks was the Stuxnet attack (2010), allegedly deployed by the U.S. and Israel to sabotage Iran's nuclear program. Stuxnet was a highly sophisticated and stealthy malware that specifically targeted industrial control systems (ICS) used in Iran's uranium enrichment facilities at Natanz. The worm exploited multiple zero-day vulnerabilities in Microsoft Windows to infiltrate the air-gapped networks of the facility, spreading undetected through USB drives.

Once inside, Stuxnet manipulated Siemens programmable logic controllers (PLCs), subtly altering the rotational speeds of uranium centrifuges while displaying normal readings to monitoring equipment. This caused mechanical degradation over time, leading to the destruction of nearly 1,000 centrifuges, significantly delaying Iran's nuclear program. The attack marked the first known case of cyber warfare causing real-world physical destruction, demonstrating how digital sabotage could serve as a strategic alternative to traditional military strikes.

Stuxnet's discovery in 2010 by cybersecurity firms such as Symantec and Kaspersky sparked global discussions on the militarization of cyberspace and the risks of cyber weapons proliferation. The attack also inspired subsequent cyber operations, including Triton (2017)—a malware targeting industrial safety systems in critical infrastructure. Stuxnet set a precedent for cyber warfare, highlighting its potential to disrupt national security, industrial processes, and global geopolitics.

Another significant case was the SolarWinds cyberattack (2020), attributed to Russian-backed hackers who infiltrated U.S. government agencies, major corporations, and critical infrastructure by compromising the widely used Orion network management software. The attack, which went undetected for months, allowed the hackers to access sensitive data from agencies such as the Department of Homeland Security, the Treasury Department, and the National Nuclear Security Administration, among others.

The breach was executed using a supply chain attack, where the attackers embedded malicious code into legitimate software updates, allowing them to infiltrate thousands of high-profile organizations. This attack underscored the vulnerability of third-party software dependencies in global cybersecurity and the growing risk posed by nation-state cyber espionage operations. The sophistication of the SolarWinds hack demonstrated that traditional cybersecurity defenses were inadequate against advanced persistent threats (APTs), forcing governments and enterprises to reevaluate their cybersecurity frameworks and implement zero-trust security models to mitigate future risks.

Cyber warfare also extends into critical infrastructure attacks, where power grids, water treatment plants, financial institutions, and transportation networks are targeted. These attacks aim to cripple essential services, disrupt economies, and instill widespread panic, making them a preferred strategy for state-sponsored hackers and cybercriminal groups alike.

One of the most infamous examples is the BlackEnergy attacks on Ukraine (2015 & 2016), where Russian-backed hackers used malware to infiltrate and shut down Ukrainian power grids, leaving hundreds of thousands of citizens without electricity. These attacks showcased the vulnerability of industrial control systems (ICS) and supervisory control and data acquisition (SCADA) networks, which are commonly used to manage national utilities. The attackers employed phishing emails to gain access to control systems, manipulating them remotely to disable power substations, and even disabling backup power options to prolong outages.

Similarly, the Colonial Pipeline ransomware attack (2021) in the U.S. demonstrated how cybercriminal groups could paralyze energy distribution, causing fuel shortages across multiple states. The attack, attributed to the Russian-linked DarkSide ransomware group, exploited vulnerabilities in the pipeline's IT network, forcing the company to shut down operations as a precaution. The attack triggered panic buying of gasoline, major disruptions in supply chains, and financial losses exceeding $4 billion. Ultimately, the company paid a $4.4 million ransom in Bitcoin to regain control of its systems, though U.S. authorities were able to recover a portion of the funds.

Beyond these cases, Iranian cyber units have been accused of attempting to hack water treatment plants in Israel (2020), aiming to manipulate chemical levels in the water supply. Had this attack been successful, it could have poisoned thousands of people, demonstrating the potential for cyber warfare to have lethal consequences. Likewise, North Korea has been linked to financial cyberattacks on SWIFT banking networks, targeting international financial institutions to steal funds and destabilize economic systems.

The increasing digitization of critical infrastructure has heightened the risks of such cyberattacks. Governments and organizations are now prioritizing cyber resilience, AI-powered threat detection, and zero-trust security models to mitigate these threats. However, as cyber warfare tactics evolve, maintaining digital security remains a persistent challenge, requiring constant vigilance and proactive defense strategies to prevent large-scale disruptions.

Governments and organizations are now prioritizing cyber resilience, AI-powered threat detection, and zero-trust security models to mitigate these threats. However, as cyber warfare tactics evolve, maintaining digital security remains a persistent challenge.

Modern-Day Media Manipulation: The Role of Digital Platforms

The digital revolution has transformed the landscape of media manipulation, making it more efficient, pervasive, and difficult to detect. The rise of social media platforms, 24-hour news cycles, and algorithm-driven content distribution has enabled state and non-state actors to spread disinformation, amplify divisive narratives, and exert control over public perception with unprecedented precision. Today's digital environment allows for rapid dissemination of targeted propaganda, leveraging data analytics and artificial intelligence to maximize impact and engagement.

Governments, intelligence agencies, and politically motivated groups deploy state-controlled media, selective information dissemination, algorithmic bias, and AI-generated content to reinforce their narratives while suppressing dissenting voices. Traditional propaganda has evolved into sophisticated influence campaigns that use deepfake videos, bot-driven engagements, and psychological manipulation techniques to create convincing and deceptive narratives.

State-Controlled Media plays a crucial role in modern information warfare. Governments fund and operate media outlets to shape domestic and international narratives, ensuring that public discourse aligns with state interests. Networks such as Russia Today (RT), China's CCTV and Global Times, and Iran's Press TV serve as strategic tools for broadcasting government-approved perspectives while countering opposition narratives. These platforms often use a mix of factual reporting and biased storytelling to create a distorted but seemingly credible version of global events.

In Russia, RT and Sputnik News have been accused of spreading disinformation, particularly in the context of geopolitical conflicts such as the Ukraine crisis, Syrian civil war, and U.S. elections. These outlets have been instrumental in advancing pro-Russian narratives while discrediting Western policies. Similarly, China's CCTV and Global Times have been at the forefront of state-sponsored influence operations, presenting an idealized view of China's economic and technological achievements while omitting discussions on human rights violations, censorship, and domestic protests.

Selective Information Dissemination is another method by which governments and intelligence agencies manipulate public perception. By strategically releasing or withholding information, state actors can shape geopolitical discussions, control the narrative around controversial topics, and mislead audiences. A notable example is the Pentagon Papers (1971), which exposed how the U.S. government selectively reported information about the Vietnam War to maintain public support. Similarly, intelligence reports on Weapons of Mass Destruction (WMDs) were manipulated in the lead-up to the Iraq War (2003), influencing public and political backing for military intervention.

China and Russia also extensively engage in information suppression and narrative control. The Chinese government's censorship of the Tiananmen Square Massacre (1989) prevents open discussion of the event within China, where history is rewritten to fit government-approved narratives. Likewise, during the 2014 annexation of Crimea, Russian media presented a sanitized version of events, suppressing evidence of military involvement while amplifying narratives of "Crimean self-determination."

Algorithmic Bias and AI-Generated Content have further enhanced the effectiveness of media manipulation. Social media platforms use proprietary algorithms to determine which content reaches wider audiences, a mechanism that can be exploited by political actors and intelligence agencies to prioritize state-sponsored narratives while downplaying alternative viewpoints. Governments and cyber influence groups take advantage of these biases by creating sensationalist, emotionally charged content that spreads virally, reinforcing ideological positions and intensifying societal divisions.

The emergence of **deepfake technology and AI-generated media** has further complicated the information battlefield. Deepfake videos, synthetic audio clips, and AI-generated news articles allow bad actors to fabricate realistic but entirely false content. These tools have been used to impersonate political leaders, manipulate financial markets, and spread false information about crises, elections, and military conflicts. The challenge of identifying and countering these deceptive tactics grows as AI technology becomes more sophisticated.

As the digital landscape continues to evolve, the battle for control over information is intensifying. Efforts to counter media manipulation now include fact-checking initiatives, AI-powered misinformation detection, stricter platform regulations, and digital literacy programs. However, as state and non-state actors refine their tactics, the future of information warfare will likely become even more complex and unpredictable, requiring continuous vigilance and adaptation to safeguard truth and transparency in the digital age.

Case Studies of Modern Media Manipulation

Modern media manipulation has played a crucial role in shaping global perceptions, swaying political decisions, and influencing societal attitudes. From state-sponsored disinformation campaigns to corporate-controlled media narratives, strategic information warfare has evolved significantly in the digital age. The following case studies highlight key instances of media manipulation and its profound impact on global events.

One of the most well-documented examples is Russia's Disinformation Campaigns, where the Kremlin has been accused of using troll farms, bot networks, and state-controlled media to spread disinformation globally. The Internet Research Agency (IRA), a Kremlin-linked organization, has orchestrated multiple influence operations, notably during the 2016 U.S. Presidential Election. Through the use of fake social media accounts, misleading advertisements, and AI-generated content, Russia sought to polarize American voters, intensify social divisions, and discredit political opponents. These tactics have since been adapted for other geopolitical conflicts, including Russia's efforts to control narratives around its actions in Ukraine and Syria.

Another significant case is China's Media Control and Censorship, which highlights the Chinese Communist Party's (CCP) dominance over domestic and international media. Domestically, China censors unfavorable news through the Great Firewall, suppressing political dissent and blocking foreign platforms like Google, Twitter, and Facebook. Internationally, China has expanded its "Media Influence Strategy", acquiring stakes in foreign news organizations, sponsoring pro-China narratives in international media, and leveraging social media platforms such as WeChat and TikTok to propagate state-approved messages. The CCP also funds Confucius Institutes, which exert subtle influence over academic and cultural narratives abroad.

The Cambridge Analytica Scandal (2018) exposed how private companies manipulate media content to influence elections and social movements. Cambridge Analytica harvested personal data from millions of Facebook users without consent to build psychographic profiles for micro-targeted political advertising. This data-driven approach was used to influence voting behavior in events such as Brexit and the 2016 U.S. Presidential Election, demonstrating how digital platforms can be weaponized for political engineering.

The COVID-19 Disinformation Campaigns further illustrate how media manipulation can fuel global crises. During the pandemic, various state and non-state actors engaged in misinformation warfare, spreading contradictory narratives about vaccine safety, virus origins, and public health policies. Chinese, Russian, and Iranian media outlets amplified conspiracy theories blaming Western governments for the virus, while Western think tanks countered with accusations of Chinese negligence. The pandemic became a battleground for media manipulation, with governments and private entities using information warfare to deflect blame, shape public sentiment, and push political agendas.

Social media has also been a key battleground in ongoing conflicts such as the Israel-Palestine dispute and the Ukraine-Russia war. Both sides have engaged in sophisticated online campaigns, utilizing bot-driven hashtag trends, manipulated imagery, and AI-enhanced misinformation to control the narrative. Governments, political activists, and intelligence agencies have actively shaped digital discourse, leveraging viral content to garner international support or demonize adversaries.

These case studies underscore how media manipulation has become an essential component of modern geopolitical strategies. The ability to control narratives, suppress dissent, and manufacture public opinion through media has made information warfare a powerful tool in statecraft, elections, and international diplomacy.

The Future of Media Manipulation and Countermeasures

As media manipulation tactics become increasingly sophisticated, fact-checking organizations, digital literacy programs, and AI-driven detection tools are being developed to combat misinformation. Governments and tech companies are also introducing policies to identify and remove fake news, deepfake content, and algorithmic manipulation. However, the battle for information supremacy continues, with new technological advancements creating both opportunities and challenges in the fight against media manipulation.

The modern information environment remains highly contested, and media manipulation will continue to play a central role in geopolitical and ideological conflicts. Nations that can control narratives, counter disinformation, and effectively leverage media will maintain an edge in the ever-evolving landscape of Information Warfare.

Media has long been a battleground for controlling narratives, shaping public perception, and influencing geopolitical outcomes. Governments, intelligence agencies, and political entities use state-controlled media, selective information dissemination, and censorship to reinforce their agendas.

During the Cold War, the United States and the Soviet Union engaged in extensive media propaganda campaigns to promote their ideologies. The U.S. funded Radio Free Europe and Voice of America, while the Soviet Union used Pravda and Radio Moscow to counter Western influence. In modern times, Russia Today (RT) and China's Global Times serve as state-controlled platforms that push government-approved narratives while suppressing dissenting voices.

The rapid expansion of digital media has given rise to AI-generated news articles, deepfake-enhanced disinformation, and algorithm-driven censorship that make it easier to manipulate audiences. Governments now invest heavily in digital propaganda units to sway elections, undermine adversaries, and control public discourse.

Social Media Warfare and Disinformation Campaigns

Social media platforms have become the modern battlegrounds of information warfare, where political entities, intelligence agencies, and non-state actors engage in digital conflicts to shape narratives, influence public opinion, and destabilize societies. These platforms serve as powerful instruments for political manipulation, psychological operations, and disinformation warfare, enabling actors to bypass traditional media and directly influence audiences.

Platforms such as Facebook, X (formerly Twitter), Instagram, YouTube, and TikTok are widely exploited for covert influence operations, election interference, and information suppression, often leveraging sophisticated algorithms to amplify propaganda, drown out dissenting voices, and manipulate public perception. Through AI-generated misinformation, bot-driven amplification, and deepfake-enhanced deception, state and non-state actors can systematically spread false narratives, fuel social divisions, and undermine trust in democratic institutions. The rapid evolution of artificial intelligence and machine learning further enhances these tactics, making disinformation campaigns more targeted, persuasive, and difficult to detect.

Governments and intelligence agencies have recognized the strategic importance of social media in modern conflicts, integrating digital influence campaigns, hashtag manipulation, and algorithmic warfare into their geopolitical arsenals. While these platforms offer opportunities for transparency and free expression, they are also increasingly weaponized to disrupt societies, influence elections, and escalate geopolitical tensions. The battle for information supremacy is now being waged in real-time, with digital narratives shaping the course of political events, public discourse, and global conflicts.

The Role of Social Media in Information Warfare

Social media has become a primary battleground for modern information warfare, where governments, intelligence agencies, and non-state actors deploy sophisticated digital strategies to shape public perception, influence political outcomes, and destabilize societies. The ability of social media to disseminate information instantaneously and engage billions of users worldwide has transformed it into a potent tool for disinformation campaigns, propaganda, and psychological operations. The open nature of social media platforms allows malicious actors to manipulate narratives, promote ideological agendas, and incite unrest with unprecedented speed and precision.

State-sponsored entities and political organizations use bot networks, troll farms, and coordinated hashtag campaigns to amplify divisive narratives, interfere in elections, and manufacture the illusion of widespread support for specific ideologies. Automated accounts (bots) and paid human operatives (trolls) generate and spread false or misleading content, drowning out legitimate discourse and creating an environment where misinformation thrives. Russia's Internet Research Agency (IRA) is one of the most well-documented examples, having deployed thousands of fake social media accounts to manipulate discussions and polarize debates in multiple countries.

The rise of deepfake technology and synthetic media has further intensified social media warfare. AI-generated deepfake videos and synthetic audio can be used to impersonate political figures, fabricate scandals, and distort reality, making it increasingly difficult for the public to distinguish between genuine and manipulated content. These technologies have been leveraged to spread false statements, manipulate financial markets, and even create fabricated news reports to sway public sentiment.

Another critical element in social media warfare is hashtag manipulation and trending topic hijacking. Intelligence agencies, propaganda units, and cyber-influence groups use carefully timed disinformation campaigns to hijack social media algorithms, ensuring that certain narratives gain widespread visibility while opposing viewpoints are suppressed. These operations can shape public perception, influence global political discourse, and control narratives around key geopolitical events.

Social media platforms themselves play a role in shaping the information landscape through algorithmic amplification and shadow banning. The algorithms that determine content visibility can be exploited by political actors to ensure that emotionally charged and sensationalist content spreads virally. Conversely, platforms may shadow-ban or suppress content that challenges prevailing narratives, effectively limiting the reach of dissenting opinions without outright censorship. The result is an ecosystem where information is filtered and manipulated to serve strategic interests, often without users realizing they are being influenced.

As social media continues to evolve, it remains at the forefront of information warfare. Governments, intelligence agencies, and private organizations are investing heavily in digital influence campaigns, AI-powered misinformation detection, and cybersecurity countermeasures to combat the growing threats posed by disinformation operations. However, the rapid advancement of artificial intelligence and deep learning technologies means that the tactics used in social media warfare will continue to evolve, making it an ongoing challenge to safeguard truth, democracy, and public trust in the digital information age.

Major Case Studies in Social Media Warfare

Social media has played a pivotal role in modern conflicts, shaping public opinion, influencing political discourse, and driving geopolitical narratives. Various state and non-state actors have leveraged social media platforms to execute coordinated disinformation campaigns, influence elections, incite unrest, and manipulate global perceptions. The following case studies illustrate the profound impact of social media warfare in recent years.

One of the most significant examples is Russia's interference in the 2016 U.S. Presidential Election, where Russian-backed operatives utilized fake social media accounts, misleading advertisements, and AI-generated content to manipulate American voters. The Internet Research Agency (IRA), a Kremlin-linked organization, systematically spread divisive messages across Facebook, Twitter, and other platforms, fueling social and political polarization. By deploying thousands of automated bots and troll accounts, Russian cyber operatives created the illusion of grassroots support for specific ideologies, shaping discussions on controversial topics such as race relations, gun control, and immigration.

China has also demonstrated its expertise in social media influence campaigns through the use of the "50 Cent Army", a government-funded initiative that employs thousands of individuals to flood digital platforms with pro-Beijing narratives. This strategy is particularly evident in discussions about Tibet, Hong Kong, Taiwan, and the South China Sea dispute. China's influence operations extend beyond censorship and propaganda, as seen in the widespread suppression of online dissent during the 2019–2020 Hong Kong protests, where pro-democracy activists were systematically targeted, their content removed, and opposing views amplified by government-sponsored accounts.

The COVID-19 pandemic further illustrated how social media could be weaponized to spread disinformation. Competing narratives about the virus's origins, vaccine efficacy, and global response were pushed by various governments and conspiracy groups. State actors such as Russia, China, and Iran strategically disseminated conflicting reports about the virus to undermine public trust in Western health institutions, promote their own vaccines, and sow discord among global populations. The rapid proliferation of false information during the pandemic demonstrated how easily public opinion can be manipulated through algorithmic amplification and emotionally charged messaging.

The Israel-Palestine conflict has also been a key battleground for social media propaganda. Both sides have engaged in digital campaigns using bot-driven hashtag trends, manipulated imagery, and AI-enhanced misinformation to control narratives and garner international support. Israeli and Palestinian factions have employed thousands of coordinated accounts to push specific political messages, influence foreign policy decisions, and mobilize supporters worldwide. Social media platforms, struggling to maintain neutrality, have faced backlash for alleged bias in content moderation, further complicating the digital battleground.

Similarly, the Ukraine-Russia war has been defined by real-time digital information warfare, with both nations leveraging social media to discredit opponents, rally public support, and shape global perceptions. Ukrainian officials have utilized platforms like X (formerly Twitter) and Telegram to document war crimes, counter Russian narratives, and gain international backing, while Russia has engaged in deepfake propaganda, AI-generated war footage, and bot-driven misinformation campaigns to justify its actions and obscure battlefield realities.

These case studies underscore how social media has become a central weapon in modern conflicts, influencing perceptions, driving political outcomes, and shaping the course of history. As artificial intelligence and algorithmic manipulation continue to evolve, the role of social media in global warfare will only grow, demanding greater vigilance from governments, technology companies, and civil society to combat digital disinformation and preserve the integrity of information ecosystems.

Defensive Measures and Counter-Disinformation Strategies

As social media warfare and digital disinformation campaigns become more advanced, governments, social media platforms, and international organizations have been forced to adapt and implement a range of countermeasures to protect democratic institutions, national security, and public discourse. These strategies include artificial intelligence-driven misinformation detection, platform regulations, public awareness campaigns, and cybersecurity advancements, all aimed at mitigating the spread of false information and ensuring the integrity of online ecosystems.

One of the most critical tools in countering disinformation is the development of AI-Powered Fact-Checking Systems. These machine learning-based algorithms can analyze vast amounts of digital content in real time, identifying inconsistencies, detecting fabricated narratives, and flagging misleading information before it goes viral. Organizations such as Google, Meta, and Twitter have invested in automated fact-checking tools that use natural language processing (NLP) to verify news articles and user-generated content. However, as AI-generated disinformation continues to evolve, these systems must constantly adapt to detect increasingly sophisticated falsehoods, including deepfake videos and synthetic media.

Social media platforms have also introduced Platform Policies Against Misinformation to curb the proliferation of fake news and propaganda. These measures include flagging potentially misleading content, adding warning labels, demonetizing accounts that repeatedly spread false information, and suspending networks of coordinated disinformation actors. Meta (formerly Facebook), for example, has taken steps to remove state-backed disinformation campaigns, while YouTube has refined its algorithm to prioritize authoritative sources during crises. However, these policies have faced criticism for either being too lenient, allowing false information to persist, or too aggressive, suppressing free speech and leading to allegations of bias.

Digital Literacy Campaigns have emerged as a key defensive strategy, aimed at educating the public on how to identify misinformation, verify sources, and critically assess online content. Many governments, non-governmental organizations (NGOs), and academic institutions have launched programs that teach individuals how to differentiate between legitimate journalism and manipulated media. These initiatives emphasize the importance of verifying multiple sources, recognizing common disinformation tactics, and understanding the psychological techniques used to manipulate emotions and biases in online narratives.

Another significant approach is Collaboration Between Governments and Tech Companies, which has led to the creation of multi-stakeholder alliances to counter foreign interference, remove malicious content, and protect democratic processes. The EU Code of Practice on Disinformation and the Global Internet Forum to Counter Terrorism (GIFCT) are examples of such cooperative efforts, where tech giants work alongside governments to disrupt coordinated misinformation campaigns and enhance cybersecurity frameworks. Intelligence agencies have also strengthened their focus on cyber threat intelligence, enabling early detection of digital influence operations and better coordination in responding to cyber threats.

Despite these efforts, the rapid advancement of AI, deepfake technology, and algorithmic manipulation means that disinformation tactics will continue to evolve. Cyber adversaries are constantly refining their strategies, making it a continuous challenge to safeguard information integrity. Governments and private organizations must remain proactive, investing in next-generation cybersecurity defenses, advanced forensic tools for digital verification, and international frameworks to counteract emerging threats in the ever-expanding landscape of social media warfare and digital disinformation.

Economic and Technological Information Warfare

Economic and technological warfare has become a cornerstone of global conflicts, allowing nations to exert influence, cripple adversaries, and secure geopolitical dominance without engaging in conventional military operations. The ability to control trade, impose economic sanctions, manipulate financial systems, and dominate technological innovation has given states powerful tools to undermine rivals and shape global events. Unlike traditional warfare, which relies on direct combat, economic and technological information warfare is a slow, strategic battle that plays out in international trade agreements, investment strategies, cyber operations, and scientific advancements.

Economic sanctions have long been a preferred method of coercion, used to pressure nations into compliance with political demands. The U.S.-China trade war is a prime example of how tariffs, restrictions on technology transfers, and economic blacklisting can be used as weapons. The U.S. has sought to curb China's technological expansion by restricting access to advanced semiconductor technologies and prohibiting key firms like Huawei from participating in Western infrastructure projects. In retaliation, China has strengthened its domestic supply chains, investing in semiconductor production and reducing its reliance on Western technology.

The use of financial cyberattacks and currency manipulation has also become a weapon in economic warfare. State-backed hacking groups, such as North Korea's Lazarus Group, have engaged in large-scale cyber heists, targeting banks and cryptocurrency exchanges to evade sanctions and fund their government's military programs. The Bangladesh Bank Heist (2016), where North Korean hackers attempted to steal nearly $1 billion, showcased how cyber financial warfare could be used to fund national operations. Likewise, the growing adoption of Central Bank Digital Currencies (CBDCs) has opened new avenues for economic control, as countries develop digital currencies to reduce dependence on the U.S. dollar and shift global financial power dynamics.

Technological dominance has also emerged as a key element of modern information warfare. The race to control artificial intelligence (AI), 5G networks, and quantum computing has become a priority for global superpowers. The Huawei 5G controversy illustrated concerns over cybersecurity risks associated with allowing foreign nations to control critical infrastructure. The global semiconductor shortage (2020-2023) further underscored the strategic importance of chip manufacturing, with the U.S. CHIPS Act (2022) aiming to reduce reliance on foreign semiconductor production. Similarly, China's control over rare earth minerals, which are essential for electronics manufacturing, has given Beijing leverage over supply chains, forcing the U.S. and Europe to explore alternative sources to maintain technological independence.

Cyberattacks targeting financial institutions and supply chains have intensified as part of economic information warfare. The SolarWinds cyberattack (2020), attributed to Russian-backed hackers, infiltrated software supply chains, affecting thousands of companies and government agencies. Such attacks demonstrate how digital vulnerabilities in global commerce can be exploited to destabilize economies and influence political outcomes. The rise of AI-driven cyber warfare has further escalated threats, with algorithms now capable of executing real-time financial disruptions, manipulating stock markets, and executing complex cyber-economic strategies.

As the global power struggle intensifies, the intersection of economic and technological information warfare will play a decisive role in shaping the future. Nations that fail to secure their financial systems, supply chains, and technological assets risk falling behind in the modern geopolitical arena. To counter these threats, governments must invest in economic resilience, cybersecurity infrastructure, and strategic technology partnerships while anticipating the next evolution of digital and economic warfare in an era where information is the ultimate weapon.

Economic and technological dominance is now a key aspect of Information Warfare. Nations leverage trade wars, economic sanctions, currency manipulation, and control over critical technologies to weaken adversaries, gain geopolitical influence, and maintain global supremacy. Unlike conventional warfare, economic and technological warfare operates through financial leverage, cyber economic espionage, supply chain disruptions, and the strategic use of emerging technologies to achieve national security objectives.

Economic Warfare: Sanctions, Trade Wars, and Financial Manipulation

Economic warfare has become a dominant tool in global geopolitics, allowing nations to exert influence, weaken adversaries, and achieve strategic objectives without engaging in direct military conflict. The use of sanctions, tariffs, trade restrictions, and financial policies enables countries to manipulate economic conditions to pressure opponents into compliance, disrupt supply chains, and control access to critical resources. These tactics are often used in combination with diplomatic measures and cyber operations to maximize impact.

One of the most high-profile examples of economic warfare is the U.S.-China Trade War (2018–Present), in which the United States imposed high tariffs on Chinese goods, citing concerns over intellectual property theft, forced technology transfers, and unfair trade practices. In retaliation, China introduced its own tariffs on American exports and pursued alternative trade alliances, such as strengthening economic ties with countries in Africa, Latin America, and the European Union. The ongoing battle for technological supremacy, particularly in semiconductors, artificial intelligence, and telecommunications, has added another layer of economic conflict between the two superpowers.

Another significant example is Western Sanctions on Russia (2014 & 2022), following its annexation of Crimea and its full-scale invasion of Ukraine. These sanctions targeted Russia's financial sector, energy exports, and key industries, restricting access to global banking systems like SWIFT and freezing assets of Russian oligarchs. As a result, Russia pivoted towards alternative financial networks, increasing trade with China, India, and other non-Western economies. The long-term effects of these sanctions have reshaped global energy markets, particularly in Europe, which sought to reduce dependence on Russian gas by expanding investments in renewable energy and securing alternative suppliers.

Economic sanctions have also been widely used against Iran and North Korea to curtail their nuclear programs and military expansion. The United States and its allies have imposed restrictions on these nations' energy exports, banking systems, and international trade, significantly impacting their economic stability. However, both countries have adapted by developing alternative revenue streams, including cyber theft, cryptocurrency fraud, and illicit trade networks to bypass restrictions. North Korea's Lazarus Group has been linked to major cyber heists, stealing hundreds of millions from banks and cryptocurrency exchanges to finance state operations.

Beyond traditional sanctions and tariffs, currency manipulation and economic sabotage have become tools of economic warfare. Some nations engage in competitive devaluation of their currencies to make exports more competitive while hurting rival economies.

As economic warfare continues to evolve, nations are adopting new strategies, including the weaponization of supply chains, financial cyberattacks, and the creation of alternative economic systems. The expansion of Central Bank Digital Currencies (CBDCs), blockchain-based financial systems, and strategic trade alliances is reshaping the global economic order. To maintain economic sovereignty and resilience, countries must invest in secure financial infrastructures, diversify supply chains, and develop economic countermeasures to mitigate the impact of economic warfare in an increasingly interconnected world.

Cyber Economic Warfare: Digital Sabotage and Financial Cyberattacks

With the increasing reliance on digital financial systems, cyberattacks targeting banking infrastructure, stock markets, and cryptocurrency networks have emerged as potent tools for economic warfare. Cybercriminal organizations and state-sponsored hacking groups now employ sophisticated cyber operations to manipulate financial markets, steal national assets, disrupt trade flows, and bypass international sanctions. These attacks are designed not only to inflict financial damage but also to erode confidence in economic stability and governance.

One of the most striking examples of cyber economic warfare is the Bangladesh Bank Heist (2016), where North Korean hackers, allegedly from the Lazarus Group, infiltrated Bangladesh's central bank and attempted to steal nearly $1 billion by exploiting vulnerabilities in the SWIFT banking system. The hackers infiltrated the bank's network months before the heist, carefully studying transaction protocols and security measures to execute their plan with precision. Using compromised credentials, they sent fraudulent requests to the Federal Reserve Bank of New York to transfer funds to various accounts in the Philippines and Sri Lanka.

While most of the fraudulent transactions were blocked after an alert was raised due to a typo in one of the payment instructions, the attackers still managed to successfully transfer $81 million before being detected. The stolen funds were funneled through casinos and shell companies, making it difficult to trace and recover the money. This attack not only showcased the vulnerabilities of global financial systems to cyber-enabled economic sabotage but also demonstrated how sophisticated state-sponsored hacking groups exploit weaknesses in interbank communication networks to conduct large-scale heists. The incident forced financial institutions worldwide to reassess their cybersecurity measures, leading to significant upgrades in banking security frameworks, including stricter authentication protocols and enhanced transaction monitoring systems.

The SolarWinds Cyberattack (2020) served as a stark reminder of the scale and sophistication of financial and economic cyber espionage. The attack, attributed to Russian-backed cyber units, infiltrated the global supply chain by embedding malicious code within a routine software update for the Orion network management platform, which was widely used by U.S. government agencies, major corporations, and financial institutions. This supply chain attack went undetected for months, allowing the hackers to establish persistent access to sensitive systems, exfiltrate classified data, and monitor communications across multiple industries.

The attack exposed critical vulnerabilities in digital infrastructure, illustrating how cyber adversaries could use third-party software dependencies to gain widespread access to high-value targets. The breach affected thousands of organizations, including the Department of Homeland Security, the Treasury Department, and major tech firms like Microsoft. Beyond espionage, the operation had economic consequences, as the revelation of the attack led to a decline in stock values for affected companies, massive remediation costs, and a heightened distrust in global supply chain security.

The SolarWinds attack underscored the growing threat of supply chain cyber warfare, where infiltrating a single trusted vendor could compromise multiple downstream entities. This incident triggered urgent reforms in cybersecurity frameworks, leading governments and businesses to adopt zero-trust security models, advanced endpoint detection systems, and stricter regulations on third-party software integrations. The attack also intensified calls for global cybersecurity cooperation, as it highlighted the challenges of defending against state-sponsored cyber threats that exploit the interconnected nature of modern digital economies.

Cyber warfare has also expanded into the realm of cryptocurrency-based financial manipulation. State-sponsored hacking groups from North Korea, Russia, and Iran have been accused of hijacking cryptocurrency exchanges, laundering illicit funds, and using digital assets to circumvent international sanctions. By exploiting decentralized financial systems, these actors can channel stolen digital currencies into state-funded projects, including nuclear programs, military expansion, and intelligence operations. North Korea, in particular, has used cryptocurrency heists to fund its weapons programs, effectively turning cyber theft into a tool of state survival.

Beyond theft and sabotage, algorithmic trading manipulation and economic cyberattacks on financial institutions have emerged as advanced tactics in cyber economic warfare. Malicious actors have deployed automated bot networks to manipulate stock prices, execute flash crashes, and create artificial inflation or deflation in cryptocurrency markets. These tactics not only cause immediate financial losses but also contribute to long-term instability, eroding public confidence in digital financial systems and the broader global economy.

As cyber economic warfare intensifies, nations are being forced to harden their financial cybersecurity defenses, establish cyber threat intelligence networks, and implement stricter regulations on digital financial transactions. The rise of quantum computing, AI-driven cyber threats, and decentralized finance (DeFi) presents both opportunities and new challenges in defending against cyber-enabled economic sabotage. Without proactive measures, the increasing digitization of financial markets and banking systems will only expand the attack surface for cyber adversaries, making economic cyber warfare one of the most critical threats to national security in the 21st century.

Technological Warfare: The Race for AI, 5G, and Quantum Supremacy

Technological warfare has become one of the most critical battlegrounds in the modern era, where nations aggressively compete for dominance in cutting-edge advancements that will define global power structures. From artificial intelligence (AI) and quantum computing to 5G networks, semiconductor production, and space technologies, technological superiority has become a strategic imperative for national security, economic growth, and military capability. The ability to control, regulate, and restrict the development of these emerging technologies provides nations with a powerful tool to exert influence over adversaries while safeguarding their own digital and physical infrastructure.

The rapid evolution of artificial intelligence has led to its integration into multiple sectors, including cybersecurity, surveillance, autonomous weapons, and economic forecasting. AI-powered systems are now being deployed for real-time battlefield analysis, drone-based reconnaissance, cyber threat detection, and automated hacking operations, making AI one of the most sought-after technologies in military and intelligence applications. Countries like the United States, China, and Russia are investing billions into AI-driven warfare capabilities, while also implementing AI regulations to maintain control over its deployment. China's AI-driven surveillance state, which utilizes facial recognition, big data analytics, and predictive policing, demonstrates how AI can be weaponized not just for external conflicts but for domestic control as well.

At the heart of technological warfare is the global semiconductor industry, which underpins the entire digital economy, from consumer electronics to advanced military systems. The global chip shortage (2020-2023) exposed critical vulnerabilities in supply chains, as Taiwan and South Korea emerged as the dominant manufacturers of high-end semiconductors. The United States responded by introducing the CHIPS Act (2022) to boost domestic semiconductor production and reduce dependence on foreign suppliers. Simultaneously, China has intensified efforts to develop its own semiconductor industry, investing heavily in self-sufficiency to circumvent U.S. sanctions and trade restrictions. The struggle for semiconductor dominance has triggered a tech arms race, with both nations seeking to control the production and distribution of these essential components.

The 5G network battle has become another focal point of technological warfare, as control over global telecommunications infrastructure translates to power over data, cybersecurity, and intelligence operations. The Huawei 5G controversy highlighted how the U.S. and its allies have restricted Chinese companies from participating in their critical communications infrastructure, citing espionage concerns. The exclusion of Huawei from Western markets has escalated technological decoupling between the U.S. and China, leading to the creation of separate digital ecosystems that are increasingly fragmented along geopolitical lines.

Beyond terrestrial technologies, space warfare and quantum computing are emerging as the next frontiers of technological dominance. Countries are developing satellite-based surveillance, anti-satellite weapons, and space-based cyber capabilities to control information and military assets beyond Earth's atmosphere. Meanwhile, quantum computing has the potential to revolutionize cryptography and break current encryption protocols, raising concerns about data security in a post-quantum world. The United States, China, and the European Union are racing to achieve quantum supremacy, recognizing that the nation that first masters quantum technology could decrypt classified intelligence, disrupt financial systems, and establish an unbreakable cybersecurity infrastructure.

As technological warfare continues to evolve, nations must prioritize research and development, intellectual property protection, cybersecurity resilience, and international collaboration to maintain an advantage. The race for dominance in AI, semiconductors, 5G, quantum computing, and space technology will shape the future of global power dynamics, determining which nations emerge as leaders in the next generation of digital and military innovation.

Weaponizing Supply Chains: Economic Leverage through Global Dependencies

The weaponization of supply chains has become a key strategy in economic and technological warfare, where nations manipulate dependencies on essential goods and resources to exert geopolitical influence. By controlling the production and distribution of critical commodities such as rare earth minerals, energy supplies, semiconductors, and medical products, countries can gain strategic leverage over their rivals, disrupt economies, and exert political pressure without resorting to direct military confrontation. This tactic has been employed by major global powers to consolidate economic dominance, retaliate against adversaries, and shape the balance of international trade.

One of the most significant examples of supply chain weaponization is China's dominance in rare earth materials, which are essential for manufacturing high-tech products, including smartphones, electric vehicles, and military equipment. China controls over 60% of the world's rare earth mineral supply and nearly 85% of the global refining capacity, making it the dominant player in this sector. In past disputes, China has restricted rare earth exports to countries such as Japan and the U.S., leveraging its monopoly to exert political pressure. In response, the U.S. and Europe are now investing in alternative rare earth extraction and processing facilities to reduce dependence on Chinese suppliers and secure their technological supply chains.

Another prime example of supply chain weaponization occurred during the COVID-19 pandemic, when vaccine production and distribution became a tool for diplomatic influence. Countries that successfully developed vaccines, including the U.S., China, and Russia, used their control over vaccine exports to strengthen alliances, expand geopolitical influence, and negotiate favorable trade agreements. China's vaccine diplomacy saw it supplying vaccines to developing nations in Africa, Latin America, and Southeast Asia in exchange for economic partnerships and political concessions. Similarly, the U.S. leveraged vaccine shipments to reinforce alliances with European and Asian nations, while Russia's Sputnik V vaccine became an instrument of soft power in countries seeking alternatives to Western medical supplies.

Energy has also been a significant battleground in supply chain warfare, particularly through OPEC+ and oil price manipulation. The Russia-Saudi Arabia oil price war (2020) caused massive economic instability, as both nations flooded global markets with oil to undermine competitors, including U.S. shale producers. At the same time, European reliance on Russian natural gas became a major vulnerability, especially during the Russia-Ukraine war, when Moscow used energy supplies as leverage against Western sanctions. The push to reduce dependency on Russian energy has accelerated the global transition toward renewable energy sources, energy diversification, and LNG (liquefied natural gas) imports from alternative suppliers.

Semiconductor supply chains have emerged as another critical front in economic warfare. The global chip shortage (2020-2023) exposed the world's heavy reliance on Taiwan and South Korea for semiconductor production, with Taiwan's TSMC (Taiwan Semiconductor Manufacturing Company) alone producing over 50% of the world's advanced chips. The U.S. has responded with initiatives like the CHIPS Act (2022) to bring semiconductor manufacturing back to domestic soil and reduce vulnerabilities in its tech industry. Meanwhile, China is heavily investing in domestic semiconductor production to bypass Western restrictions and counter U.S. sanctions aimed at limiting its access to cutting-edge technology.

As global interdependencies grow, the manipulation of supply chains will remain a crucial tactic in geopolitical strategy. Nations are increasingly focusing on securing critical resources, diversifying supply routes, and strengthening domestic production capacities to mitigate risks associated with economic coercion. The future of global power struggles will be defined not just by military might, but by a nation's ability to control, secure, and weaponize essential supply chains to influence economic and political outcomes on a global scale.

Conclusion: The Future of Economic and Technological Information Warfare

Economic and technological warfare will continue to evolve as nations seek dominance in finance, trade, and emerging technologies. With the increasing digitization of economies, cybersecurity threats, supply chain dependencies, and AI-driven economic strategies will become central to national security considerations. Countries that fail to adapt to these changing dynamics risk economic subjugation, digital vulnerabilities, and geopolitical disadvantages.

To counter these threats, nations must invest in economic resilience, technological self-sufficiency, cybersecurity frameworks, and strategic global partnerships to protect their economic interests and maintain their sovereignty in an era of information-driven warfare.

Economic and technological dominance is now a key aspect of Information Warfare. Nations leverage trade wars, economic sanctions, and control over critical technologies to weaken adversaries. The U.S.-China trade war has demonstrated how economic strategies can be weaponized to exert political and technological influence.

China's Belt and Road Initiative (BRI) has been used as a geopolitical tool to create economic dependencies, while the Huawei 5G controversy highlighted concerns over technological security and espionage. Similarly, cyberattacks targeting stock markets, financial institutions, and cryptocurrency exchanges have shown how economic disruptions can be engineered as a form of warfare.

CHAPTER III

Cyber and Cognitive Warfare in the 21st Century

The evolution of warfare in the 21st century has extended beyond conventional military strategies, bringing cyber and cognitive warfare to the forefront of global conflicts. Unlike traditional kinetic warfare, these modern forms of warfare focus on information dominance, psychological manipulation, and digital disruption, creating new battlefields where data, algorithms, and human perception become the primary targets and weapons.

The rapid advancements in artificial intelligence (AI), big data, and behavioral analytics have transformed the nature of warfare, enabling state and non-state actors to launch precision-targeted influence campaigns, perception manipulation strategies, and cyber-enabled attacks at an unprecedented scale. Cyber warfare operations now extend far beyond simple hacking attempts; they include sophisticated deepfake technology, synthetic media, automated disinformation networks, and AI-driven cognitive attacks designed to destabilize governments, corporations, and entire societies.

Meanwhile, cognitive warfare, sometimes referred to as psycho-informational warfare, manipulates human perceptions through memetic engineering, psychological operations (PSYOPS), and algorithmic propaganda. The ability to influence populations in real-time through social media manipulation, sentiment analysis, and psychographic profiling has blurred the lines between truth and deception, making disinformation one of the most potent weapons of modern conflict. The battlefield is no longer limited to physical terrain—it has expanded into the digital and cognitive domains, where algorithms dictate narratives, data is weaponized, and perception itself becomes the target.

The Rise of AI-Driven Warfare

Artificial intelligence has revolutionized warfare, providing autonomous decision-making capabilities, predictive analytics, and deep learning algorithms that enhance cyber and cognitive warfare operations. AI-powered tools are being used to automate cyberattacks, generate synthetic content, analyze vast datasets for intelligence gathering, conduct psychological profiling, and optimize disinformation campaigns. Machine learning models can now detect behavioral patterns, predict responses, and adjust narratives in real-time, making AI an indispensable tool in modern information warfare.

The use of AI-driven cyber warfare extends beyond conventional hacking; it incorporates self-learning malware, AI-powered phishing attacks, and adversarial machine learning, where cyberattacks dynamically adapt to their targets' defensive measures. Governments and non-state actors deploy AI-enhanced cybersecurity offense and defense mechanisms, leveraging AI to predict cyber threats, infiltrate systems, and deploy malware that autonomously evolves to bypass detection.

In influence operations, AI is harnessed to create highly personalized disinformation campaigns by leveraging psychographic profiling and sentiment analysis. Social media manipulation, bolstered by AI-generated personas and automated content distribution, allows for the rapid spread of false narratives, deepfake videos, and synthetic news articles, making it increasingly difficult for audiences to distinguish between authentic and fabricated information. AI also enables the hyper-personalization of propaganda, where messages are tailored based on individual users' online behavior, increasing engagement and psychological impact.

Furthermore, AI enhances real-time battlefield decision-making, where it aids in intelligence analysis, deep reconnaissance, and target acquisition. AI-integrated drones, autonomous weapons, and smart surveillance systems now function with minimal human intervention, revolutionizing military strategy, intelligence gathering, and cyber-kinetic operations. As AI continues to evolve, its application in both cyber and cognitive warfare will redefine global security landscapes, raising ethical concerns about the weaponization of artificial intelligence and the future of autonomous warfare.

Deep Fakes, Synthetic Media, and Influence Campaigns

The emergence of deepfake technology and synthetic media has dramatically transformed influence campaigns, enabling adversarial actors to create hyper-realistic fake videos, audio recordings, and images that can deceive audiences and manipulate perceptions. These advancements have fundamentally altered the landscape of information warfare, making it increasingly difficult to distinguish between authentic and fabricated content. Deepfake-generated materials have been widely used for political subversion, corporate fraud, and psychological operations (PSYOPS), demonstrating the profound implications of synthetic media on global stability.

One of the most alarming aspects of deepfake technology is its role in political warfare. State-sponsored influence campaigns have weaponized deepfakes to fabricate scandalous statements, misrepresent political figures, and simulate real-world events to discredit opponents or shape public opinion. In 2019, a deepfake video of Gabon's President Ali Bongo surfaced, sparking rumors about his health and leading to an attempted coup. Similarly, in the lead-up to the 2024 U.S. Presidential Election, AI-generated deepfake robocalls impersonating political leaders misled voters about polling dates, showcasing the threat of synthetic deception in democratic processes.

Beyond politics, corporate espionage and financial fraud have also been transformed by synthetic media. In 2020, criminals used an AI-generated voice deepfake to impersonate a CEO, instructing an employee to transfer $35 million into fraudulent accounts. This incident highlights how deepfake-enabled fraud can bypass traditional security measures, undermining financial stability and corporate governance. Additionally, deepfakes have been exploited in phishing attacks, where AI-generated faces and voices convincingly impersonate high-ranking officials or business executives, compromising cybersecurity protocols.

Deepfake technology also plays a pivotal role in cyber warfare and military deception. AI-powered disinformation campaigns have used synthetic media to fabricate false military victories, staged surrender announcements, and manipulated battlefield footage to demoralize enemy forces and mislead intelligence agencies. In 2022, during the Russia-Ukraine conflict, deepfake videos surfaced portraying Ukrainian President Volodymyr Zelensky calling for surrender, attempting to erode Ukrainian resistance and confuse both military and civilian populations.

The rapid proliferation of deepfake content is further amplified by AI-powered bot networks, algorithmic content manipulation, and micro-targeted disinformation campaigns. Malicious actors deploy these techniques to ensure that deceptive narratives reach highly specific audiences, exploiting social media algorithms to spread falsehoods at unprecedented speeds. The combination of synthetic media and social engineering creates an environment where trust in information ecosystems is systematically eroded, paving the way for large-scale cognitive manipulation.

To combat the rising threat of deepfake-driven influence campaigns, governments, tech companies, and cybersecurity firms are investing in deepfake detection algorithms, blockchain-based content verification, and AI-powered forensic analysis. Researchers are developing advanced countermeasures such as digital watermarking techniques, deepfake-resistant authentication protocols, and legislative frameworks to regulate synthetic media production and dissemination. However, as generative AI models continue to evolve, the challenge of differentiating between real and fake content remains an ongoing arms race in the domain of information warfare.

The consequences of deepfake technology extend beyond immediate deception—they erode public trust in institutions, disrupt financial and political systems, and contribute to the increasing weaponization of digital misinformation. As synthetic media capabilities become more advanced and accessible, influence campaigns leveraging deepfake technology will continue to challenge national security, economic stability, and democratic governance worldwide.

Cognitive Hacking and Perception Manipulation

Cognitive hacking represents one of the most insidious threats in modern warfare, where adversaries manipulate human perception and decision-making processes to alter reality. Unlike traditional cyberattacks that target digital systems, cognitive hacking focuses on the human mind as the primary battlefield, leveraging advanced psychological and technological tactics to reshape beliefs, manipulate emotions, and control behaviors.

By exploiting cognitive biases, social engineering tactics, and psychological warfare techniques, attackers can influence public opinion, destabilize political systems, and erode societal trust. Techniques such as memetic warfare, where carefully crafted narratives and visual propaganda spread virally across social media, have been used to embed falsehoods deeply into public consciousness. Cambridge Analytica's psychological micro-targeting in the 2016 U.S. Presidential Election and Russia's disinformation campaigns in the Ukraine conflict exemplify how tailored misinformation can alter political landscapes and public sentiment.

Cognitive hacking also utilizes AI-driven sentiment analysis, which detects emotional vulnerabilities in targeted populations, allowing adversaries to fine-tune propaganda campaigns to maximize impact. Deepfake technology further exacerbates the threat, as hyper-realistic synthetic media can be used to create deceptive videos of leaders making false statements, triggering unrest or diplomatic crises.

A notable example of large-scale cognitive hacking was the COVID-19 misinformation campaigns, where false narratives about vaccine safety, virus origins, and global conspiracies were strategically amplified to sow distrust in governments and scientific institutions. These efforts successfully fragmented societies, creating ideological echo chambers where misinformation thrived and scientific consensus was undermined.

As cognitive hacking techniques evolve, they pose an existential challenge to democratic governance, corporate security, and social cohesion. Countermeasures such as media literacy programs, AI-powered misinformation detection, and cognitive resilience training are essential to safeguarding societies against the manipulation of perception in this new era of digital warfare.

Techniques such as memetic warfare, emotionally charged narratives, and AI-driven sentiment manipulation are used to create self-reinforcing echo chambers that radicalize audiences and intensify social divisions. These tactics exploit cognitive biases, social media algorithms, and hyper-personalized digital content to manipulate emotions and reinforce ideological extremism. By targeting individuals with content that aligns with their existing beliefs and fears, attackers can deepen polarization and make audiences more susceptible to misinformation.

The ability to engineer psychological operations (PSYOPS) at scale, using AI-driven behavioral analysis, has led to highly targeted disinformation campaigns that can predict, manipulate, and control individual thought processes. AI-powered tools can analyze users' social media interactions, browsing habits, and emotional triggers to craft narratives that resonate deeply with specific demographic groups. These campaigns often employ automated bot networks, deepfake videos, and synthetic personas to increase engagement and create the illusion of grassroots support for a given agenda.

These attacks are particularly effective in influencing voter behavior, as seen in numerous election cycles where false narratives about candidates, voting processes, or political events have been strategically disseminated to sway public opinion. Similarly, disinformation campaigns are used to sow discord among ethnic or ideological groups, intensifying social fragmentation and civil unrest. In some cases, governments or non-state actors use coordinated smear campaigns to discredit opposition figures, journalists, or activists, effectively silencing dissent and controlling the political narrative.

The consequences of these tactics are far-reaching, as manipulated populations often act on false information, leading to real-world political instability, economic disruptions, and erosion of democratic institutions. Addressing these threats requires advanced AI-driven misinformation detection, cross-platform fact-checking initiatives, and greater public awareness of cognitive hacking techniques to build resilience against psychological manipulation in the digital age.

Role of Big Data and Behavioral Analytics in Information Warfare

Big data analytics has become a cornerstone of modern cyber and cognitive warfare, enabling actors to collect, process, and weaponize vast amounts of information to manipulate societies. Governments, corporations, and intelligence agencies utilize behavioral analytics, predictive modeling, and psychometric profiling to gain deep insights into individual and group behavior. This allows for the development of micro-targeted influence operations, real-time propaganda adaptation, and precision-guided digital psychological attacks. The ability to analyze massive datasets in real time has transformed information warfare into a science, where narratives can be strategically deployed to alter public opinion, destabilize societies, and influence decision-making at scale.

Social media platforms, search engines, and e-commerce websites continuously collect user data, creating detailed behavioral profiles that can be exploited for personalized manipulation tactics. These platforms leverage sophisticated machine learning algorithms to track online behavior, purchasing habits, emotional triggers, and ideological leanings. Political campaigns, intelligence agencies, and foreign adversaries have weaponized these insights to craft emotionally compelling narratives, adjust propaganda in real time, and influence the collective consciousness of entire populations. The infamous Cambridge Analytica scandal demonstrated how psychographic profiling could be used to influence elections, as vast amounts of Facebook data were harvested to create psychological profiles of voters, allowing political campaigns to deliver highly personalized and emotionally charged messaging that influenced voting behavior.

The integration of AI-driven sentiment analysis and predictive analytics has made it possible to detect social trends, public dissatisfaction, and ideological shifts before they fully manifest. Governments and private entities utilize these insights to manipulate stock markets, sway public opinion on policy issues, and forecast potential unrest. For example, China's social credit system integrates big data analytics with behavioral scoring, allowing the state to reward or punish citizens based on their online and offline behavior. Similarly, intelligence agencies use predictive analytics to identify potential threats, radicalization patterns, and early signs of cyber or terrorist attacks.

Beyond psychological manipulation, big data is used in financial warfare, where adversaries analyze financial transactions, cryptocurrency flows, and market fluctuations to engage in economic sabotage, cyber-heists, and currency manipulation. North Korea's Lazarus Group, for instance, has employed sophisticated AI-driven tactics to steal billions from financial institutions and cryptocurrency exchanges, funding state operations while destabilizing international financial systems.

The ability to process massive data streams from social networks, online interactions, and digital footprints has transformed information warfare into a sophisticated science of influence. Psychographic profiling, which classifies individuals based on their psychological traits, enables adversaries to deliver highly personalized disinformation, manipulate voting behavior, and shape ideological beliefs with precision. As technological advancements continue, the ethical implications of mass surveillance, algorithmic bias, and AI-powered persuasion raise significant concerns.

To counter these threats, nations must invest in advanced AI-driven misinformation detection, cross-platform fact-checking initiatives, and public awareness campaigns. Cyber resilience strategies, ethical AI frameworks, and stricter regulations on data privacy and algorithmic transparency will be crucial in preventing the misuse of big data and behavioral analytics in information warfare. The growing power of big data as a tool for cognitive and cyber warfare means that without proactive measures, societies risk falling into a future where information is weaponized, truth is subjective, and perception is controlled by those who command the data.

Big data analytics has become a cornerstone of modern cyber and cognitive warfare, enabling actors to collect, process, and weaponize vast amounts of information to manipulate societies. Governments, corporations, and intelligence agencies utilize behavioral analytics, predictive modeling, and psychometric profiling to gain deep insights into individual and group behavior. This allows for the development of micro-targeted influence operations, real-time propaganda adaptation, and precision-guided digital psychological attacks.

Social media platforms, search engines, and e-commerce websites continuously collect user data, creating detailed behavioral profiles that can be exploited for personalized manipulation tactics. Political campaigns, intelligence agencies, and foreign adversaries have weaponized these insights to craft emotionally compelling narratives, adjust propaganda in real-time, and influence the collective consciousness of entire populations.

The ability to process massive data streams from social networks, online interactions, and digital footprints has transformed information warfare into a sophisticated science of influence. Psychographic profiling, which classifies individuals based on their psychological traits, enables adversaries to deliver highly personalized disinformation, manipulate voting behavior, and shape ideological beliefs with precision.

CHAPTER IV

The Digital Battlefield: Tools and Tactics of Modern Information Warfare

The methodologies employed in information warfare have undergone a dramatic transformation with the rise of digital platforms and communication technologies. The ever-expanding digital ecosystem offers malicious actors a fertile ground to exploit tools like news portals, social media platforms, video-sharing sites, and encrypted messaging apps to conduct sophisticated disinformation campaigns, amplify propaganda, and manipulate public perceptions. These methods are strategically designed to exploit the inherent vulnerabilities of these platforms, leveraging their speed, reach, and algorithmic amplification to maximize impact.

News portals, whether legitimate or fabricated, serve as key vehicles for disseminating false narratives, often exploiting search engine optimization (SEO) techniques to ensure wide visibility. Social media platforms are particularly potent, given their ability to create echo chambers, foster polarization, and artificially amplify content through bots and fake accounts. Meanwhile, video platforms like YouTube have emerged as major battlegrounds, with deepfake technology and AI-generated content blurring the lines between reality and fabrication. AI-generated deepfake videos are now being used to manipulate public perception at an unprecedented scale, allowing malicious actors to fabricate speeches, create fake endorsements, and even alter historical records to suit ideological or political goals. These deepfakes have been deployed in election campaigns, geopolitical conflicts, and smear campaigns, often with devastating consequences. In global politics, deepfake technology has been used to impersonate world leaders, generating fake statements to incite diplomatic tensions or discredit opponents. During the 2020 U.S. elections, fabricated videos were circulated to misrepresent candidates' positions on key issues, misleading voters and influencing public opinion. Similarly, deepfakes have been weaponized in India to create deceptive narratives during regional elections, manipulating voter sentiment and spreading misinformation.

Countermeasures to detect and prevent deepfake-driven disinformation are being developed through AI-powered forensic analysis, real-time content verification, and regulatory measures mandating the identification of AI-generated media. Tech companies are investing in automated detection tools to analyze inconsistencies in video and audio content, while governments are working on legislative frameworks to penalize the malicious use of deepfake technology. However, as deepfake generators become more advanced and accessible, countering their influence remains a significant challenge. Encrypted messaging apps add another layer of complexity by enabling the rapid, untraceable spread of disinformation within private groups and regional networks, making the detection and containment of manipulated content even more difficult.

This chapter delves deeply into these tools, platforms, and strategies, analyzing their mechanics, the implications of their misuse, and proposing robust countermeasures to mitigate their effects. The discussion underscores the necessity of technological innovation, regulatory action, and public awareness in countering the evolving threats of information warfare.

News Portals as Propaganda Tools

News portals, both legitimate and fabricated, serve as critical instruments in disseminating false narratives. The rise of digital journalism and the ease of creating online news outlets have given malicious actors an effective platform to spread misinformation. These portals exploit the trust placed in journalistic entities, making their content appear credible to unsuspecting audiences. Examples from recent global events underline the scale and sophistication of such efforts.

Disseminating Fabricated News Stories: Malicious actors carefully design stories to resonate with the biases, fears, and expectations of their target audiences, ensuring maximum engagement and virality. These narratives often exploit contentious issues such as politics, religion, and public health, making them emotionally compelling and harder for audiences to dismiss. For instance, during the 2016 U.S. presidential election, websites masquerading as legitimate news outlets circulated blatantly fabricated stories to influence voter perceptions. These stories included allegations of illegal activities and conspiracy theories involving candidates, such as the infamous "Pizzagate" scandal, which falsely claimed that a political figure was involved in a child trafficking ring. Such articles were widely shared on social media platforms, reinforcing pre-existing biases and creating echo chambers where false information spread unchecked.

A more recent example includes misinformation during the COVID-19 pandemic, where fabricated news about vaccine side effects circulated on pseudo-news portals. These articles used scientific jargon and fabricated expert quotes to appear credible, leading to widespread vaccine hesitancy. Malicious actors also tailored these stories for specific demographics, amplifying fears in vulnerable communities.

These fabricated stories, often accompanied by doctored images or videos, thrive on their ability to evoke strong emotional reactions. This emotional engagement drives clicks, shares, and discussions, further entrenching the false narratives within public discourse. Countering this phenomenon requires coordinated efforts, including algorithmic detection of misinformation, robust fact-checking, and widespread public education to enhance digital literacy.

Amplifying State-Sponsored Narratives: Authoritarian governments strategically utilize controlled news portals to craft and disseminate propaganda that aligns with their geopolitical goals. Russia's RT and Sputnik exemplify such platforms, often accused of framing international events in ways that discredit Western policies while bolstering Russia's global image. These outlets operate under the guise of legitimate journalism, blending factual reporting with carefully curated biases to make their narratives appear credible. For example, during the annexation of Crimea in 2014, RT extensively broadcast narratives portraying the move as a defensive action to protect Russian-speaking populations, sidelining the global consensus condemning it as an act of aggression.

Similarly, China's state-sponsored platforms like CGTN and Xinhua News use similar tactics to promote the Belt and Road Initiative (BRI) as a benevolent global development strategy while downplaying criticisms of debt diplomacy. These platforms frequently highlight the economic benefits of BRI projects without addressing concerns about environmental degradation or financial burdens on participating countries.

By leveraging these news portals, state actors ensure that their messages reach international audiences, influencing public opinion and policy-making in target nations. The challenge lies in distinguishing between legitimate state media and propaganda outlets, as the latter often use the same channels of distribution and professional presentation techniques, making detection and counteraction particularly challenging. Addressing these influences requires concerted efforts involving regulatory measures, media literacy programs, and transparency initiatives to expose the true origins and intent of such narratives.

Exploiting Search Engine Optimization (SEO): Fake news portals have mastered the use of SEO techniques to manipulate search engine algorithms, ensuring their stories rank prominently in search results. These portals strategically embed keywords, craft clickbait headlines, and build intricate networks of backlinks to other sites, all designed to increase their visibility and credibility. The aim is to deceive unsuspecting audiences into believing their content is authentic and trustworthy.

During the COVID-19 pandemic, this tactic reached alarming levels. Numerous pseudo-news portals optimized their articles with terms like "vaccine safety," "COVID cure," and "side effects," ensuring they appeared at the top of search results for concerned readers. Many of these articles included fabricated scientific claims, false expert quotes, and exaggerated statistics, creating confusion and fueling vaccine hesitancy. For instance, some portals falsely claimed vaccines caused infertility, leveraging fear and misinformation to drive traffic to their sites.

This phenomenon is not limited to health-related topics. Political misinformation has also benefited from SEO manipulation. Fake news stories about election fraud, scandals involving political figures, or conspiracies are strategically optimized to dominate search engines during critical moments, such as elections or geopolitical crises. These tactics amplify the reach of disinformation and distort public discourse.

Counteracting this misuse of SEO requires collaborative efforts between search engine companies, fact-checkers, and governments. Search engines must refine their algorithms to prioritize verified and credible sources, while educational initiatives should empower users to critically evaluate search results. By addressing these vulnerabilities, the impact of SEO manipulation on misinformation can be significantly reduced.

Monetization of Propaganda: Many fabricated news portals are economically driven, using sensationalized and divisive content to generate substantial revenue. These portals craft emotionally charged stories, often utilizing clickbait headlines that are designed to attract high traffic volumes. By capitalizing on the virality of their content, these actors monetize public engagement through ad networks, affiliate marketing, and even direct sponsorships from groups with vested interests.

For instance, during the political unrest in Myanmar, certain fabricated stories about the Rohingya crisis garnered widespread attention on social media. These articles, filled with inflammatory rhetoric and graphic imagery, not only deepened societal tensions but also generated significant ad revenue for the portals hosting them. Similarly, during the 2020 U.S. elections, sensational stories about election fraud and partisan scandals were circulated widely, driving millions of clicks to fake news websites, which profited from the resulting advertising revenue.

Another example can be drawn from the COVID-19 pandemic. Portals promoting conspiracy theories about the virus's origins or vaccine side effects gained massive traction online. These stories often led readers to purchase "alternative cures" or subscribe to newsletters, further increasing profits for their creators. By exploiting fears and misinformation, these portals created a self-sustaining cycle of disinformation and revenue generation.

Addressing the monetization of propaganda requires a multi-faceted approach. Ad networks need to vet publishers more rigorously, ensuring that they do not inadvertently support disinformation campaigns. Public awareness campaigns must educate users about the financial motives behind clickbait content, encouraging more responsible online behavior. Regulatory measures targeting the advertising practices of such portals can also serve as a deterrent, reducing the economic incentives for spreading harmful narratives.

These examples underscore the power of news portals in shaping narratives and influencing societal behaviors. By leveraging trust and visibility, they serve as potent tools in the arsenal of information warfare. Countering their influence requires rigorous fact-checking, promoting media literacy, and holding creators accountable for propagating harmful content.

Exploitation of Social Media Platforms

Social media platforms, including Facebook, Twitter, Instagram, and TikTok, are among the most potent tools for conducting information warfare. These platforms combine global reach, real-time interaction, and sophisticated algorithmic amplification, making them highly effective for disseminating misinformation, fostering polarization, and manipulating public discourse. Their design prioritizes engagement and virality, often inadvertently creating opportunities for malicious actors to exploit.

Fake Accounts and Bot Networks: Malicious actors deploy extensive networks of fake profiles and automated bots to manipulate social media platforms and amplify their narratives artificially. These accounts are designed to mimic real users by posting comments, sharing content, and engaging in discussions, creating the illusion of widespread support or outrage around specific topics. The influence of such networks extends beyond casual online interactions, as they can sway public opinion, distort political discourse, and escalate societal tensions.

One prominent example occurred during the 2019 Hong Kong protests, where bot networks actively spread misinformation to delegitimize the protest movement. These bots flooded social media with posts portraying protesters as violent extremists and disseminated fabricated narratives to confuse and divide public opinion. By saturating the digital space with falsehoods, the bot networks aimed to erode local and international support for the protests.

A similar phenomenon was observed during the 2020 U.S. presidential elections, where fake accounts were instrumental in propagating conspiracy theories about voter fraud. These networks systematically targeted specific demographic groups with tailored messages, exploiting existing political divisions to deepen polarization and foster distrust in the electoral process.

The effectiveness of fake accounts and bots lies in their ability to exploit algorithms that prioritize engagement. By generating high levels of activity, these networks ensure that manipulated content gains visibility, reaching audiences who may not actively seek out such information. Combating these threats requires platforms to enhance their detection mechanisms, such as deploying AI-driven tools to identify patterns of coordinated activity, verifying account authenticity, and implementing stricter user verification protocols. Public education campaigns are equally critical, empowering users to recognize and report suspicious online behavior.

Hashtag Campaigns: Hashtag campaigns are a critical tactic in information warfare, leveraging the architecture of social media platforms to amplify disinformation and shape public narratives. Malicious actors orchestrate these campaigns by exploiting algorithms that prioritize trending content, creating the illusion of widespread organic support or outrage. These campaigns often combine bots, fake accounts, and real user engagement to maximize reach and legitimacy.

One of the most notable examples is the "#StopTheSteal" campaign during the 2020 U.S. presidential elections. This campaign systematically spread baseless claims of election fraud, polarizing the electorate and undermining trust in democratic institutions. The hashtag trended across multiple platforms, inciting protests and culminating in the January 6th Capitol riots. By tapping into existing political divisions, the campaign effectively amplified disinformation and fostered real-world consequences.

In the Indian context, politically charged hashtags such as "#IndiaAgainstPropaganda" and "#ToolKitExposed" have been utilized to shape public opinion and manipulate discourse during sensitive events. These campaigns often emerge during times of heightened political or social tension, aiming to polarize opinions and suppress dissent. A notable example is the controversy surrounding the "toolkit" allegedly linked to the farmers' protests in 2021. This document, which purportedly outlined strategies to mobilize international support for the protests, was tied to hashtags like "#ToolKitExposed."

The hashtag gained massive traction on social media, suggesting a coordinated global conspiracy against the Indian government. The narrative shifted focus from the core issues raised by the protesting farmers to allegations of foreign interference. This campaign polarized opinions, with one side emphasizing the legitimate concerns of the farmers and the other branding the protests as orchestrated attempts to destabilize the nation.

Similarly, hashtags like "#IndiaAgainstPropaganda" were used to counter international criticism following tweets by global personalities supporting the farmers. These hashtags, often backed by influential entities and coordinated groups, served to rally nationalist sentiments and discredit opposing viewpoints. These examples highlight how hashtags can be weaponized to redirect public attention and shape national and international narratives.

Similarly, hashtags like "#FreeKashmir" have been used in the Indian context to create divisive narratives aimed at undermining the government and the Indian Army. This hashtag, often circulated during protests or events related to Jammu and Kashmir, has been used to frame the situation as a human rights crisis while ignoring the historical and geopolitical complexities of the region.

Many posts under this hashtag were part of coordinated campaigns designed to incite unrest, gain international attention, and delegitimize India's position. These campaigns often included misinformation about military operations or exaggerated claims about civilian conditions, accompanied by emotionally charged visuals and unverified statistics to provoke strong reactions.

By leveraging the algorithmic nature of platforms like Twitter, such hashtags gained quick traction, influencing not just domestic discourse but also shaping perceptions internationally. Countering these narratives requires proactive measures, including real-time fact-checking, algorithmic transparency from platforms, and fostering digital literacy among users to critically assess viral content.

These examples highlight how coordinated hashtag campaigns can be weaponized to drive specific agendas and deepen societal rifts. Countering such tactics requires robust fact-checking mechanisms, algorithmic transparency from social media platforms, and public awareness campaigns to help users critically evaluate trending topics.

In geopolitical scenarios, hashtags like "#UkraineNazis" and "#IStandWithRussia" have been utilized to spread pro-Kremlin propaganda. These campaigns, often state-backed, aim to justify aggressive policies and polarize international audiences. The strategic use of emotionally charged language in these hashtags ensures virality and engagement, further complicating efforts to debunk them.

To counteract the misuse of hashtag campaigns, several measures are essential:

Advanced Detection Tools: Social media platforms must deploy AI-driven systems to identify coordinated hashtag activity, such as sudden surges in usage or repetitive posting patterns.

Transparency in Algorithms: Platforms should disclose how trending topics are determined and take proactive measures to prevent the amplification of manipulated trends.

Public Awareness: Educating users about how hashtags are exploited in information warfare can foster critical engagement and reduce susceptibility to disinformation.

Collaborative Efforts: Governments, platforms, and civil society organizations must work together to identify and mitigate harmful hashtag campaigns in real time.

Hashtag campaigns remain a potent tool in information warfare, capable of distorting public discourse and driving divisive agendas. Addressing their misuse requires a multi-pronged approach that combines technological innovation, regulatory oversight, and public education.

These campaigns thrive due to their ability to blend real user interactions with orchestrated efforts from bots and fake accounts, creating a snowball effect that makes narratives go viral. Combating their misuse involves transparency in platform algorithms, public education to raise awareness of manipulation tactics, and collaborative efforts between governments, platforms, and civil society to ensure accurate information dissemination.

Algorithmic Manipulation:

Algorithmic manipulation refers to the strategic exploitation of algorithms used by digital platforms to prioritize and amplify specific content. Malicious actors design misinformation campaigns to exploit these algorithms, ensuring that their content appears prominently in user feeds. By crafting sensationalist, emotionally charged, or polarizing content, these actors achieve higher engagement levels, which in turn prompts algorithms to further promote their messages.

One notable example is the false narrative linking 5G technology to the spread of COVID-19. This misinformation campaign spread rapidly as social media algorithms prioritized engaging posts. Videos and articles claiming that 5G signals weakened immune systems or directly caused the virus gained significant traction, leading to real-world consequences such as vandalism of telecommunications infrastructure in several countries.

Algorithms are also manipulated to polarize societies during political events. For instance, disinformation campaigns during elections often exploit trending keywords to amplify divisive content, ensuring their narratives dominate public discourse. The use of targeted advertisements and micro-targeting further deepens this manipulation by tailoring content to specific demographic or ideological groups, increasing its persuasive impact.

To combat algorithmic manipulation, platforms need greater transparency in how their algorithms function. Measures like promoting verified content, reducing the reach of unverified or misleading posts, and enabling users to understand why certain content is shown can mitigate these risks. Additionally, educating users about the dynamics of algorithmic prioritization empowers them to critically evaluate the content they encounter, reducing the overall effectiveness of such manipulation strategies.

Manipulation via YouTube and Video Platforms

YouTube and other video-sharing platforms have emerged as critical battlegrounds in information warfare due to their visual and auditory appeal, ease of access, and global reach. Videos are particularly effective in influencing audiences by evoking strong emotional responses, making them an ideal medium for spreading propaganda, misinformation, and divisive content. The increasing sophistication of video production technologies, including AI-generated content, has further amplified their role in modern information warfare.

Targeting Public Figures: Malicious actors use deep fake videos and heavily edited clips to tarnish the reputations of public figures, spread false claims, or manipulate public perception. For instance, during the 2019 Indian general elections, a deep fake video of a political leader was circulated, misrepresenting their stance on key issues. Similarly, fabricated speeches of international leaders have been used to incite unrest or discredit governments, creating a ripple effect of mistrust and confusion among the public.

Promoting Conspiracy Theories: Video platforms are frequently used to propagate conspiracy theories that exploit mistrust in official narratives. During the COVID-19 pandemic, videos claiming that 5G technology caused the virus gained significant traction, leading to real-world consequences such as the vandalism of 5G infrastructure. These videos often combine pseudoscientific jargon with emotionally charged visuals, making them appear credible and compelling to viewers.

Exploiting Monetization Systems: Sensationalized and misleading videos often benefit from the ad-based revenue models of platforms like YouTube. Creators of such content capitalize on high viewership by using clickbait titles and thumbnails that attract attention. For example, during the Russia-Ukraine conflict, several channels monetized fabricated narratives, such as exaggerated casualty figures or false claims about military operations, to generate income while spreading disinformation.

Use of AI-Generated Content: Advanced AI tools enable the creation of highly convincing yet entirely fabricated videos at scale. These tools allow propagandists to produce content with minimal resources, blurring the lines between reality and fabrication. For instance, AI-generated videos depicting false events or synthetic personas delivering messages have been used to sway public opinion and undermine trust in authentic sources. These advancements pose significant challenges for verification and content moderation.

Algorithmic Amplification: YouTube's recommendation algorithms often prioritize engaging and sensational content, inadvertently amplifying harmful narratives. This creates a feedback loop where users are continuously exposed to similar misinformation, deepening their biases and reinforcing echo chambers. For instance, individuals searching for vaccine-related information might be directed to anti-vaccine propaganda due to algorithmic preferences for high-engagement content.

To combat the manipulation of video platforms, several strategies must be employed:

Improved Content Moderation: Platforms need to invest in advanced detection systems to identify and remove misleading or harmful videos swiftly. AI-driven tools can analyze metadata, visual cues, and audio patterns to flag suspicious content.

Transparency in Algorithms: Video platforms must ensure transparency in how their recommendation algorithms function and take proactive measures to prevent the amplification of harmful content.

Collaboration with Fact-Checkers: Fact-checking organizations should work closely with video platforms to verify viral content and provide context through disclaimers or corrections.

Digital Literacy Campaigns: Educating users about the risks of misinformation and how to critically evaluate video content is essential to reducing the impact of manipulated narratives.

Messaging Apps as Disinformation Hubs

Encrypted messaging platforms, such as WhatsApp, Telegram, and Signal, have emerged as significant vectors for the dissemination of disinformation. These platforms, designed to prioritize user privacy, have become prime tools for malicious actors to spread false narratives, manipulate opinions, and incite social divisions. The private and often encrypted nature of these apps makes it difficult to monitor or regulate the spread of harmful content, presenting unique challenges in the fight against information warfare.

Forwarded Misinformation: One of the most effective ways disinformation spreads on messaging apps is through the forwarding feature, which enables users to pass along messages to large groups or individual contacts rapidly. During the COVID-19 pandemic, WhatsApp became a hotbed for misinformation, with widely forwarded messages promoting fake remedies, conspiracy theories, and exaggerated fears about vaccine safety. These messages often included phrases like "forwarded as received," lending a veneer of credibility while absolving the sender of responsibility. Such unchecked forwarding allows harmful narratives to reach millions within hours, leaving little time for fact-checking or counteraction.

Closed Groups and Channels: Private groups and channels on apps like Telegram are often breeding grounds for targeted disinformation campaigns. These groups cater to specific audiences, such as ideological communities or regional populations, making the misinformation highly tailored and impactful. For example, during the 2019 Indian general elections, WhatsApp groups were extensively used to spread divisive narratives, including fake news about political candidates and communal tensions. The closed nature of these groups allows disinformation to propagate without scrutiny, making it challenging for authorities to intervene.

Localized Campaigns: Messaging apps are increasingly used to execute localized disinformation campaigns in regional languages. This tactic is particularly effective in countries with diverse linguistic and cultural demographics. For instance, in multilingual nations like India, false information tailored to local dialects and cultural sensitivities has been used to incite violence or sway voter opinions during elections. These localized campaigns exploit the trust that people place in messages received in their native language, amplifying their reach and impact.

Anonymity and Encryption Challenges: The end-to-end encryption offered by platforms like WhatsApp and Signal ensures user privacy but also shields malicious actors from detection. This encryption makes it nearly impossible to trace the origins of disinformation or hold perpetrators accountable. While these features are vital for protecting legitimate communication, they also complicate efforts to curb the misuse of these platforms for nefarious purposes.

Addressing Disinformation on Messaging Apps

Combatting the misuse of messaging platforms requires a multifaceted approach combining technological, regulatory, and educational measures:

Fact-Checking Integrations: Messaging apps should integrate fact-checking features directly into their platforms, allowing users to verify the authenticity of forwarded messages quickly. For instance, WhatsApp has introduced measures to limit the number of times a message can be forwarded and partnered with fact-checking organizations to debunk viral misinformation.

Localized Moderation Efforts: Platforms must invest in moderation systems tailored to regional languages and cultural contexts. By deploying AI tools that understand local dialects and idiomatic expressions, companies can identify and mitigate the spread of region-specific disinformation.

User Reporting Mechanisms: Strengthening reporting tools can empower users to flag suspicious messages or groups. Platforms should ensure that reported content is reviewed promptly and, if necessary, acted upon to prevent further dissemination.

Public Awareness Campaigns: Educating users about the risks of misinformation on messaging apps is critical. Awareness initiatives should focus on teaching individuals how to identify false information, verify sources, and exercise caution before forwarding messages.

Regulatory Oversight: Governments must balance privacy concerns with the need for accountability. Policies that mandate transparency in platform operations, such as requiring platforms to identify viral content origins without compromising encryption, could provide a middle ground.

Partnerships with Civil Society: Collaborating with NGOs and advocacy groups can help amplify efforts to counter disinformation, particularly in vulnerable communities where messaging apps are the primary source of information.

Messaging apps represent a unique and growing challenge in the landscape of information warfare. While their encryption and private communication features are vital for legitimate use, they also facilitate the rapid spread of harmful narratives. Addressing these issues requires innovative solutions, proactive platform policies, and informed user behavior to preserve the integrity of information in these digital spaces.

Deepfake Technology in Disinformation Campaigns

Deep fakes represent one of the most transformative yet contentious advancements in artificial intelligence, fundamentally altering how media is created, shared, and interpreted. Leveraging Generative Adversarial Networks (GANs), deep fakes fabricate hyper-realistic yet entirely synthetic videos, audio, and images. While these advancements unlock unprecedented creative potential, they also introduce severe risks in the form of deception, disinformation, and societal manipulation. This chapter provides a detailed exploration of how deep fakes function, their application in political and propaganda domains, global and Indian case studies, and the tools and strategies for their detection and mitigation.

Deepfake technology has emerged as a powerful tool in the arsenal of information warfare, enabling malicious actors to create hyper-realistic, AI-generated videos that manipulate public perception. These AI-generated deepfake videos are increasingly being used to distort reality, spread misinformation, and influence political, social, and economic outcomes. By leveraging deep learning algorithms, deepfake creators can fabricate videos of public figures appearing to say or do things they never actually did, making it increasingly difficult for the average viewer to discern fact from fiction.

How AI-Generated Deepfake Videos Are Used to Manipulate Public Perception

Deepfake technology is often used to manipulate political discourse, sow confusion, and erode trust in credible institutions. Political adversaries deploy deepfakes to spread misleading narratives, impersonate leaders, or generate fabricated scandals. One of the most concerning aspects of deepfakes is their ability to create entirely fabricated speeches or actions by politicians, celebrities, and other influential figures, which can be used to incite unrest, provoke backlash, or alter public opinion. These synthetic media tools are also widely used for character assassination, where manipulated videos falsely depict individuals engaging in illegal or unethical activities. The viral nature of deepfakes ensures that misinformation spreads rapidly before the truth can catch up, significantly damaging reputations and trust.

Case Studies of Deepfake Influence on Elections and Global Politics

The impact of deepfake technology on elections has been evident in multiple instances around the world. During the 2020 U.S. presidential election, deepfake videos surfaced, showing manipulated footage of candidates making controversial statements. Although these videos were later debunked, they had already spread widely across social media, leading to increased polarization and confusion among voters. Another instance occurred in Myanmar, where deepfake content was used to spread disinformation during the country's political unrest, exacerbating ethnic tensions and justifying military crackdowns. In India, during state and general elections, deepfake technology has been weaponized to create fake speeches of political leaders endorsing rival parties or making inflammatory remarks, leading to heightened communal tensions.

Beyond elections, deepfakes have been employed in global politics as part of broader disinformation campaigns. Russia has been accused of using AI-generated videos to spread false narratives about Ukraine in the ongoing Russia-Ukraine conflict. Similarly, in the Middle East, deepfake videos have been circulated to create fake statements by diplomats and military officials, influencing negotiations and diplomatic relations.

Countermeasures for Deepfake Detection and Prevention

Detecting and mitigating the impact of deepfake technology is a significant challenge for governments, tech companies, and cybersecurity experts. Several countermeasures are being developed and deployed to combat the spread of deepfake misinformation. AI-powered detection tools, such as deepfake forensic analysis, are being integrated into social media platforms to identify inconsistencies in videos and flag suspicious content. Advanced deepfake detection algorithms analyze subtle inconsistencies in facial expressions, lighting, and audio synchronization to differentiate AI-generated content from authentic videos.

Fact-checking organizations and media houses play a crucial role in debunking deepfake misinformation by conducting rigorous verification before amplifying news stories. Governments are also introducing stricter regulations and policies to penalize the malicious use of deepfake technology. Several countries, including India, the U.S., and the EU, have begun drafting laws to criminalize the creation and distribution of deepfake content intended to mislead or harm individuals.

Public awareness and media literacy programs are essential to help individuals critically evaluate the content they consume. Educating the public about the risks associated with deepfake technology and providing them with the tools to identify manipulated media can help build societal resilience against digital deception. Collaboration between governments, tech companies, and academia is crucial in developing and implementing robust defense mechanisms against the growing threat of AI-generated misinformation.

As deepfake technology becomes more sophisticated and accessible, the risks associated with disinformation campaigns will only escalate. Proactive measures, technological advancements, and global cooperation are necessary to safeguard information integrity in the digital era. The battle against deepfake-driven information warfare is ongoing, requiring continuous innovation and vigilance to protect democratic institutions and public trust.

Cyber Troops and State-Sponsored Online Manipulation

The increasing digitization of global communications has led to the rise of cyber troops—state-sponsored actors who engage in online manipulation to influence political discourse, disrupt adversaries, and control public perception. Governments have recognized the power of digital platforms in shaping narratives and have deployed troll armies, bot farms, and coordinated disinformation campaigns to advance their strategic interests. These efforts are often aimed at sowing discord, amplifying propaganda, and suppressing dissent while maintaining plausible deniability.

Governments Using Troll Armies and Bot Farms for Digital Propaganda

Many nations have established cyber troops to execute large-scale influence operations. These state-backed actors operate through coordinated social media accounts, online forums, and messaging platforms to push government-approved narratives, attack opposition voices, and manipulate search engine results. Troll armies—human-operated social media accounts that engage in spreading state propaganda—are frequently used to discredit journalists, academics, and activists who challenge government policies. These trolls flood comment sections, harass dissidents, and amplify misleading information to distort reality.

Bot farms, on the other hand, use automated accounts to artificially boost engagement metrics, making specific content appear more popular than it is. These bots can generate thousands of likes, shares, and retweets within minutes, creating an illusion of widespread support for a particular ideology or policy. For example, during the Hong Kong protests, Chinese state-sponsored bots flooded Twitter with anti-protester propaganda, attempting to discredit the pro-democracy movement and shift public perception in favor of the Chinese government.

Examples from China, Russia, and India's Adversaries

China has been one of the most prolific users of cyber troops for online manipulation. The Chinese Communist Party (CCP) employs the "50 Cent Army," a vast network of paid internet commentators who promote pro-government views and suppress dissent. These operatives are deployed across Chinese and international platforms to counter negative narratives about China, especially regarding issues like human rights abuses in Xinjiang, Hong Kong protests, and Taiwan's sovereignty. China has also used fake accounts to manipulate discourse on global crises such as COVID-19, spreading misinformation about the virus's origins and the effectiveness of Western vaccines.

Russia's cyber warfare operations are among the most sophisticated in the world. The Russian government, through agencies like the Internet Research Agency (IRA), has conducted influence campaigns targeting elections in the United States, European Union, and neighboring countries. During the 2016 U.S. presidential election, Russian bots and trolls flooded social media with divisive content, pushing false narratives about candidates and exacerbating political polarization. In Ukraine, Russian cyber troops have waged an ongoing information war by spreading fake news about the conflict, portraying Ukraine's government as corrupt, and fabricating stories to justify military aggression.

India has also faced cyber warfare threats from adversarial nations such as Pakistan and China. State-sponsored bot networks have been used to manipulate narratives about Kashmir, Indo-Pak relations, and border conflicts. Fake social media accounts originating from Pakistan have spread propaganda designed to incite communal tensions and destabilize India's internal security. During periods of heightened tension, these accounts amplify fake news, creating confusion and distrust among the population. Similarly, China has been accused of using cyber troops to spread misinformation about India's economic policies and border disputes, attempting to weaken India's strategic position on the global stage.

The Role of Artificial Intelligence in Automated Disinformation Warfare

Artificial intelligence has significantly enhanced the capabilities of cyber troops, making online manipulation more efficient and scalable. AI-powered bots can generate realistic human-like interactions, responding to trending topics in real-time and adapting their messaging based on audience sentiment. These bots use machine learning algorithms to analyze social media behavior, identify key influencers, and target specific demographics with tailored propaganda.

AI-driven deepfake technology further complicates the information warfare landscape. State actors can now produce highly realistic video and audio clips of political figures, fabricating statements and actions that never occurred. These deepfake materials are then distributed through cyber troop networks to create confusion and undermine trust in public institutions. For example, deepfake videos of world leaders making inflammatory remarks have been used to manipulate diplomatic relations and incite public outrage.

To counter AI-driven disinformation, governments and technology companies are developing advanced detection tools capable of identifying coordinated bot activity, fake profiles, and AI-generated media. Social media platforms are implementing stricter verification processes, while cybersecurity agencies are investing in AI-powered defense mechanisms to detect and neutralize cyber troop operations. However, the rapid evolution of AI technology means that disinformation tactics will continue to adapt, requiring constant vigilance and innovation to safeguard information integrity in the digital age.

Cyber troops and AI-driven disinformation campaigns represent one of the most pressing challenges in modern information warfare. As governments increasingly weaponize digital platforms to advance their geopolitical agendas, the global community must prioritize transparency, regulation, and technological countermeasures to mitigate the threats posed by state-sponsored online manipulation.

Influencer-Based Disinformation and Covert Influence Operations

Social media influencers have become a critical tool in modern disinformation campaigns, where they are used to amplify narratives, push propaganda, and manipulate public opinion. These influencers, often unknowingly or deliberately, promote misleading content that aligns with the interests of governments, corporations, or political groups. As influencers hold substantial sway over public perception, their involvement in disinformation campaigns raises significant concerns regarding media ethics and accountability.

Social Media Influencers Being Used as Covert Propaganda Tools

Governments and interest groups strategically collaborate with influencers to push specific agendas, often under the guise of organic content creation. These influencers may receive financial incentives, exclusive access to events, or other perks in exchange for promoting politically motivated messages. Unlike traditional news media, influencer-driven disinformation operates in a more subtle and engaging manner, making it difficult for audiences to detect manipulation. This technique has been used in geopolitical conflicts, elections, and crisis situations to sway public sentiment and create artificial consensus on divisive issues.

The appeal of social media influencers stems from their perceived authenticity and relatability. Many influencers build strong parasocial relationships with their followers, making their endorsements appear more credible than traditional advertisements or state-sponsored media. When influencers disseminate misleading narratives, whether knowingly or unknowingly, their reach ensures that the message spreads organically, often bypassing traditional fact-checking mechanisms. This is particularly effective when governments or interest groups collaborate with influencers who already cater to a specific ideological demographic, reinforcing existing biases and increasing susceptibility to propaganda.

Additionally, state actors and interest groups have been known to create entire influencer networks to shape public discourse. These networks may include micro-influencers—individuals with smaller but highly engaged audiences—who can push coordinated narratives in a way that feels more organic and less like overt propaganda. By leveraging these influencers, disinformation campaigns gain an air of legitimacy that is difficult to combat through traditional countermeasures. This tactic has been observed in conflicts such as the Russia-Ukraine war, where influencers and bloggers have been used to spread pro-Russian or anti-Western narratives under the guise of independent journalism.

One of the most concerning aspects of influencer-driven disinformation is its potential to undermine democratic institutions. During election seasons, influencers have been used to spread misleading information about candidates, voting procedures, and political movements, often sowing distrust in the electoral process. The 2016 and 2020 U.S. elections saw coordinated disinformation efforts involving influencers and pseudo-news pages spreading false narratives about voter fraud, foreign interference, and political scandals. Similarly, in India, influencers have played a significant role in spreading divisive narratives during political campaigns, often amplifying fake news stories that serve partisan interests.

Furthermore, the use of influencers for disinformation is not limited to politics. During the COVID-19 pandemic, influencers were instrumental in spreading vaccine misinformation, promoting unverified treatments, and fueling conspiracy theories about the virus's origins. This had real-world consequences, as misinformation led to vaccine hesitancy and public health risks. The effectiveness of influencer-driven propaganda highlights the need for greater scrutiny, regulation, and media literacy to counter its influence in the digital age.

Fake Influencers and AI-Generated Personas

The emergence of AI-generated influencers has further complicated the landscape of digital propaganda. AI-driven personas, which appear as real people on social media, can produce content, interact with users, and build large followings while being entirely fabricated. These AI-generated influencers are programmed to disseminate specific narratives, engage in political discussions, and even counter opposing viewpoints in a way that appears authentic. By leveraging sophisticated deep learning models, these synthetic influencers can mimic human-like engagement patterns, respond to trending topics in real time, and tailor their content to appeal to specific demographics.

State-sponsored and interest-driven organizations have used such tactics to spread misinformation while avoiding legal accountability, as no human entity can be held responsible for the content being disseminated. These AI-generated personas often employ emotional appeal and controversy to maximize engagement, influencing public perception in ways that traditional propaganda cannot. The effectiveness of these synthetic influencers has been demonstrated in geopolitical conflicts, where fabricated personas have been deployed to spread pro-government narratives, discredit opposition groups, and create artificial social movements. For example, during the Russia-Ukraine conflict, AI-generated profiles were used to spread false narratives about battlefield developments, frame political dissidents as foreign agents, and manipulate public discourse about the legitimacy of the war.

Additionally, AI-driven influencers have found their way into corporate and commercial disinformation campaigns, where companies or lobbying groups use them to sway public opinion on environmental, political, or economic issues. In some instances, these personas have been used to attack competitors, promote misleading research, or fabricate customer testimonials. The combination of machine learning, sentiment analysis, and targeted advertising enables these artificial influencers to adapt their messaging dynamically, making them more persuasive than traditional bot-driven campaigns.

The widespread use of AI-generated influencers poses a unique regulatory challenge, as traditional measures such as content moderation, account verification, and legal accountability are difficult to enforce against non-human entities. Efforts to curb this phenomenon require advances in AI-detection tools, enhanced platform transparency, and increased collaboration between technology companies, regulators, and cybersecurity experts. Without proactive intervention, AI-generated influencers will continue to erode trust in digital communications, blur the lines between reality and fabrication, and reshape the landscape of global disinformation.

Regulatory Challenges in Tracking and Controlling Paid Propaganda

Regulating influencer-based disinformation is challenging due to the decentralized nature of social media platforms. Many influencers operate outside traditional journalism ethics, and their content is not subject to the same fact-checking and editorial standards as news organizations. Additionally, financial transactions between governments, organizations, and influencers often occur through indirect channels, making it difficult to track payments and sponsorship deals. Efforts to impose stricter transparency requirements for sponsored content, mandatory disclaimers, and AI-driven monitoring tools are being explored as countermeasures. However, without global regulatory cooperation, influencer-driven propaganda will remain a significant threat in digital information warfare.

To combat this growing issue, increased public awareness, platform accountability, and regulatory interventions are necessary. Governments and social media platforms must work together to enforce transparency in influencer collaborations and develop detection mechanisms for AI-generated personas. Strengthening digital literacy programs will also play a crucial role in helping users identify and critically assess content promoted by influencers, ensuring a more informed and resilient society against covert influence operations.

The Role of Dark Web and Anonymous Channels in Misinformation

The dark web and encrypted platforms serve as critical enablers of misinformation, providing anonymity and protection for individuals and organizations that engage in disinformation campaigns. These platforms facilitate the global spread of fake news, extremist propaganda, and politically motivated falsehoods, often making it difficult for intelligence agencies and regulators to track the sources and mitigate the damage. The dark web is particularly notorious for hosting marketplaces where fabricated news articles, fake social media accounts, and disinformation services are bought and sold, fueling large-scale information warfare campaigns.

How Encrypted and Dark Web Platforms Facilitate Global Disinformation

Encrypted messaging services and dark web forums allow disinformation operatives to collaborate, share misinformation tactics, and disseminate propaganda without the risk of exposure. These platforms provide an ideal ecosystem for cybercriminals, rogue states, and extremist groups to coordinate attacks on political opponents, fabricate conspiracy theories, and launch social engineering campaigns. Unlike traditional social media platforms that implement moderation policies, the dark web operates outside conventional regulatory frameworks, making it nearly impossible to take down harmful content once it is disseminated. Encrypted messaging services such as Telegram and Signal have been used to spread fake news and orchestrate real-world disruptions by enabling anonymous coordination among malicious actors.

Anonymous Groups Spreading Radical Ideologies and Fabricated News

The dark web has become a breeding ground for extremist narratives, allowing anonymous groups to organize disinformation campaigns that incite violence, political instability, and ethnic conflicts. Radical organizations use these platforms to recruit members, spread extremist propaganda, and discredit legitimate news sources. Additionally, conspiracy theories thrive in these spaces, as misinformation spreads unchecked, gaining credibility among isolated online communities. Political and ideological extremist groups manipulate discussions, leveraging anonymity to target specific demographics with misleading content designed to polarize society and disrupt democratic institutions.

Countermeasures for Intelligence Agencies in Tracking and Mitigating Risks

Intelligence agencies and cybersecurity experts are continuously developing new strategies to combat the spread of misinformation on the dark web and encrypted platforms. AI-driven content monitoring tools are being deployed to detect patterns of misinformation and trace the digital footprint of bad actors. Law enforcement agencies collaborate with international cyber units to dismantle disinformation networks and intercept encrypted communications linked to propaganda campaigns. Governments are also working towards enforcing stricter regulations on encrypted services, requiring platforms to cooperate in identifying and removing misinformation threats.

Public education and awareness campaigns play a crucial role in mitigating the risks posed by dark web misinformation. Encouraging digital literacy and critical thinking helps individuals recognize unreliable sources and resist manipulation. Furthermore, advanced AI-based tracking systems are being integrated into intelligence operations to counteract deep-rooted disinformation efforts. The challenge, however, remains in balancing national security concerns with online privacy rights, as heavy-handed regulation could lead to concerns regarding censorship and surveillance.

Psychological Warfare through Digital Platforms

In the digital age, psychological warfare has evolved into an intricate strategy that leverages online platforms to manipulate emotions, beliefs, and behaviors. Governments, corporations, and interest groups use digital media to exploit psychological vulnerabilities, spreading misinformation and propaganda to influence public opinion, destabilize adversaries, and achieve strategic objectives. Unlike conventional military tactics, psychological warfare in the digital realm does not rely on physical confrontation but instead on the ability to control narratives, instill doubt, and create widespread confusion.

How Fear, Uncertainty, and Doubt (FUD) Are Weaponized

One of the most effective tools in psychological warfare is the strategic deployment of fear, uncertainty, and doubt (FUD). By amplifying real or fabricated threats, disinformation campaigns can create panic, erode trust in institutions, and manipulate public perception. Fear-based messaging is often used to target specific demographics, leveraging their anxieties about security, economic stability, or public health.

For example, during the COVID-19 pandemic, misinformation campaigns exploited public fear by spreading conspiracy theories about vaccine safety, government overreach, and false remedies. These narratives not only fueled vaccine hesitancy but also deepened political and ideological divisions within societies. Similarly, cyber adversaries have used FUD tactics to discredit political opponents, creating an atmosphere of distrust that weakens democratic processes.

Political campaigns frequently use uncertainty to influence voter behavior. Disinformation campaigns introduce conflicting narratives about candidates, policies, and election procedures, making it difficult for the electorate to discern fact from fiction. During elections in the United States, Russia, and India, foreign and domestic actors have deployed misinformation strategies to create confusion about voting mechanisms, ultimately discouraging voter participation or skewing public perception in favor of specific candidates.

Doubt is another powerful psychological tool in digital warfare. By seeding doubt about the legitimacy of governments, law enforcement agencies, and media institutions, adversaries can erode public confidence in democratic systems. The spread of fake news about election fraud, judicial corruption, or media bias is a prime example of how doubt is used to weaken democratic structures and create societal discord.

Cognitive Biases Exploited in Digital Disinformation Campaigns

Psychological warfare capitalizes on inherent cognitive biases to make disinformation more persuasive and effective. Confirmation bias, the tendency for individuals to seek out information that aligns with their existing beliefs, plays a crucial role in the spread of propaganda. Disinformation campaigns exploit this bias by targeting specific groups with tailored messaging that reinforces their ideological stance, making it more difficult for them to accept alternative viewpoints.

Availability bias is another cognitive vulnerability leveraged in digital warfare. People tend to judge the likelihood of events based on readily available information. Disinformation campaigns flood social media with sensationalized or emotionally charged content to dominate the information landscape, ensuring that their narrative becomes the most accessible and believable.

The bandwagon effect, where individuals conform to prevailing opinions, is also widely exploited. Coordinated bot networks and cyber troops artificially inflate the popularity of misleading narratives by generating massive engagement through likes, shares, and comments. This creates the illusion of widespread consensus, pressuring individuals to adopt certain viewpoints without critically assessing their validity.

Emotional manipulation is another key tactic in psychological warfare. Misinformation campaigns often rely on outrage, anger, or nostalgia to provoke strong emotional reactions, making it more likely that falsehoods will be shared and believed. Political and social movements are frequently targeted with emotionally charged content designed to radicalize opinions, deepen polarization, and foster divisions within communities.

The Impact on Elections, Social Movements, and Policy Decisions

The ability to control digital narratives through psychological warfare has profound implications for elections, social movements, and policymaking. Electoral processes are particularly vulnerable to digital disinformation, as misinformation can shape voter perceptions, suppress turnout, and delegitimize results. In recent elections across the world, psychological warfare tactics have been used to polarize electorates, manipulate public discourse, and sway voter sentiment in favor of specific candidates or parties.

Social movements have also been significantly affected by psychological warfare through digital platforms. Governments and adversaries use misinformation to discredit activist groups, disrupt organizing efforts, and sow internal divisions among movements advocating for political, social, or economic change. For example, during global protests such as the Black Lives Matter movement and Hong Kong's pro-democracy demonstrations, disinformation campaigns sought to delegitimize protestors, create internal rifts, and shift public opinion against them.

Policy decisions are increasingly shaped by digital psychological warfare, as governments and policymakers respond to online narratives and public pressure. Misinformation campaigns influence legislative priorities, shape diplomatic relations, and alter national security strategies. Governments and corporate entities have been known to manipulate online discourse to justify controversial policies, such as increased surveillance measures, censorship laws, or military interventions, often using psychological manipulation to gain public approval.

In response to these threats, governments, tech companies, and civil society organizations must implement comprehensive strategies to counter psychological warfare in the digital space. Strengthening digital literacy, promoting fact-checking initiatives, and enhancing regulatory oversight are crucial steps in mitigating the impact of disinformation campaigns. Artificial intelligence and machine learning tools must be leveraged to detect and neutralize coordinated disinformation efforts before they can influence public discourse.

Psychological warfare through digital platforms represents one of the most insidious threats to modern society. As the tools of digital manipulation become more sophisticated, safeguarding the integrity of information and ensuring the resilience of democratic institutions must be a top priority. The battle against disinformation is not just a technological challenge but a societal one, requiring collective action to preserve truth, trust, and stability in the digital age.

The Future of AI-Driven Disinformation and Countermeasures

As artificial intelligence continues to advance, its applications in disinformation campaigns are becoming more sophisticated, posing significant challenges to information integrity and digital security. AI-driven disinformation tools are evolving rapidly, enabling malicious actors to create hyper-realistic fake content, automate large-scale influence campaigns, and manipulate digital ecosystems with unprecedented precision. The increasing accessibility of AI-powered tools means that disinformation campaigns are no longer limited to state-sponsored actors but can now be orchestrated by private entities, political groups, and individuals.

Emerging Trends in AI-Powered Misinformation Tools

One of the most concerning developments in AI-driven disinformation is the rise of deepfake technology, which allows for the creation of highly realistic synthetic videos, audio recordings, and images. AI-generated deepfakes can be used to fabricate statements from political figures, impersonate individuals for fraudulent activities, and create false narratives to manipulate public opinion. The deployment of AI-powered chatbots, which can generate human-like responses and engage in political discourse, further complicates efforts to detect and counter misinformation.

AI is also being used to generate hyper-personalized disinformation. Machine learning algorithms analyze vast amounts of user data to create tailored propaganda designed to influence specific demographics. By leveraging behavioral insights, AI can craft messages that appeal to individual biases, making disinformation more persuasive and harder to recognize. Additionally, AI-driven sentiment analysis tools enable disinformation campaigns to adapt their strategies in real-time, amplifying content that resonates with target audiences while suppressing counter-narratives.

Another emerging trend is the use of AI to manipulate search engine results and social media algorithms. By generating vast amounts of misleading content, disinformation campaigns can flood digital spaces with fabricated stories, making it difficult for users to find accurate information. AI-powered SEO manipulation ensures that false narratives gain traction, ranking higher in search engine results and appearing more frequently in user feeds.

Ethical Concerns and Regulatory Measures Against AI-Driven Propaganda

The rapid proliferation of AI-driven disinformation raises significant ethical concerns regarding truth, trust, and accountability. The ability to generate highly realistic but entirely fabricated content undermines public trust in digital media, erodes confidence in democratic institutions, and makes it increasingly difficult to distinguish between authentic and manipulated information. The ethical dilemma extends to technology companies, which must balance innovation with the responsibility to prevent the misuse of AI for malicious purposes.

Regulatory measures are being developed to address these challenges, with governments and international organizations exploring policies to mitigate the risks associated with AI-driven propaganda. Some countries have introduced laws criminalizing the use of deepfake technology for malicious intent, while others are considering transparency requirements for AI-generated content. Social media platforms are also implementing stricter content moderation policies, requiring users to disclose AI-generated media and enhancing detection systems to flag manipulated content.

The ethical implications of AI-driven disinformation also extend to journalism and media ethics. News organizations must adapt to the evolving landscape by investing in AI detection tools, strengthening editorial standards, and prioritizing investigative journalism to debunk false narratives. Media literacy programs are essential to equip the public with the skills needed to critically evaluate digital content and recognize AI-generated disinformation.

The Role of Cybersecurity and AI-Powered Detection Systems

As AI-driven disinformation threats escalate, cybersecurity and AI-powered detection systems are playing a crucial role in combating digital deception. Cybersecurity experts are developing machine learning models that can identify deepfake videos, detect coordinated bot activity, and analyze suspicious content patterns. AI-driven anomaly detection systems are being integrated into social media platforms to flag inauthentic behavior and prevent the spread of manipulated content.

Governments and technology companies are investing in AI-powered defense mechanisms to counteract disinformation campaigns. These include blockchain-based verification systems to authenticate digital content, watermarking techniques to distinguish real media from AI-generated fabrications, and automated fact-checking tools that cross-reference claims with verified sources. Cybersecurity agencies are also collaborating with AI researchers to improve real-time monitoring capabilities, enabling faster response times to emerging disinformation threats.

International cooperation is essential in addressing the global challenge of AI-driven disinformation. Collaborative efforts between governments, tech companies, and research institutions can lead to the development of standardized frameworks for AI regulation, ensuring that ethical considerations are integrated into technological advancements. AI-driven disinformation poses a persistent threat to information integrity, but with proactive countermeasures, transparency, and technological innovation, societies can build resilience against digital manipulation.

The future of AI-driven disinformation will continue to evolve, necessitating continuous adaptation of countermeasures and regulatory policies. While artificial intelligence holds immense potential for positive applications, its misuse in disinformation campaigns underscores the importance of ethical AI development, public awareness, and global coordination in preserving the integrity of digital information ecosystems.

The Global Information Battlefield

CHAPTER V

China's Information Warfare Doctrine

China's information warfare doctrine is an intricate and multi-layered strategy that integrates cyber capabilities, psychological operations, media influence, and legal maneuvers to achieve its geopolitical objectives. Unlike traditional warfare, where physical force determines victory, China prioritizes asymmetric tactics, perception control, and cognitive dominance to weaken adversaries without direct confrontation. This doctrine reflects the increasing reliance on non-kinetic warfare, where disinformation, cyber offensives, and psychological operations (PSYOPS) play a crucial role in shaping global conflicts.

The foundation of this strategy is deeply embedded in the People's Liberation Army (PLA) and its Three Warfares Strategy, which comprises public opinion warfare, psychological warfare, and legal warfare as its three primary pillars. These elements work cohesively to influence both domestic and international narratives, ensuring that China's strategic goals are advanced while its actions remain veiled behind layers of propaganda and legal justifications.

Public opinion warfare focuses on controlling the narrative through state-run media, diplomatic rhetoric, and disinformation campaigns that project China's strategic interests while discrediting opponents. This extends beyond traditional media into the digital realm, where AI-powered content amplification, bot-driven engagement, and social media manipulation ensure that China's messaging reaches and influences targeted audiences across the world. China has mastered the art of perception management, ensuring that its actions appear justified while simultaneously discrediting adversarial positions.

Psychological warfare is another key pillar, aimed at undermining enemy morale, exploiting social divisions, and influencing decision-making through misinformation and coercion. China actively employs deepfake technology, false narratives, and psychological coercion to manipulate how adversaries perceive events. A notable example was China's use of fabricated videos and AI-generated propaganda during conflicts such as the 2020 Galwan Valley standoff with India, where social media platforms were flooded with manipulated content aimed at confusing and demoralizing

Indian forces and civilians alike.

The third component, legal warfare (lawfare), involves using international legal frameworks to advance China's territorial and economic interests while weakening the legal standing of its rivals. Beijing frequently deploys lawfare tactics in disputes over the South China Sea, border conflicts, and trade negotiations, often positioning itself as a victim while aggressively pursuing its geopolitical objectives. Through strategic treaty interpretations, diplomatic lobbying, and leveraging international institutions, China has been able to shape global policies in its favor, ensuring that its adversaries face legal and diplomatic roadblocks when countering its expansionist moves.

By seamlessly integrating these three pillars, China's information warfare doctrine represents a comprehensive and evolving strategy that blends cyber warfare, cognitive manipulation, and legal instruments to project influence and maintain dominance in the global information landscape. As this doctrine continues to expand, adversaries must develop robust countermeasures, enhanced cyber defenses, and strategic alliances to counteract the growing reach of China's non-kinetic warfare operations.

People's Liberation Army (PLA) and Its Three Warfares Strategy

At the core of China's information warfare doctrine is the Three Warfares (San Zhan) Strategy, formulated by the People's Liberation Army (PLA) in 2003. This strategy represents a comprehensive approach to non-kinetic warfare, allowing China to influence global narratives, shape public perception, and achieve strategic dominance without engaging in direct military confrontation. By leveraging public opinion warfare, psychological warfare, and legal warfare, China seeks to gain long-term strategic advantages over its adversaries through control of information, perceptions, and legal interpretations.

Public Opinion Warfare

Public opinion warfare is a fundamental pillar of China's information strategy, focused on shaping domestic and international narratives to align with Beijing's objectives. The PLA and Chinese Communist Party (CCP) tightly control state-run media, diplomatic messaging, and online discourse to promote a pro-China worldview while undermining opposing perspectives.

China's state-controlled media outlets, including Xinhua, CGTN, Global Times, and CCTV, are instrumental in amplifying pro-China narratives worldwide. These media platforms produce strategic messaging that highlights China's achievements, downplays domestic issues, and aggressively counters narratives critical of Beijing. By systematically influencing global think tanks, academic institutions, and foreign policymakers, China ensures that its strategic interests are presented favorably.

Beyond traditional media, China has embraced digital propaganda through AI-driven content amplification, algorithmic manipulation, and social media influence campaigns. The CCP employs bot networks, content farms, and coordinated troll operations to shape online discourse, ensuring that pro-China content is prioritized and widely shared, while suppressing or discrediting critical viewpoints. This was evident during the Hong Kong protests (2019-2020), where Chinese-backed social media campaigns sought to delegitimize pro-democracy activists and frame the movement as "foreign interference."

China has also established strategic partnerships with international media outlets and content platforms to soften its global image and influence foreign reporting. Through media acquisitions, financial investments, and diplomatic pressure, China has been able to insert pro-China narratives into foreign news coverage, ensuring that global discussions align with its strategic interests.

Psychological Warfare

Psychological warfare is aimed at undermining the morale of adversaries, fostering internal discord, and exploiting cognitive biases to weaken opposition forces from within. The PLA has developed highly sophisticated disinformation and psychological manipulation techniques, utilizing AI-generated misinformation, deepfake technology, and fear-based narratives to achieve its objectives.

One prominent example of psychological warfare was seen during the 2020 Galwan Valley conflict between China and India, where fabricated videos, manipulated satellite imagery, and social media disinformation were widely circulated to intimidate Indian forces and create confusion among policymakers. Chinese state-backed operatives spread false narratives about casualty figures, territorial gains, and India's military readiness, aiming to lower public confidence in the Indian government's handling of the crisis.

In addition to military conflicts, China employs psychological coercion against political dissidents, journalists, and foreign officials. Reports have surfaced of Chinese authorities engaging in doxxing campaigns, cyber harassment, and digital blackmail to pressure critics into silence. High-profile cases include coordinated attacks against pro-Taiwanese independence activists and Uyghur human rights organizations, where intimidation tactics, smear campaigns, and false accusations were systematically deployed to discredit opposition groups.

Psychological operations also extend to economic and diplomatic coercion, where China uses trade restrictions, economic boycotts, and diplomatic isolation to pressure nations into compliance with its policies. Countries that criticize China's policies on Tibet, Hong Kong, Taiwan, or the South China Sea often find themselves economically penalized or diplomatically marginalized.

Legal Warfare (Lawfare)

Legal warfare, or lawfare, is China's use of international law, regulatory frameworks, and legal loopholes to advance its territorial claims and economic interests while undermining its adversaries. This strategy allows China to exploit legal ambiguities and international institutions to justify its actions and delay or weaken countermeasures from rival states.

One of the most well-documented examples of lawfare is China's approach to the South China Sea dispute, where Beijing has used historical claims, selective treaty interpretations, and strategic legal maneuvering to justify its territorial expansion. Despite a 2016 ruling by the Permanent Court of Arbitration rejecting China's claims, Beijing has continued to assert sovereignty over vast areas of the South China Sea by manipulating legal narratives, establishing artificial islands, and challenging international maritime laws.

China also employs lawfare in trade disputes, cybersecurity regulations, and diplomatic negotiations. By strategically delaying legal proceedings, launching counterclaims, and exploiting international legal gaps, Beijing ensures that it maintains legal and regulatory leverage in economic conflicts. For instance, China has repeatedly used trade sanctions and legal retaliations against countries that restrict Chinese technology companies like Huawei and ZTE, portraying itself as a victim of unfair trade policies.

Furthermore, China actively influences international regulatory bodies and legal organizations to shape global norms in its favor. Through its participation in the United Nations, World Trade Organization (WTO), and International Telecommunication Union (ITU), China has worked to rewrite standards on cybersecurity, digital governance, and trade regulations, ensuring that its interests are institutionally embedded in global policy frameworks.

China's Cyber Attacks and Influence Operations Against India

China's cyber warfare capabilities have become a significant strategic challenge for India, with Beijing leveraging cyber espionage, influence operations, and advanced hacking campaigns to target India's national security infrastructure. Chinese state-sponsored hacking groups, often referred to as Advanced Persistent Threats (APTs), have systematically targeted Indian government agencies, military networks, critical infrastructure, financial institutions, and technology firms to steal sensitive data and disrupt essential services. The aim of these cyber operations is to weaken India's strategic positioning, gain intelligence superiority, and expand China's geopolitical influence.

Major Cyber Attacks Against Indian Infrastructure

Chinese cyberattacks against India have intensified over the past decade, focusing on critical sectors such as power grids, defense establishments, communication networks, and research institutions. One of the most prominent cyber intrusions was the RedEcho cyber attack (2021), where Chinese hackers targeted India's power grid infrastructure, regional load dispatch centers, and oil & gas companies. The attack was an example of cyber-enabled economic coercion, demonstrating China's ability to cripple essential services and exert pressure on India during geopolitical tensions.

During the Doklam standoff (2017) and the Galwan Valley clashes (2020), Indian cybersecurity agencies detected a surge in cyber intrusions originating from China, particularly aimed at Indian Army networks, government email servers, and think tanks involved in national security research. These cyber intrusions focused on gathering intelligence on troop movements, military strategies, and diplomatic communications between Indian officials and allied nations.

Another critical incident involved Stone Panda (APT10), a Chinese hacking group, which was linked to cyberattacks on Indian pharmaceutical companies during the COVID-19 pandemic. The group targeted Serum Institute of India and Bharat Biotech, attempting to steal research data, vaccine formulations, and production strategies. These attacks underscored China's intent to gain a competitive edge in biotechnology and medical advancements while simultaneously disrupting India's global role in vaccine distribution.

China's Cyber-Enabled Influence Operations Against India

China's cyber-enabled influence operations against India have evolved into a sophisticated and multi-layered strategy, integrating disinformation campaigns, social media manipulation, AI-driven propaganda, and psychological warfare tactics. The goal of these operations is to exploit political, social, and ideological divisions, weaken India's national unity, and erode trust in democratic institutions.

One of the most effective tools in China's cyber influence arsenal is strategic disinformation, which involves the systematic spread of false narratives, doctored images, deepfake videos, and misleading news reports across digital platforms. Chinese state-backed actors use bot networks, troll farms, and algorithmic amplification techniques to ensure that these falsehoods reach a vast audience. This was particularly evident during the border tensions in Ladakh (2020), where Chinese-backed propaganda channels disseminated fake reports of massive Indian military casualties, falsified videos showing supposed Indian troop surrenders, and misleading news articles to shape global perceptions and demoralize Indian troops.

China has also leveraged WeChat, TikTok (before its ban in India), and other digital platforms as vehicles for influence operations. Before India banned TikTok, Chinese intelligence agencies exploited its massive user base to spread pro-China narratives, suppress critical content, and gather intelligence on Indian users. WeChat, which was widely used by Indian business and diplomatic communities, was similarly weaponized to track conversations, conduct digital espionage, and spread misinformation among policymakers and influential circles.

Another key aspect of China's influence operations is the use of AI-powered cognitive warfare. Chinese intelligence agencies have developed sophisticated AI-driven psychological profiling systems that analyze social media behavior, political affiliations, and emotional triggers to craft highly personalized disinformation campaigns. These AI-driven tactics were employed during Indian general elections, where pro-China networks worked to amplify divisive issues, inflame religious tensions, and manipulate political discourse to weaken Indian democratic processes.

China's influence operations also extend to economic and trade-related disinformation, where false narratives are spread to disrupt investor confidence in India's markets and promote dependency on Chinese supply chains. By leveraging covert financial investments in Indian digital media platforms, China has attempted to subtly control narratives surrounding India's trade policies, economic growth, and foreign relations.

Additionally, China's cyber influence strategy includes diplomatic and academic infiltration, where Chinese government-backed think tanks,

Confucius Institutes, and research collaborations with Indian universities are used as tools for ideological persuasion, intelligence gathering, and indirect narrative control. Reports indicate that Chinese-linked scholars and media professionals have been involved in shaping academic debates in Indian institutions, promoting narratives that align with Beijing's strategic interests.

The weaponization of social media algorithms is another powerful tool in China's information warfare strategy. Chinese state-sponsored actors manipulate platforms like YouTube, Twitter, and Facebook to ensure that pro-China narratives are boosted through artificial engagement metrics, while dissenting voices are shadow-banned or algorithmically suppressed. A key example of this was seen during the COVID-19 pandemic, where China actively worked to control global narratives about the virus's origins by flooding Indian and international media spaces with counter-narratives designed to deflect blame away from Beijing.

Use of Social Media Platforms for Psychological Manipulation

Social media has become one of the most powerful weapons in China's psychological warfare arsenal, enabling Beijing to shape narratives, suppress dissent, and artificially amplify pro-China sentiment. By leveraging state-controlled influencers, automated bot networks, algorithmic manipulation, and artificial intelligence (AI)-driven content dissemination, China has created a highly sophisticated ecosystem for influencing public opinion across India and beyond.

Chinese psychological operations rely on bot-driven propaganda campaigns, troll farms, and AI-enhanced disinformation techniques that create the illusion of widespread public sentiment. These tactics were particularly evident during the Ladakh border conflict, where China-backed social media networks spread fabricated reports of Indian military casualties, exaggerated battlefield setbacks, and manipulated satellite images to sow discord and demoralize Indian forces. By exploiting existing ideological and political divisions, China ensures that its narratives create internal conflicts and public distrust in Indian leadership.

China also employs AI-driven psychological profiling to understand public sentiment, political leanings, and emotional triggers. This data is then used to craft hyper-targeted disinformation campaigns that resonate with specific social groups. During Indian general elections, for example, Chinese state-sponsored actors were found using automated misinformation networks to amplify religious and caste-based divisions, inflame political tensions, and manipulate trending hashtags to shift electoral discourse in favor of China's strategic interests.

Another major component of China's social media-based psychological warfare is the exploitation of banned digital platforms like TikTok, WeChat, and UC Browser, which were previously widely used in India. Before their ban, these platforms were utilized for large-scale data collection, intelligence gathering, and social engineering. AI-driven content moderation algorithms ensured that anti-China posts were suppressed, while pro-China narratives were artificially boosted, shaping digital conversations in Beijing's favor.

Beyond India, China has deployed similar psychological manipulation tactics on a global scale, targeting Western democracies, Asian geopolitical rivals, and international institutions. Through a combination of strategic censorship, cyber harassment, narrative engineering, and diplomatic coercion, Beijing has sought to discredit activists, silence dissenting voices, and control international perception of its policies on Hong Kong, Tibet, Taiwan, and the Uyghur genocide. Reports indicate that state-backed Chinese cyber units actively target media organizations, academic researchers, and government officials who challenge China's narratives, deploying coordinated disinformation attacks and cyber harassment campaigns to intimidate critics.

To counter China's psychological warfare tactics, India has strengthened its digital forensics, AI-driven misinformation detection, and social media monitoring mechanisms. Intelligence agencies now actively track and neutralize bot networks, while Indian policymakers have pushed for stricter content regulations on social media platforms to prevent foreign manipulation of digital discourse. Additionally, public awareness campaigns on misinformation detection and cyber hygiene are being promoted to enhance digital resilience among Indian citizens.

As psychological warfare continues to evolve, China's ability to manipulate social media will remain a formidable challenge for India's national security and information integrity. The battle for narrative dominance in the digital age requires India to continuously enhance its cyber capabilities, strengthen its digital policy frameworks, and invest in advanced AI-driven countermeasures to safeguard against China's expansive psychological influence operations.

Use of Bot Networks and AI-Driven Disinformation

China's cyber influence operations extend beyond traditional propaganda techniques, utilizing AI-powered bot networks, automated troll farms, and algorithmic disinformation campaigns to infiltrate Indian social media, manipulate public discourse, and create artificial narratives. These operations are designed to exploit political, social, and economic vulnerabilities within India by spreading misinformation, polarizing debates, and influencing electoral processes.

One of the most sophisticated elements of China's cyber influence strategy is the deployment of bot-driven propaganda campaigns, where automated accounts—often controlled by artificial intelligence—are used to flood social media platforms with fabricated content, pro-China narratives, and misinformation targeted at India. These bot networks can create an illusion of grassroots movements, amplifying narratives that align with China's strategic goals while silencing dissenting voices through mass reporting and algorithmic manipulation.

During Indian general elections, China-linked bot networks were detected spreading disinformation, inflaming religious and caste-based tensions, and promoting divisive political agendas. AI-generated bot accounts operated in multiple languages, making them difficult to detect and counter. These automated accounts used deepfake videos, doctored images, and emotionally charged hashtags to manufacture social unrest, shift public focus from real issues, and indirectly influence voter behavior.

China's use of automated content farms and troll networks is another key component of its AI-driven disinformation strategy. These troll farms, operated by state-sponsored cyber units, deploy coordinated attacks against Indian policymakers, journalists, and activists who criticize Beijing's policies. By spreading false accusations, defaming individuals, and orchestrating large-scale online harassment campaigns, China aims to intimidate and silence opposition voices. These attacks have been particularly evident in India's debates on Tibet, Hong Kong, the South China Sea, and the Ladakh border conflict, where pro-China bot networks have attempted to shape digital narratives in Beijing's favor.

Furthermore, China has mastered algorithmic disinformation techniques, where its cyber operatives manipulate YouTube, Twitter, Facebook, and Indian social media platforms to boost pro-China narratives while suppressing critical content. By exploiting recommendation algorithms and engagement metrics, China ensures that propaganda content is prioritized in search results and social media feeds, while anti-China content is downranked or shadow-banned. This tactic was evident during the COVID-19 pandemic, where China actively sought to control global narratives about the virus's origins by overwhelming Indian and international media platforms with state-sponsored counter-narratives that deflected blame away from Beijing.

Another concerning aspect of AI-driven disinformation is the weaponization of deepfake technology, where Chinese cyber units have created fake videos of Indian politicians, fabricated speeches, and altered military communications to spread confusion and undermine public trust in government institutions. These deepfakes, often indistinguishable from real footage, have been deployed during critical geopolitical moments, such as border conflicts and trade negotiations, to erode India's international credibility and foster internal discord.

Cyber Espionage Targeting Indian Institutions

China's cyber espionage campaigns against Indian institutions reflect a long-term strategy aimed at gaining economic, military, and technological dominance through systematic cyber intrusions. Chinese Advanced Persistent Threat (APT) groups have been implicated in sustained cyber operations targeting Indian defense networks, government agencies, financial institutions, space research facilities, and critical infrastructure. These operations are designed to steal classified intelligence, disrupt strategic programs, and gain economic leverage over India.

One of the most damaging cyber espionage incidents was the breach of India's National Informatics Centre (NIC), where Chinese hackers gained unauthorized access to classified government documents, defense procurement records, and diplomatic communications. The compromised data provided China with valuable insights into India's national security strategies, foreign policy frameworks, and cybersecurity capabilities. Intelligence reports suggest that PLA-linked hacking groups infiltrated highly secured networks using advanced malware, spear-phishing tactics, and zero-day vulnerabilities to gain sustained access.

China's intellectual property theft and technology espionage extend beyond government institutions to Indian academic and scientific research centers. Chinese cyber operatives have systematically targeted universities, AI research labs, and semiconductor manufacturing firms to steal research on space technology, quantum computing, biotech advancements, and artificial intelligence. Universities and think tanks involved in strategic policy analysis, cyber defense research, and advanced materials development are prime targets, as Beijing seeks to extract cutting-edge knowledge that aligns with its military and industrial ambitions.

A notorious example of China's cyber espionage activities was the RedFoxtrot campaign, where Chinese-linked APT groups targeted Indian telecommunications firms, defense contractors, and aerospace research institutions. Reports indicate that the group used social engineering tactics and advanced persistent malware to infiltrate mission-critical networks, enabling long-term surveillance and intelligence gathering. Another significant case was the breach of India's Kudankulam Nuclear Power Plant in 2019, where malware linked to Chinese hackers was detected on internal systems. While the Indian government downplayed the breach, cybersecurity experts confirmed that it was part of an espionage attempt to extract sensitive information on India's nuclear capabilities.

China's cyber activities are also deeply embedded in supply chain infiltration, where Chinese firms and digital infrastructure are used as potential backdoors for cyber espionage. Reports have indicated that Chinese manufacturers supplying telecommunication equipment, surveillance systems, and electronic components to India have embedded covert surveillance software and hidden data-exfiltration capabilities. India's concerns over Chinese tech giants like Huawei and ZTE stem from fears that their equipment could facilitate cyber espionage, leading the Indian government to impose severe restrictions on their participation in India's 5G network infrastructure.

India's Countermeasures and Cyber Defense Strategies

India has taken a multi-layered approach to counteract the persistent cyber espionage and influence operations conducted by China. Given the scale and sophistication of Chinese cyber threats, India has significantly expanded its cybersecurity infrastructure, strengthened its regulatory frameworks, and increased strategic collaboration with international allies to defend against state-sponsored cyber intrusions. These countermeasures span technological advancements, policy interventions, legislative reforms, and global partnerships, ensuring a comprehensive response to the evolving cyber threats posed by Beijing.

One of India's primary responses has been strengthening its cybersecurity institutions, particularly the National Cyber Security Coordinator (NCSC), Defence Cyber Agency (DCA), and Indian Computer Emergency Response Team (CERT-In). These agencies have been tasked with monitoring cyber threats, analyzing attack patterns, and deploying rapid-response measures against cyber intrusions targeting Indian government and military infrastructure. India has also established sector-specific cybersecurity frameworks, ensuring that critical infrastructure sectors such as energy, defense, finance, and healthcare are fortified against potential cyberattacks.

Recognizing the long-term risks of Chinese cyber espionage, India has imposed strict restrictions on Chinese digital infrastructure and technology companies. In one of its most decisive moves, India banned over 200 Chinese apps, including TikTok, WeChat, UC Browser, and Baidu, citing concerns over data security and potential intelligence-gathering activities. Furthermore, the Indian government has placed severe limitations on Chinese telecom firms like Huawei and ZTE, preventing them from participating in India's 5G rollout and other key digital infrastructure projects. These bans and restrictions have helped mitigate China's ability to access sensitive Indian user data, conduct digital surveillance, and exploit vulnerabilities in India's communication networks.

To further enhance cyber resilience, India has been investing heavily in indigenous cybersecurity technologies, AI-driven threat intelligence, and quantum-safe cryptography. The government is actively promoting local innovation in cybersecurity through initiatives such as Cyber Surakshit Bharat and Make in India, encouraging the development of secure, India-made hardware and software solutions that reduce reliance on foreign technology. AI-powered cyber defense mechanisms are now being integrated into India's cybersecurity strategies, enabling real-time threat detection, malware analysis, and predictive analytics to preempt cyberattacks before they occur.

India has also strengthened its cyber defense cooperation with global allies, forming strategic partnerships with countries such as the United States, Japan, Australia, and the European Union. As part of the Quad Cybersecurity Partnership, India is working closely with its allies to share intelligence on cyber threats, conduct joint cyber drills, and enhance cross-border cybersecurity cooperation. In addition, India has signed bilateral agreements with Israel, France, and the UK to further bolster its cyber defense capabilities and exchange expertise on countering state-sponsored cyber warfare.

On the legislative front, India has introduced new cybersecurity and data protection laws aimed at securing national digital infrastructure and protecting citizens' personal data from foreign cyber threats. The Personal

Data Protection Bill (PDPB) and the proposed National Cybersecurity Strategy outline strict regulations on data storage, cross-border data transfers, and cybersecurity compliance, ensuring that sensitive Indian data is safeguarded from unauthorized foreign access. Additionally, the Indian government has been expanding offensive cyber capabilities, allowing agencies to conduct proactive cyber operations against hostile state actors when necessary.

Recognizing the role of public awareness in cyber defense, India has also launched large-scale digital literacy and cyber hygiene campaigns to educate citizens about the risks of cyber espionage, misinformation, and phishing attacks. Initiatives such as Cyber Swachhta Kendra promote the use of secure digital practices, multi-factor authentication, and secure communication protocols to mitigate individual and corporate vulnerabilities to cyber intrusions.

As cyber warfare continues to evolve, India's ability to counter China's aggressive cyber operations will depend on its capacity to stay ahead of emerging threats, invest in cybersecurity innovation, and foster strong global alliances. By integrating advanced cybersecurity infrastructure, robust policy measures, and international cooperation, India is positioning itself to effectively defend against Chinese cyber espionage while ensuring long-term digital sovereignty and national security.

In response to China's persistent cyber espionage campaigns, India has taken several proactive steps to strengthen its cybersecurity defenses and digital sovereignty:

India has implemented a comprehensive and multi-layered cybersecurity strategy to counteract the escalating cyber threats posed by China. With China's persistent cyber intrusions, influence operations, and espionage campaigns targeting Indian military, government, critical infrastructure, and private sector organizations, India has developed a proactive approach combining technological advancements, legal frameworks, military cyber operations, and international partnerships.

CHAPTER VI

Pakistan's Information Warfare Tactics

The long-standing **Indo-Pakistani conflict** has been shaped by historical animosities, territorial disputes, and ideological differences, fueling a sustained rivalry between the two nations. Since the partition of British India in 1947, Pakistan has consistently sought to undermine India's geopolitical and military standing, particularly over the Kashmir, which has been a flashpoint for multiple wars and skirmishes. In addition to conventional military confrontations, cross-border terrorism, and diplomatic standoffs, Pakistan has increasingly relied on information warfare as a means of destabilizing India without engaging in direct armed conflict.

Pakistan has developed a sophisticated information warfare strategy aimed at influencing narratives, spreading disinformation, and destabilizing India's geopolitical position. This strategy operates through a combination of proxy propaganda networks, cyber-enabled influence campaigns, and psychological operations, creating an extensive ecosystem for digital warfare, media manipulation, and **cross-border cyber attacks**. Unlike traditional military operations, which have a visible and direct impact, information warfare operates in the digital and cognitive domains, where perceptions, beliefs, and narratives can be shaped subtly over time.

Pakistan's Inter-Services Public Relations (ISPR), the media arm of its military, plays a central role in orchestrating anti-India narratives, mobilizing digital assets, and executing psychological campaigns targeting Indian security forces and civilians. ISPR's influence extends beyond traditional media, as it actively engages in coordinated propaganda efforts on social media platforms, deepfake technology, and artificial intelligence-driven misinformation campaigns. These efforts are designed to undermine Indian national unity, erode trust in democratic institutions, and manipulate international perceptions about India's internal policies.

Given the history of hostility and proxy conflicts, Pakistan has weaponized digital spaces, cyber networks, and information platforms to project itself as a victim while portraying India as an aggressor. This has been particularly evident in the aftermath of key events such as the 2001 Indian Parliament attack, the 2008 Mumbai attacks, the 2016 Uri attack, and the 2019 Pulwama suicide bombing, all of which were followed by aggressive anti-India propaganda campaigns orchestrated by Pakistan's information warfare apparatus. By exploiting ethnic, religious, and political fault lines, Pakistan aims to weaken India from within while gaining diplomatic leverage on the global stage.

As technology advances and the digital battlefield evolves, Pakistan's information warfare tactics continue to grow in sophistication, requiring India to remain vigilant, proactive, and adaptive in countering these persistent threats. Understanding the historical and geopolitical context of Indo-Pakistani relations is essential in formulating effective countermeasures and strategic defenses against Pakistan's evolving digital aggression.

Proxy Propaganda Networks and Fake News Factories

Pakistan has systematically built an extensive proxy propaganda network, employing fake news websites, bot-controlled social media accounts, and coordinated digital influence campaigns to shape global perceptions and destabilize India's internal discourse. These networks operate through fabricated media houses, pseudo-NGOs, and paid social media influencers, creating a deceptive information ecosystem that enables Pakistan to influence international bodies, foreign policymakers, and global public opinion.

A significant example of Pakistan's information warfare tactics was revealed in 2020, when the EU DisinfoLab, an independent Brussels-based investigative organization, uncovered a massive pro-Pakistan disinformation operation. This operation, known as the Indian Chronicles, exposed a 15-year-long covert influence operation orchestrated to malign India's global reputation, manipulate international institutions, and exert diplomatic pressure on New Delhi.

Investigators found that over 750 fake media outlets, 550 domain names, and dozens of fictitious NGOs were engaged in spreading anti-India propaganda across Europe, North America, and international platforms such as the United Nations Human Rights Council (UNHRC). These sites functioned under the guise of legitimate news portals, think tanks, and humanitarian organizations, creating a facade of authenticity. Their primary focus was to fabricate reports on human rights violations in Kashmir, exaggerate religious intolerance in India, and distort narratives around Indian military operations, presenting these falsehoods as credible journalism.

What made this operation particularly effective was its ability to exploit dormant identities of deceased individuals, manipulate Western media narratives, and use European political institutions as platforms to amplify propaganda. The DisinfoLab report highlighted that several Members of the European Parliament (MEPs) were unknowingly involved in spreading disinformation, with fake NGOs presenting themselves as credible human rights organizations advocating for the Kashmiri cause. By leveraging artificial credibility and digital influence, these networks successfully manipulated policy discussions within international organizations such as the European Parliament, the United Nations, and global media platforms.

Further analysis revealed that the operation repurposed legitimate-sounding domain names, including hijacked defunct newspapers from various countries, to add legitimacy to their false narratives. The scale of the operation extended to coordinating online attacks against Indian diplomats, weaponizing social media hashtags, and using deepfake accounts to simulate popular dissent within India.

This meticulously crafted disinformation network underscores the growing sophistication of Pakistan's proxy propaganda efforts, demonstrating how state-backed influence operations can manipulate global discourse and interfere in the sovereignty of nations through digital warfare. India has since increased diplomatic engagements to expose these tactics, tightened cybersecurity measures, and leveraged AI-based counter-disinformation tools to counteract the growing threat of influence operations targeting its global standing.

Additionally, Pakistan has aggressively leveraged social media platforms such as Twitter, Facebook, YouTube, and Instagram to manufacture discontent within India. Fake news campaigns—often designed to coincide with significant political or military events—aim to polarize public opinion, incite communal tensions, and undermine faith in Indian governance. One of the most notorious instances was observed during the abrogation of Article 370 in 2019, when Pakistani social media operatives flooded digital platforms with fabricated images and videos depicting mass protests and alleged human rights violations in Jammu and Kashmir. Many of these materials were later proven to be doctored or sourced from unrelated conflicts.

Pakistan also utilizes YouTube-based propaganda channels and Telegram groups to circulate anti-India content, create false historical narratives, and push conspiracy theories. These campaigns frequently collaborate with

Chinese and Turkish-backed networks, amplifying narratives that paint India in a negative light, particularly concerning its treatment of minorities, human rights policies, and foreign relations. Fake fact-checking websites are also a tool frequently deployed by Pakistani digital operatives, where fabricated "debunking" of genuine Indian narratives is presented as fact-based reporting, further misleading global audiences.

Moreover, Pakistan has relied on AI-generated deepfake videos, synthetic voice recordings, and AI-manipulated images to create highly convincing disinformation campaigns. In 2021, intelligence reports surfaced that Pakistani agencies were using AI-generated deepfake videos impersonating Indian officials, military leaders, and diplomats to spread false narratives about India's defense policies and international relations. These tactics have been particularly effective in diplomatic forums, where such misinformation is weaponized to exert pressure on India in global negotiations.

Another concerning aspect is the financial backing that these proxy networks receive. Intelligence agencies have traced funding from Pakistan's intelligence services (ISI) to digital content creators, influencers, and media channels specifically tasked with pushing pro-Pakistan and anti-India narratives. This financial model ensures that Pakistan's information warfare remains persistent, adaptable, and scalable, making it a continuous threat to India's national security and international reputation.

The cumulative impact of these fake news factories and proxy propaganda networks has been significant, affecting international policymaking, influencing public debates, and creating long-term reputational damage for India on global platforms. Recognizing this challenge, India has ramped up efforts to counter misinformation, identify and de-platform fake accounts, and expose Pakistan-backed disinformation operations through intelligence collaborations with global allies. However, the constantly evolving nature of Pakistan's information warfare means that countermeasures must remain dynamic, technologically advanced, and strategically proactive.

ISPR's Role in Anti-India Narratives

The Inter-Services Public Relations (ISPR), the media wing of the Pakistan Army, plays a central role in Pakistan's information warfare and psychological operations (PSYOPS) against India. Unlike conventional military engagements, ISPR's focus is on controlling narratives, manipulating digital spaces, and influencing domestic and international perceptions through coordinated disinformation campaigns, propaganda dissemination, and cyber-based influence operations.

ISPR operates as a hybrid media and intelligence apparatus, directly overseeing state-controlled media networks, social media operatives, digital content creators, and cyber propaganda units to amplify Pakistan's strategic objectives. The organization functions as the nerve center for crafting and disseminating anti-India narratives, particularly in areas related to Kashmir, cross-border conflicts, and India's domestic policies. By leveraging mass media, social media algorithms, and psychological tactics, ISPR seeks to erode India's global reputation, destabilize internal cohesion, and mobilize international sentiment against New Delhi's policies.

A key element of ISPR's strategy is controlling Pakistan's domestic narrative while simultaneously projecting an anti-India stance to global audiences. This is achieved through state-backed news outlets such as PTV, Dawn News, and The Express Tribune, which serve as primary vehicles for spreading state-sanctioned disinformation. Beyond traditional media, ISPR has aggressively expanded its digital influence operations, employing AI-driven content generation, bot networks, and troll farms to dominate social media discussions, amplify pro-Pakistan narratives, and suppress dissenting voices.

One of ISPR's most effective disinformation tools is its network of state-sponsored YouTube channels, Twitter handles, and coordinated WhatsApp groups that systematically disseminate false narratives about India's military operations, human rights records, and internal affairs. ISPR-backed digital influencers, operating under pseudonyms, engage in manipulating hashtags, fabricating news stories, and creating viral misinformation campaigns aimed at fueling unrest and sowing distrust within Indian society.

ISPR's involvement in deepfake technology and AI-generated propaganda has significantly enhanced its capabilities in psychological manipulation. During the Pulwama terror attack (2019) and the abrogation of Article 370 (2019), ISPR executed large-scale misinformation campaigns, fabricating video clips, AI-generated protest visuals, and exaggerated casualty figures to stoke tensions within India and influence global opinion. Indian intelligence agencies uncovered several instances of Pakistani-controlled social media accounts impersonating Indian citizens, journalists, and activists to amplify divisive content and exploit religious and political sensitivities.

Beyond India, ISPR's influence extends into Western and Middle Eastern media landscapes, where it actively cultivates alliances with global think tanks, foreign journalists, and lobbying groups to push anti-India narratives at international forums. The organization has been instrumental in creating diplomatic pressure on India regarding Kashmir, often fabricating reports of alleged Indian military excesses and presenting them at the United Nations, the European Parliament, and human rights councils.

Additionally, ISPR has pioneered meme-based warfare and psychological operations targeted at the Indian Armed Forces. Pakistani cyber units routinely create satirical memes, propaganda videos, and morale-damaging content aimed at undermining the confidence of Indian military personnel. These psychological tactics are designed to instill doubt, lower morale, and induce panic among Indian troops deployed in conflict zones.

India has taken several countermeasures to neutralize ISPR's digital influence operations, including monitoring Pakistani misinformation networks, blocking hostile social media accounts, and exposing false narratives through diplomatic channels. Indian cybersecurity agencies have also enhanced their AI-driven detection mechanisms to track and dismantle bot-driven influence campaigns originating from ISPR-backed networks.

As Pakistan's information warfare infrastructure continues to evolve, ISPR remains at the forefront of covert digital propaganda and narrative manipulation. Countering its influence requires India to enhance cybersecurity capabilities, invest in strategic communication efforts, and engage in proactive counter-narratives to safeguard national security in the era of digital warfare.

Cross-Border Cyber Attacks and Fake Social Media Accounts

Pakistan's information warfare extends beyond propaganda into coordinated cyber-enabled attacks and large-scale social media manipulation. The objective of these operations is to compromise Indian government institutions, defense networks, financial systems, and public trust by launching cyberattacks and spreading misinformation on digital platforms. Pakistan's cyber offensive is primarily executed by state-backed hacking groups such as APT36 (Transparent Tribe), Gorgon Group, and SideCopy, which are directly or indirectly linked to Pakistan's intelligence services, particularly the Inter-Services Intelligence (ISI) and the Pakistan Army Cyber Command.

In recent years, Pakistan-based cyber operatives have launched a series of high-profile cyber intrusion attempts against Indian government agencies, strategic installations, and private enterprises. These attacks have targeted critical infrastructure, diplomatic communications, military networks, and financial institutions. Key cyberattacks include:

- **The 2019 cyberattack on Indian defense research institutions**, where hackers used spear-phishing techniques and sophisticated malware to attempt data extraction related to missile technology and classified defense projects.
- **APT36's targeting of Indian government networks**, where Pakistani hackers used remote-access trojans (RATs), spyware, and zero-day vulnerabilities to infiltrate sensitive military communications and steal intelligence reports.
- **Malware campaigns targeting Indian banking infrastructure**, with cybercriminals attempting to disrupt digital payment systems, compromise ATM networks, and exfiltrate sensitive financial data.
- **Phishing campaigns impersonating Indian military officials**, where attackers created fake defense email accounts and WhatsApp messages to trick personnel into revealing classified information.

Apart from cyberattacks, Pakistan has built an extensive network of fake social media accounts used for disinformation campaigns, inciting communal hatred, and influencing public discourse within India. Pakistani operatives, often working under the guise of Indian activists, journalists, and influencers, infiltrate Indian digital spaces to amplify anti-India narratives, hijack social movements, and create artificial outrage. Indian cybersecurity agencies have identified thousands of bot-controlled Twitter accounts, Facebook pages, and Instagram handles that actively push anti-India hashtags, conspiracy theories, and fabricated news reports.

One of the most well-documented cases of this cyber-enabled disinformation was observed in 2019, following the abrogation of Article 370 in Jammu and Kashmir. Pakistani-controlled digital operatives flooded social media with fake videos, altered images, and misinformation aimed at creating panic, instigating protests, and fueling tensions between religious and political groups. Many of these accounts were later traced back to bot networks operating from Pakistan's Rawalpindi and Lahore regions.

Pakistan's cyber-enabled psychological operations also extend to targeting India's military and intelligence personnel. Several cases have emerged where Pakistani intelligence agencies used fake social media profiles of women to entrap Indian defense personnel into leaking sensitive information. In 2020, the Honey Trap scandal revealed that Pakistani cyber operatives had created fake female identities on Facebook and Instagram to lure Indian soldiers into compromising conversations, eventually extracting classified military details. The intelligence agencies of India, including the National Technical Research Organisation (NTRO) and Defence Intelligence Agency (DIA), have since strengthened their surveillance mechanisms to prevent such breaches.

Additionally, Pakistani operatives have used deepfake technology and AI-generated content to spread fabricated messages attributed to Indian leaders, attempting to create diplomatic tensions, spread internal discord, and mislead the public. This was evident when deepfake videos of Indian military officers making false statements about India's defense readiness were circulated on social media platforms, attempting to lower morale among armed forces and create doubt within Indian political circles.

Psychological Operations Targeting Indian Armed Forces

Pakistan has consistently used psychological operations (PSYOPS) as a strategic tool to target the Indian Armed Forces, aiming to weaken their morale, create internal discord, and manipulate public perception regarding India's military capabilities. These operations are executed using a combination of disinformation campaigns, cyber infiltration, social media manipulation, and direct psychological attacks on serving personnel and their families.

A significant aspect of these psychological operations involves spreading false narratives about the Indian military's effectiveness, leadership, and internal cohesion. Pakistani intelligence-backed digital operatives systematically create and disseminate fabricated news, deepfake videos, and doctored images to push an anti-India agenda. This was prominently observed during the 2016 Uri attack, where Pakistani digital operatives circulated fake casualty figures, manipulated war footage, and misleading battlefield images to distort reality and demoralize Indian troops.

Similarly, during the Balakot airstrikes (2019), Pakistan's Inter-Services Public Relations (ISPR) and state-backed social media operatives launched an aggressive disinformation campaign claiming that multiple Indian fighter jets were shot down, a claim that was later debunked by independent global agencies. These psychological tactics were aimed at instilling doubt within the Indian military hierarchy, creating confusion in public perception, and influencing global narratives about India's airstrike efficacy.

Pakistan has also weaponized encrypted messaging platforms like WhatsApp, Telegram, and Signal to infiltrate Indian military communication channels. Intelligence reports have confirmed that Pakistani operatives have been creating fake recruitment messages, impersonating senior Indian military officials, and spreading misleading information within defense circles to gain unauthorized access to confidential data. One of the most sophisticated cyber-psychological attacks occurred in 2020, when the Honey Trap scandal revealed how Pakistani intelligence agents, disguised as women on social media, successfully extracted classified military details from unsuspecting Indian soldiers. This operation exposed the vulnerability of human-based intelligence (HUMINT) breaches through psychological manipulation.

Beyond direct military targets, Pakistan's PSYOPS also focus on eroding public confidence in India's defense capabilities. By leveraging AI-generated propaganda, troll networks, and coordinated social media narratives, Pakistan attempts to fuel public dissent, exaggerate border skirmishes, and incite communal tensions linked to India's military operations. During the abrogation of Article 370 in 2019, Pakistan orchestrated a massive digital misinformation campaign, spreading rumors of large-scale human rights violations by the Indian Army in Jammu & Kashmir, despite global agencies confirming otherwise.

Pakistan's deepfake technology and AI-powered psychological warfare capabilities have further enhanced its ability to manipulate reality and craft misleading narratives. Indian cybersecurity agencies have detected deepfake videos impersonating Indian defense officials, falsely showing them making anti-government statements, criticizing military leadership, or discussing fabricated operational failures. These highly realistic AI-generated videos are intended to foster internal dissent, create rifts between military leadership and the government, and demoralize defense personnel.

India's Countermeasures Against Psychological Warfare

Recognizing the growing threat of psychological operations, India has significantly strengthened its counter-PSYOPS mechanisms, digital security awareness programs, and intelligence-based preventive measures. The Indian Armed Forces have introduced cyber hygiene training, social media awareness workshops, and psychological resilience programs for personnel and their families to combat these threats.

Additionally, India's Defence Cyber Agency (DCA) and National Technical Research Organisation (NTRO) have implemented real-time AI-based disinformation detection systems that monitor and neutralize Pakistani PSYOPS before they gain traction. Intelligence agencies have also exposed and countered bot-driven campaigns by working with global cybersecurity organizations and social media platforms to deplatform fake accounts spreading propaganda.

Moreover, India has launched coordinated strategic communication efforts, where military and government spokespersons swiftly debunk misinformation, clarify disinformation narratives, and present factual reports to neutralize false Pakistani claims. These initiatives are crucial in strengthening national resilience against external psychological manipulation, preserving military morale, and maintaining a stable information environment.

As psychological operations continue to evolve in sophistication, India must remain proactive in countering information warfare threats, ensuring that its armed forces, intelligence agencies, and citizens are well-equipped to detect and mitigate psychological manipulation tactics used by adversarial forces.

A key aspect of Pakistan's information warfare doctrine is psychological operations (PSYOPS) targeting the Indian Armed Forces. These operations focus on undermining soldier morale, spreading distrust within the military ranks, and influencing public perception of India's defense capabilities.

One of the most infamous psychological warfare campaigns was seen during the 2016 Uri attack, where Pakistani digital operatives spread fake narratives about Indian troop movements, false casualty figures, and misinformation about internal military conflicts. Similar operations were carried out during the Balakot airstrikes (2019), when ISPR and Pakistani social media handlers created fabricated reports about Pakistan shooting down multiple Indian fighter jets, a claim that was later debunked.

Pakistan has also weaponized WhatsApp, Telegram, and other encrypted messaging platforms to infiltrate Indian military communication networks. Pakistani intelligence agencies have previously launched fake recruitment drives, impersonated military officers, and used social engineering tactics to extract sensitive data from Indian defense personnel. In 2020, the Honey Trap scandal exposed how Pakistani cyber operatives, masquerading as women on social media, lured Indian soldiers into sharing classified military information.

India's Countermeasures Against Pakistan's Information Warfare

India has developed a comprehensive counter-information warfare strategy to counteract Pakistan's persistent disinformation campaigns, cyber intrusions, and psychological operations. Recognizing the growing sophistication of Pakistan's information warfare tactics, India has implemented multi-layered security measures, combining cyber defense enhancements, intelligence-gathering advancements, counter-disinformation mechanisms, and strategic diplomatic efforts.

Strengthening Cybersecurity Agencies and National Cyber Defense

To counter Pakistan's cyber-enabled influence operations, India has significantly strengthened its cybersecurity institutions. Agencies such as the National Technical Research Organisation (NTRO), Defence Cyber Agency (DCA), National Critical Information Infrastructure Protection Centre (NCIIPC), and CERT-In have been tasked with monitoring, detecting, and neutralizing cyber threats originating from Pakistani networks.

- **Real-time Cyber Threat Intelligence:** These agencies operate advanced cyber intelligence programs that monitor dark web activities, hacking groups, and bot networks linked to Pakistan's cyber warfare teams.
- **Cyber Hardening of Strategic Infrastructure:** The Indian government has implemented zero-trust architecture and enhanced cyber resilience frameworks for military, nuclear, banking, and critical infrastructure systems to prevent cyber espionage and hacking attempts.
- **AI-Powered Cyber Surveillance:** India has deployed AI-driven anomaly detection systems that track real-time threats, deepfake content, and manipulated videos aimed at disrupting India's internal stability.

Counter-Disinformation and Fact-Checking Mechanisms

To counter Pakistan's fake news factories and proxy propaganda networks, India has implemented fact-checking and counter-narrative mechanisms to prevent the spread of false information targeting Indian institutions and social harmony.

- **Dedicated Counter-Disinformation Units:** Indian intelligence agencies have set up specialized teams to track, expose, and dismantle fake news networks, propaganda websites, and bot-driven influence campaigns.
- **Collaboration with Social Media Platforms:** India has partnered with Twitter, Facebook, YouTube, Instagram, and Telegram to identify and

remove thousands of Pakistani-operated fake accounts that spread disinformation.

- **Legal Frameworks Against Digital Misinformation:** The Indian government is strengthening cyber laws and misinformation policies to hold foreign operatives accountable for digital interference.
- **Public Awareness and Media Literacy Initiatives:** Indian authorities have launched cyber awareness campaigns to educate citizens, journalists, and policymakers on identifying disinformation, AI-generated fake content, and malicious narratives.

Blocking Fake Social Media Accounts and Digital Manipulation

Pakistan's bot-driven influence operations have been a major tool for destabilizing India's political landscape, military morale, and economic stability. In response, India has developed multi-tiered countermeasures to detect, track, and block fake accounts operated from Pakistan.

- **AI-Based Detection of Fake Social Media Accounts:** Indian cybersecurity teams have deployed machine learning models to identify fake engagements, artificial amplification, and bot-driven narratives.
- **Rapid Response Teams for Narrative Correction:** Indian cyber units work closely with defense analysts and media strategists to counter and correct false narratives in real time.
- **Cross-Border Digital Monitoring:** Indian intelligence services track Pakistan-backed disinformation campaigns and deepfake video production labs, neutralizing them before they gain traction.

Psychological Resilience Programs for Armed Forces

Given Pakistan's persistent psychological warfare against Indian security forces, the Indian military has introduced several countermeasures to protect troop morale, operational secrecy, and psychological resilience.

- **Cyber Hygiene and Social Media Awareness Workshops:** The Indian Army, Navy, and Air Force have made training in cyber hygiene, digital footprint reduction, and phishing attack prevention mandatory for all personnel.
- **Psychological Warfare Training for Soldiers:** Indian soldiers are trained in counter-PSYOPS techniques, ensuring they can identify, resist, and report psychological manipulation attempts.

- **Monitoring of Encrypted Communication Channels:** Intelligence agencies have increased surveillance on WhatsApp, Telegram, and Signal, which have been used for Pakistani honey trap operations and misinformation targeting Indian personnel.
- **National Military Resilience Programs:The Indian government has expanded mental health initiatives within the armed forces, ensuring psychological stability and operational focus.**

Diplomatic Engagement and International Exposure of Pakistan's Information Warfare

India has actively leveraged diplomatic platforms, cybersecurity forums, and international coalitions to expose Pakistan's state-sponsored disinformation operations and cyber warfare tactics.

- **Presenting Evidence at International Forums:** India has systematically presented reports at the United Nations (UN), G20 summits, and global cybersecurity conferences to highlight Pakistan's proxy disinformation networks and cyber warfare strategies.
- **Strategic Alliances Against Cyber Threats:** India has deepened cybersecurity collaborations with the United States, Israel, Japan, and European nations, ensuring intelligence sharing and coordinated counter-disinformation efforts.
- **Active Cyber Diplomacy Engagements:** India participates in global discussions on digital security, foreign cyber interference, and data sovereignty, advocating for stronger international mechanisms against state-sponsored cyber warfare.

CHAPTER VII

Russia, the West, and Global Disinformation Campaigns

Russia has been one of the pioneers of disinformation warfare, effectively using cyber operations, political subversion, and media manipulation to interfere in elections, sow discord, and undermine democratic institutions worldwide. In response, Western powers, including NATO and the United States, have developed countermeasures to curb the spread of propaganda and disinformation. India, too, faces growing threats from digital influence campaigns and can learn valuable lessons from global strategies in tackling cyber-enabled psychological operations. This chapter explores Russia's hybrid warfare model, the countermeasures adopted by NATO and the United States, and the lessons India can draw from these experiences to strengthen its digital resilience and national security.

Russia's Hybrid Warfare Model and Cyber Influence in Elections

Russia's hybrid warfare model is a multifaceted strategy that integrates conventional military tactics, cyber operations, psychological warfare, and political subversion to exert influence and achieve geopolitical objectives. This approach enables Russia to wage conflicts in a manner that is often ambiguous, difficult to attribute, and highly disruptive to adversaries. Unlike traditional kinetic warfare, hybrid warfare operates below the threshold of direct military confrontation, allowing Russia to destabilize nations without triggering formal declarations of war. The key components of this strategy include cyber espionage, election interference, disinformation campaigns, and the weaponization of digital platforms.

One of the most prominent examples of Russia's hybrid warfare tactics was its interference in the 2016 United States presidential election. Russian intelligence agencies, including the GRU and FSB, orchestrated a series of cyberattacks, social media influence operations, and coordinated hacking efforts to manipulate public opinion and undermine the integrity of the electoral process. The Internet Research Agency (IRA), a Kremlin-linked organization, deployed thousands of fake social media accounts posing as American citizens to amplify divisive content, spread misinformation, and fuel societal discord. These operations targeted key issues such as immigration, racial tensions, and gun control, strategically exploiting existing political divisions to influence voter sentiment. Additionally, Russian hackers infiltrated email servers of political organizations, leaking sensitive information to shape media narratives and discredit specific candidates.

Beyond the United States, Russia has employed similar tactics to influence elections across Europe. The 2017 French presidential election saw Russian-backed cyber operatives launch hacking attacks against the campaign of Emmanuel Macron, leaking internal communications to undermine his credibility. Similarly, in Germany, Russian intelligence has been implicated in cyber intrusions targeting political institutions and media outlets, attempting to sway public opinion against leaders who oppose Russian foreign policy. The United Kingdom has also been a target, with evidence suggesting Russian interference in the Brexit referendum, where disinformation campaigns were used to amplify divisive narratives surrounding immigration and national sovereignty.

Russia's disinformation operations extend far beyond electoral interference. During the annexation of Crimea in 2014, Russia orchestrated an extensive propaganda campaign across state-controlled media, social media platforms, and international forums to justify its territorial expansion while discrediting Ukraine and the West. Russian news agencies such as RT and Sputnik broadcasted misleading narratives portraying Crimea's annexation as a legitimate and popular decision, while downplaying reports of military aggression. Simultaneously, Russian cyber operatives launched digital attacks against Ukrainian government networks, further destabilizing the country and weakening its ability to respond effectively.

The Russia-Ukraine war has been another critical case study in the evolution of Russian hybrid warfare. Kremlin-backed media outlets and cyber units have flooded global digital platforms with fabricated reports, conspiracy theories, and manipulated videos portraying Russia as a victim of Western aggression. These influence operations aim to erode international support for Ukraine, shape global perceptions of the conflict, and create divisions within Western alliances. Russian troll farms and bot networks continue to amplify anti-Ukraine propaganda, while cyberattacks target Ukraine's military infrastructure, energy grids, and government databases to disrupt operations and induce chaos.

Another hallmark of Russia's hybrid warfare strategy is its use of digital platforms to cultivate political movements and extremist ideologies that serve its interests. Russian intelligence has been linked to efforts to radicalize fringe groups in the West, exacerbating ideological polarization through tailored misinformation campaigns. Social media algorithms are manipulated to push divisive content into mainstream discourse, intensifying societal fragmentation and weakening democratic institutions. By engineering distrust in governments, electoral systems, and traditional media, Russia seeks to destabilize adversaries from within, making them more vulnerable to external influence.

Russia's success in leveraging hybrid warfare has prompted nations around the world to develop countermeasures aimed at mitigating the threat of information manipulation and cyber aggression. The increasing sophistication of Russian cyber capabilities underscores the necessity for democratic states to invest in cyber defense, strategic communication, and media literacy programs to safeguard their political systems from external interference. The study of Russia's hybrid warfare model provides critical insights into the future of global conflicts, where the battle for influence is increasingly waged in the digital domain rather than on traditional battlefields.

Russia has been at the forefront of modern information warfare, employing a sophisticated hybrid warfare model that integrates cyber operations, political influence campaigns, and media manipulation to achieve its strategic objectives. Unlike traditional military confrontations, Russia's information warfare relies on deception, ambiguity, and the exploitation of digital ecosystems to manipulate public opinion and destabilize adversaries. This approach has been particularly evident in its cyber influence operations targeting elections, disinformation campaigns in conflict zones, and manipulation of social media platforms to shape global narratives.

One of the most well-documented cases of Russian disinformation campaigns was its interference in the 2016 United States presidential election. Using a network of state-backed troll farms, automated bots, and coordinated hacking efforts, Russia's intelligence agencies successfully infiltrated digital spaces to spread divisive content, amplify societal tensions, and manipulate voter behavior. The Internet Research Agency, a key player in Russia's digital influence operations, deployed thousands of fake social media accounts impersonating American citizens to create discord on controversial issues such as immigration, gun control, and racial relations. Additionally, Russian hackers breached email servers and leaked sensitive political communications, further influencing public perception. This model of cyber influence has not been limited to the United States, as similar tactics have been used to interfere in elections across Europe, including in France, Germany, and the United Kingdom.

Russia's digital disinformation campaigns extend beyond elections, influencing public perception in times of geopolitical conflicts. The annexation of Crimea in 2014 saw Russia deploying coordinated propaganda efforts across television networks, social media, and international platforms to justify its actions while discrediting Ukraine and Western nations. Similarly, during the Russia-Ukraine war, Kremlin-backed news agencies and cyber operatives flooded global platforms with fabricated reports portraying Russia as a victim of Western aggression, while downplaying war crimes and battlefield losses.

NATO's Response to Digital Warfare

NATO, recognizing the growing threat posed by Russian digital warfare, has developed a robust and multi-layered strategy to combat disinformation, cyber threats, and hybrid warfare tactics. The alliance's approach is built on four key pillars: intelligence sharing, cyber defense collaboration, public awareness campaigns, and proactive strategic communications. These efforts aim to safeguard democratic institutions, counter state-sponsored propaganda, and build resilience against foreign influence operations.

One of NATO's core responses to digital warfare has been the establishment of the Strategic Communications Center of Excellence (StratCom COE) in Latvia. This specialized agency is tasked with monitoring and analyzing Russian disinformation campaigns, identifying emerging threats, and formulating counter-strategies. The center conducts extensive research on how digital platforms are exploited for geopolitical manipulation, mapping out influence operations in real-time and recommending countermeasures to NATO member states. The agency also works closely with cybersecurity teams across NATO countries to detect and neutralize cyber threats that originate from adversarial nations.

Recognizing the role of technology companies in combating disinformation, NATO has strengthened its partnerships with major social media firms, including Google, Meta, Twitter, and TikTok. These collaborations focus on removing coordinated inauthentic behavior, deplatforming state-sponsored bot networks, and flagging misleading content. NATO has also advocated for stricter algorithmic transparency and content moderation policies to prevent the spread of foreign disinformation. Additionally, through NATO's Cyber Defence Pledge, member states have committed to enhancing their national cyber capabilities and collaborating in real-time to respond to cyber incidents linked to foreign adversaries.

Another significant aspect of NATO's response has been the implementation of cyber drills and war games designed to prepare member states for large-scale digital conflicts. Exercises such as Locked Shields, organized by the NATO Cooperative Cyber Defence Centre of Excellence (CCDCOE) in Estonia, simulate real-world cyberattacks on national infrastructure, testing the ability of allied nations to respond swiftly to coordinated cyber threats. These exercises not only help develop stronger defense mechanisms but also enable the rapid exchange of intelligence on emerging cyberattack techniques used by adversarial states.

Beyond cyber defense, NATO has launched extensive public awareness campaigns to educate citizens about digital misinformation and psychological warfare tactics. Recognizing that disinformation thrives on public trust deficits, NATO's StratCom teams actively engage in debunking false narratives, fact-checking viral claims, and amplifying truthful information. NATO-backed initiatives such as the European External Action Service's East StratCom Task Force have been instrumental in exposing Russian disinformation efforts, particularly regarding Ukraine, NATO military movements, and Western political stability.

NATO's response to digital warfare continues to evolve as adversarial states adopt more sophisticated hybrid warfare techniques. The alliance remains committed to advancing its cyber capabilities, strengthening international cooperation, and ensuring that democratic nations remain resilient against foreign information manipulation. By fostering collaboration between governments, tech firms, and civil society, NATO aims to create a unified front against the growing threat of digital warfare.

NATO, recognizing the growing threat of Russian digital warfare, has adapted its strategic posture to counter disinformation and cyber threats. The alliance has developed an extensive counter-hybrid warfare framework, which includes real-time intelligence sharing, coordinated cyber defenses, and media literacy programs aimed at strengthening democratic resilience against foreign influence. NATO has also established dedicated cyber units that actively track, expose, and neutralize state-sponsored disinformation campaigns originating from Russian sources.

The establishment of NATO's Strategic Communications Center of Excellence has been a critical step in analyzing and countering state-sponsored disinformation campaigns. Through simulated cyber drills, strategic communication efforts, and the deployment of rapid response teams, NATO seeks to mitigate the impact of Russian influence operations in member states. The organization also actively collaborates with private technology firms, including Google, Meta, and Twitter, to detect and remove fake accounts, misinformation campaigns, and coordinated influence networks tied to Russian actors. Furthermore, NATO conducts public awareness campaigns to educate citizens about digital threats, deepfake technology, and the risks of manipulated information in democratic processes.

USA's Role in Cyber Security and Information Control

The United States has positioned itself as a global leader in cybersecurity, developing advanced frameworks to protect critical infrastructure, combat cyber threats, and counter disinformation campaigns from state and non-state actors. With increasing threats from adversaries such as Russia, China, Iran, and North Korea, the U.S. has adopted a multi-pronged approach that includes cyber deterrence, legislative measures, diplomatic pressure, and partnerships with technology companies to secure the digital landscape.

One of the key institutions driving U.S. cybersecurity efforts is the Cybersecurity and Infrastructure Security Agency (CISA), which was established in 2018 to enhance the resilience of the nation's cyber infrastructure. CISA collaborates with government agencies, private corporations, and international partners to safeguard national security interests. The agency plays a vital role in monitoring cyber threats, issuing security advisories, and coordinating responses to large-scale cyberattacks on financial systems, government networks, and industrial control systems.

Another major pillar of U.S. cybersecurity strategy is the role played by intelligence agencies such as the National Security Agency (NSA) and the Federal Bureau of Investigation (FBI). The NSA, through its Cybersecurity Directorate, engages in active cyber defense, disrupting foreign espionage operations, and developing cryptographic security measures. Meanwhile, the FBI's Cyber Division focuses on investigating cybercrime, identifying cyber espionage threats, and preventing digital attacks on U.S. institutions. Both agencies work closely with CISA and the Department of Homeland Security (DHS) to combat threats from foreign cyber actors and coordinate defensive cyber operations.

The United States has also taken significant steps to deter cyber aggression through economic sanctions and diplomatic measures. In response to Russian interference in the 2016 U.S. presidential election and subsequent cyberattacks, the U.S. imposed targeted sanctions on Russian intelligence officers, cyber operatives, and organizations responsible for disinformation campaigns. Similar sanctions have been applied against Chinese and Iranian entities involved in cyber espionage and intellectual property theft. By leveraging its economic influence, the U.S. aims to impose financial costs on cyber adversaries and reduce their operational capabilities.

To strengthen cyber defenses across sectors, the United States has launched public-private partnerships, working with major technology firms such as Google, Microsoft, Meta, and Amazon to develop security solutions, threat intelligence-sharing platforms, and rapid response mechanisms to mitigate cyber threats. These collaborations have led to improved defenses against ransomware attacks, supply chain vulnerabilities, and deepfake-based misinformation campaigns. Additionally, the U.S. has pushed for stronger cybersecurity regulations, requiring companies to adopt robust security protocols and report cyber incidents in real-time.

In the realm of information control and disinformation countermeasures, the U.S. has established the Global Engagement Center (GEC) to combat foreign propaganda and state-sponsored disinformation. The GEC works with international partners to expose and neutralize influence operations that seek to manipulate public discourse, interfere in democratic processes, or spread divisive narratives. Additionally, initiatives such as the Rapid Response Team for digital misinformation work in coordination with NATO allies to identify and counter hostile information campaigns in real time.

Artificial intelligence and machine learning have also become key components of U.S. cybersecurity and disinformation defense strategies. The U.S. government has increased investment in AI-driven threat detection systems that can analyze vast amounts of data to identify cyber threats, disinformation campaigns, and deepfake-generated propaganda. These advanced technologies enable faster response times to emerging threats, preventing large-scale disruptions caused by foreign adversaries.

The role of the military in cyber defense has grown significantly, with the U.S. Cyber Command (CYBERCOM) leading offensive and defensive cyber operations. CYBERCOM conducts preemptive cyber missions against adversarial networks, disrupts cybercriminal organizations, and provides tactical support to military operations worldwide. It works in coordination with other U.S. military branches to ensure the protection of defense networks, intelligence systems, and command infrastructure.

The evolution of cyber warfare and digital disinformation has made cybersecurity a national security priority for the United States. By integrating cutting-edge technology, fostering international cooperation, and enforcing strong cyber policies, the U.S. continues to strengthen its defenses against the rapidly evolving threats of cyber-enabled influence operations. The lessons learned from U.S. cybersecurity strategies provide valuable insights for other nations, including India, in developing robust frameworks to counter cyber threats and safeguard national security in the digital age.

The United States has played a crucial role in shaping global cybersecurity policies and countering disinformation. The establishment of the Cybersecurity and Infrastructure Security Agency (CISA) has strengthened the nation's ability to detect and respond to cyber threats from state actors. This agency, alongside the National Security Agency (NSA) and the Federal Bureau of Investigation (FBI), has been instrumental in identifying foreign interference in domestic affairs and preventing cyberattacks on critical infrastructure.

The United States has also imposed sanctions on Russian entities involved in cyberattacks and disinformation campaigns, attempting to deter further aggression. These sanctions target government-backed cyber units, media outlets spreading state propaganda, and financial institutions that support disinformation networks. Additionally, diplomatic measures have been taken, with the expulsion of Russian intelligence operatives suspected of conducting cyber espionage in the United States and Europe.

Initiatives such as the Global Engagement Center focus on exposing and countering propaganda from adversarial states, working in collaboration with allies to disrupt the flow of disinformation. The United States has also implemented stricter regulations on foreign-owned media operations within its borders, requiring transparency in funding and content distribution to prevent covert influence. As part of its broader strategy, the U.S. government has increased investment in artificial intelligence-driven misinformation detection, ensuring rapid response to emerging threats in the digital space.

India's Information Warfare Landscape

CHAPTER VIII

India's Vulnerabilities and Challenges

India's emergence as a digital powerhouse has brought significant advantages, but it has also exposed the country to numerous cyber vulnerabilities and information warfare challenges. As the world's largest democracy with a rapidly growing digital infrastructure, India faces a complex set of threats ranging from cyber espionage and hacking attempts on government and private sector networks to coordinated misinformation campaigns that aim to create political and social instability. These challenges demand a robust and multi-faceted response, integrating technological advancements, legal frameworks, and public awareness initiatives.

India's Digital Infrastructure: Strengths and Weaknesses

India's digital infrastructure has experienced rapid expansion over the past decade, driven by technological advancements and policy initiatives aimed at digital inclusion. With increasing smartphone penetration, widespread internet access, and government-led digital transformation programs, India is positioned as a major player in the global digital economy. However, alongside these advancements come significant challenges, particularly in securing critical infrastructure, protecting personal data, and preventing cyber threats that exploit systemic vulnerabilities.

India's Digital India initiative has significantly improved access to e-governance, digital payments, and cloud-based public services. The widespread adoption of Aadhaar for identity verification, Unified Payments Interface (UPI) for financial transactions, and the push towards smart cities have facilitated seamless digital experiences for millions. Additionally, India has become a hub for information technology services, contributing to its status as a global outsourcing destination. These strengths have positioned India as a leader in digital innovation, but they also expose the nation to security risks stemming from an inadequate cybersecurity framework.

One of the most pressing concerns is the lack of standardized cybersecurity protocols across industries. Many government and private sector entities still rely on outdated infrastructure, making them easy targets for cyberattacks. Critical infrastructure such as power grids, banking systems, healthcare institutions, and defense networks faces heightened risks from cyber threats, particularly from state-sponsored actors. Cyber espionage targeting government databases, financial fraud in banking networks, and ransomware attacks on major corporations are increasing in frequency, underscoring the urgent need for a robust cybersecurity framework.

Another significant challenge is data protection and privacy enforcement. While India has introduced the Digital Personal Data Protection Bill to regulate how personal information is stored and processed, implementation remains a challenge. Many organizations still lack strong data security measures, leaving sensitive information vulnerable to breaches. The lack of stringent penalties for data mismanagement also makes enforcement difficult, allowing cybercriminals and malicious actors to exploit loopholes in existing laws.

India's reliance on imported digital infrastructure and foreign technology solutions adds another layer of vulnerability. With significant portions of India's telecommunications hardware, software solutions, and cloud computing infrastructure sourced from international vendors, concerns about backdoor access, cyber espionage, and supply chain vulnerabilities remain persistent. The increasing use of Chinese-made hardware and software in India's 5G rollout and IoT-based smart city projects raises concerns about potential security risks posed by foreign control over digital networks.

In addition to external threats, India's internal cybersecurity talent gap presents a significant hurdle. While India has a growing base of IT professionals, there is a shortage of highly skilled cybersecurity experts who can address advanced threats such as AI-driven cyberattacks, deepfake-based disinformation, and quantum computing vulnerabilities. Without a comprehensive talent development strategy that prioritizes cybersecurity education and workforce training, India risks falling behind in the global race to secure its digital assets.

To mitigate these vulnerabilities, India must adopt a multi-layered cybersecurity strategy that includes stronger legal frameworks, public-private partnerships, and investments in cutting-edge security technologies. Cyber resilience must become a national priority, ensuring that digital infrastructure is not only efficient and accessible but also secure and resistant to evolving cyber threats.

India's rapid digital transformation has been fueled by advancements in cloud computing, 5G networks, artificial intelligence, and data-driven governance. Initiatives such as Digital India, which aim to connect millions of citizens and businesses to the digital ecosystem, have contributed to economic growth and efficiency. However, this surge in digital adoption has also introduced significant security risks. While India has made strides in digital connectivity, many government and private sector organizations still rely on outdated security protocols, making them susceptible to cyberattacks. The lack of standardized security measures across different industries further exacerbates these vulnerabilities. Additionally, weak enforcement of data protection laws and limited cybersecurity awareness among businesses and individuals leave India exposed to large-scale cyber threats.

A major area of concern is India's critical infrastructure, including power grids, banking systems, healthcare facilities, and defense networks, which are primary targets for cyberattacks. State-sponsored adversaries, particularly from China and Pakistan, have repeatedly attempted to infiltrate these networks to disrupt essential services and steal sensitive information. The threat landscape is evolving rapidly, requiring India to adopt stronger cyber resilience strategies and upgrade national security protocols to counter emerging digital threats effectively.

Cyber Threats to Indian Government, Military, and Private Sector

India faces a growing spectrum of cyber threats that target its government institutions, military, and private sector. These threats originate from a combination of state-sponsored hacking groups, cybercriminal syndicates, and hacktivist organizations, each employing sophisticated attack methodologies to compromise national security, economic stability, and digital sovereignty. With the rapid advancement of cyber capabilities among adversarial nations, the nature of cyber threats facing India continues to evolve, necessitating a proactive and strategic approach to cybersecurity.

Government institutions have been prime targets of cyber espionage, with multiple high-profile cyber intrusions recorded over the years. Breaches in Aadhaar data, ransomware attacks on state-owned enterprises, and cyber intrusions targeting sensitive diplomatic and defense establishments highlight the scale of vulnerability. Hackers utilize various tactics, including phishing schemes, malware injections, and zero-day exploits, to infiltrate these networks. Once inside, attackers can extract classified information, manipulate government databases, or disrupt critical services. The increasing digitalization of government services, while beneficial for efficiency and transparency, also expands the attack surface available to cyber adversaries.

The Indian military has consistently been under cyber siege, with adversarial states seeking to compromise strategic intelligence, disrupt defense communication networks, and weaken operational preparedness. In recent years, Chinese cyber espionage groups have been implicated in attacks targeting India's defense infrastructure, particularly through infiltrations in satellite communications, border surveillance systems, and military command networks. Reports have also surfaced about targeted cyberattacks attempting to breach the email servers of senior defense personnel, raising concerns about potential data leaks that could compromise national security and battlefield tactics. Cyber intrusions aimed at defense suppliers and subcontractors further compound this challenge, as adversaries attempt to access sensitive military designs, technological blueprints, and classified operational data.

Beyond the public sector, India's private enterprises, particularly in industries such as pharmaceuticals, telecommunications, financial services, and e-commerce, remain prime targets for cybercriminals and foreign intelligence agencies. Cyberattacks on financial institutions have resulted in large-scale data breaches, identity theft, and fraudulent transactions. Intellectual property theft is another pressing concern, as cyber operatives attempt to steal research and development data, patents, and corporate trade secrets to gain a competitive edge. The rise of ransomware attacks has also put Indian businesses at significant risk, with cybercriminals demanding hefty ransoms to restore access to encrypted data. Supply chain attacks targeting software vendors and IT service providers have become another prevalent vector for cyber intrusions, enabling adversaries to compromise multiple organizations through a single breach.

State-sponsored actors, particularly from China and Pakistan, continue to leverage cyber warfare as a strategic tool to destabilize India. Cyberattacks linked to Pakistan-based hacking groups have focused on infiltrating government networks, conducting misinformation campaigns, and targeting financial institutions to disrupt economic activities. China's cyber operations, on the other hand, have been more sophisticated, employing advanced persistent threats (APTs) to carry out long-term surveillance, data theft, and cyber sabotage. The coordinated nature of these attacks underscores the need for India to enhance its cyber defense mechanisms through advanced threat detection systems, incident response capabilities, and robust information-sharing frameworks with allied nations.

To mitigate the risks posed by these cyber threats, India must adopt a multi-layered cybersecurity strategy that prioritizes threat intelligence gathering, real-time monitoring, and rapid response mechanisms. Strengthening public-private partnerships in cybersecurity can enhance collective resilience by integrating expertise from technology firms, defense contractors, and financial institutions. Additionally, enhancing workforce training in cyber defense, implementing stricter data protection laws, and investing in indigenous cybersecurity solutions will play a critical role in bolstering India's national security posture in the digital domain.

India faces an ever-growing array of cyber threats targeting government institutions, the military, and private sector industries. These threats originate from state-sponsored hacking groups, cybercriminal syndicates, and hacktivist organizations, each using sophisticated techniques to compromise national security. Government institutions have been prime targets of cyber espionage, with multiple high-profile cyber intrusions, including breaches of Aadhaar data, ransomware attacks on state-owned enterprises, and cyber espionage targeting diplomatic and defense establishments. Hackers often employ phishing schemes, malware infections, and zero-day vulnerabilities to infiltrate these networks, extracting classified information related to national security.

The Indian military has faced persistent cyber threats, with adversaries seeking to steal strategic intelligence, disrupt communication networks, and weaken operational readiness. In recent years, Chinese hackers have reportedly targeted Indian defense infrastructure, exploiting vulnerabilities in satellite communications, border surveillance systems, and military command networks. There have also been attempts to infiltrate email servers of senior defense personnel, raising concerns about data leaks and battlefield espionage. The private sector, particularly industries related to pharmaceuticals, telecommunications, financial services, and e-commerce, remains a significant target for cyberattacks. Cybercriminals and state-sponsored actors frequently engage in intellectual property theft, ransomware attacks, and financial fraud, making cybersecurity a crucial priority for Indian enterprises.

Fake News Ecosystem and Internal Polarization

India's digital expansion has created an environment where information flows rapidly across various platforms, but it has also given rise to an ecosystem of fake news that poses a serious threat to social cohesion and national security. The widespread use of social media, instant messaging services, and user-generated content platforms has enabled the dissemination of misinformation at an unprecedented scale. The challenge of fake news is not just its rapid spread, but also its ability to manipulate public opinion, incite violence, and deepen societal divisions.

One of the primary drivers of the fake news ecosystem is the increasing reliance on social media as a primary source of information. Platforms such as WhatsApp, Twitter, Facebook, and YouTube have become arenas for political propaganda, communal narratives, and ideological battles. These platforms provide an easy way for misinformation to be shared without verification, often reaching millions before fact-checking mechanisms can respond. This problem is exacerbated by the presence of algorithm-driven echo chambers, where users are continuously fed content that reinforces their existing beliefs, making them more susceptible to misleading narratives.

Fake news in India is often driven by coordinated campaigns involving bot networks, deepfake technology, and artificial intelligence-generated content. These sophisticated methods are used to fabricate videos, manipulate images, and create misleading narratives that can sway public opinion. In many cases, these campaigns are designed to exploit religious, social, and political fault lines to deepen polarization. Disinformation related to historical events, government policies, and communal conflicts has led to real-world consequences, including mob violence, riots, and hate crimes. Inflammatory content spread through WhatsApp forwards and social media posts has been directly linked to instances of lynching and targeted attacks in various regions of the country.

Political actors, both domestic and foreign, have leveraged fake news to delegitimize opponents, influence elections, and manipulate public perception. During election cycles, false claims about political candidates, misleading information about voting procedures, and doctored surveys are used to create confusion among voters. The ability of foreign adversaries to exploit India's social and political divisions through disinformation campaigns further complicates the issue. There have been documented cases where foreign-backed networks have amplified false narratives to create instability and undermine democratic institutions.

The regulatory challenges in addressing fake news are significant. The end-to-end encryption of messaging platforms like WhatsApp makes it difficult to track the origins of misleading content, while the vast scale of social media usage makes real-time moderation challenging. Although major technology firms have taken steps to curb misinformation through fact-checking partnerships and content moderation policies, the effectiveness of these measures remains limited. The increasing use of artificial intelligence to create hyper-realistic deepfake videos adds another layer of complexity, as detecting manipulated content becomes more difficult.

To counter the threats posed by fake news, India needs a multi-pronged approach that combines technological solutions, regulatory measures, and public awareness initiatives. Strengthening digital literacy programs to educate citizens on verifying sources, cross-checking information, and identifying false narratives is crucial. Fact-checking initiatives should be expanded and integrated into mainstream news media and online platforms. Legal frameworks must also be updated to hold individuals and organizations accountable for the deliberate spread of misinformation. Additionally, collaboration between the government, social media companies, and civil society organizations can help in developing comprehensive strategies to combat the menace of fake news and maintain social stability.

As the digital landscape continues to evolve, the challenge of fake news and internal polarization will require sustained efforts from all stakeholders. By fostering a culture of information verification and strengthening institutional resilience against disinformation, India can mitigate the risks associated with the growing fake news ecosystem.

India's vast digital landscape, combined with the widespread use of social media platforms and instant messaging services, has created an ideal environment for the rapid spread of misinformation. Fake news and disinformation campaigns are being used as tools to manipulate public opinion, incite violence, and polarize communities. Social media platforms such as WhatsApp, Twitter, Facebook, and YouTube have become battlegrounds for political propaganda, communal narratives, and ideological warfare. Bad actors leverage bot networks, deepfake technology, and AI-generated content to fabricate false narratives, often targeting sensitive religious and political issues. The challenge of regulating such content is compounded by end-to-end encryption and the inability of fact-checking mechanisms to keep pace with misinformation spread.

Disinformation campaigns often exploit existing social and religious tensions, aiming to divide communities and fuel ideological extremism. False information related to historical events, government policies, and communal conflicts has led to real-world violence, riots, and hate crimes in India. Misinformation is also being used to delegitimize political opponents and create distrust in democratic institutions, further deepening divisions within society. The increasing sophistication of disinformation tactics requires India to strengthen its digital literacy initiatives and enforce stricter social media policies to counter misinformation effectively.

Misinformation During Elections and Public Crises

Elections and public crises are particularly vulnerable to misinformation campaigns, as adversaries and vested interest groups seek to exploit uncertainty, manipulate public opinion, and disrupt governance. These periods witness a surge in disinformation tactics, including fake news, deepfake videos, artificially boosted narratives, and coordinated online influence operations. The high stakes of electoral processes and crisis management make them ideal targets for digital subversion.

During elections, misinformation is often weaponized to discredit political candidates, influence voter perception, and create confusion about the electoral process. Political parties, both domestic and foreign, engage in information manipulation by using fake news websites, misleading opinion polls, and doctored images or videos to target opposition candidates. Social media platforms become battlegrounds where political narratives are artificially amplified through bot-driven campaigns and hashtag manipulation. This often results in the spread of unverified claims about candidates' backgrounds, fabricated scandals, and false promises, influencing voter sentiment and decision-making. Misinformation about voting procedures, such as false claims of voter suppression, changes in election dates, or tampered electronic voting machines, further undermines public trust in democratic institutions and electoral integrity.

Foreign adversaries have increasingly played a role in influencing elections through cyber-enabled disinformation campaigns. Nations with geopolitical interests use state-sponsored troll farms and fake accounts to sway political outcomes, polarize communities, and weaken democratic processes. Reports have highlighted instances of foreign entities attempting to influence Indian elections by supporting divisive narratives, amplifying extremist viewpoints, and creating fake social media profiles impersonating real citizens. The emergence of artificial intelligence and deepfake technology has made election misinformation more deceptive, making it difficult for the public to distinguish between real and manipulated content.

Public crises such as pandemics, natural disasters, terrorist attacks, and economic downturns provide another opportunity for malicious actors to spread misinformation. In times of crisis, the public's reliance on digital media for real-time updates increases, creating an environment where false narratives can spread rapidly before authorities can counter them. The COVID-19 pandemic showcased the devastating impact of misinformation, with false medical advice, conspiracy theories, and vaccine hesitancy campaigns fueling confusion and panic. Claims about unproven treatments, fabricated statistics about infection rates, and misleading reports about government policies created widespread distrust in healthcare institutions and emergency response efforts. Similar misinformation trends have been observed in the aftermath of natural disasters, where fabricated reports about rescue operations, government inaction, or exaggerated casualty figures have led to unnecessary panic and chaos.

Another major concern is the use of crisis-driven misinformation to incite violence and civil unrest. False claims about religious attacks, police brutality, and economic policies have been used to mobilize protests, create communal tensions, and fuel extremist ideologies. During major protests or conflicts, misinformation campaigns often hijack social movements to push hidden agendas, manipulate facts, and intensify discord between different sections of society. Such tactics have been used to exploit political and social divisions, weakening national stability and governance.

Addressing the challenges posed by misinformation during elections and public crises requires a comprehensive and multi-pronged approach. Fact-checking mechanisms need to be integrated into mainstream media and social media platforms to identify and counter fake news in real time. Governments must collaborate with technology companies to enhance content moderation, detect bot-driven influence operations, and remove misleading content before it gains traction. Public awareness campaigns promoting media literacy should be prioritized, educating citizens on verifying sources, identifying fake news, and critically evaluating digital information.

Legal frameworks must also evolve to hold individuals and organizations accountable for spreading deliberate misinformation. Strengthening election-related cyber laws, increasing transparency in political advertising, and imposing penalties on those engaging in digital subversion can help deter manipulation attempts. Additionally, the development of artificial intelligence-powered misinformation detection tools can play a crucial role in identifying and neutralizing deceptive content before it influences public perception. By implementing these measures, India can safeguard its democratic processes, maintain public trust in governance, and ensure that misinformation does not undermine national stability during critical events.

Elections and national crises represent the most vulnerable periods for misinformation campaigns, as bad actors attempt to manipulate voter behavior, incite panic, and disrupt governance. During election cycles, coordinated disinformation campaigns are deployed to discredit political candidates, mislead voters, and spread propaganda favoring certain political agendas. Foreign adversaries and domestic political groups use fake news websites, doctored videos, and manipulated polls to influence public sentiment. Social media platforms become breeding grounds for automated bot campaigns, hashtag manipulation, and deceptive political ads, all designed to sway electoral outcomes. This form of digital manipulation not only misinforms voters but also undermines public trust in democratic institutions.

Crises such as natural disasters, pandemics, and national security emergencies provide an opportunity for malicious actors to spread fear and uncertainty. The COVID-19 pandemic witnessed an unprecedented surge in misinformation, with false medical advice, conspiracy theories, and vaccine hesitancy campaigns undermining public trust in health institutions. Similarly, false narratives about law enforcement actions, economic policies, and social movements have incited panic and mass protests, destabilizing governance efforts. These instances highlight the need for rapid response mechanisms and fact-checking frameworks to counter misinformation effectively during critical national events.

Building a Resilient Digital Ecosystem

Building a resilient digital ecosystem in India requires a multi-dimensional approach that addresses cybersecurity, regulatory frameworks, digital literacy, and international cooperation. As cyber threats and information warfare tactics continue to evolve, India must proactively enhance its cyber resilience to safeguard its national security, economic stability, and democratic integrity.

A key component of digital resilience is strengthening cybersecurity infrastructure. Investments in AI-driven threat detection, blockchain-based data protection, and quantum cryptography can enhance India's ability to counter advanced cyber threats. Real-time monitoring systems and predictive analytics should be deployed across critical infrastructure, including government institutions, defense networks, financial systems, and power grids, to detect and neutralize cyber threats before they escalate. Strengthening endpoint security, enforcing multi-factor authentication, and integrating zero-trust security frameworks can further minimize vulnerabilities in digital systems.

Regulatory frameworks play a crucial role in ensuring a secure digital environment. Enforcing the Personal Data Protection Bill and introducing stringent cybersecurity policies will help protect sensitive information and hold organizations accountable for data breaches. Legislation should be updated to regulate digital platforms, making social media companies responsible for monitoring and mitigating the spread of misinformation and deepfake content. Cybercrime laws should also be enhanced to impose stricter penalties on cybercriminals, foreign adversaries, and state-sponsored actors engaging in cyber warfare and digital subversion.

Public awareness and media literacy are fundamental to building a resilient digital society. Digital literacy campaigns should be launched to educate citizens on recognizing misinformation, verifying news sources, and adopting safe online practices. Integrating cybersecurity education into school curriculums and corporate training programs will help create a more informed population that can critically analyze digital content. Collaboration with fact-checking organizations and media watchdogs can further support efforts to counter misinformation and prevent disinformation campaigns from influencing public discourse.

International cooperation is essential in combating cyber threats and information warfare. Strengthening partnerships with global cybersecurity frameworks and intelligence-sharing networks will enable India to proactively address emerging threats. India should actively participate in global cybersecurity dialogues, contribute to international norms on responsible state behavior in cyberspace, and collaborate with allied nations to develop joint cyber defense strategies. Engaging with global tech giants, cybersecurity firms, and digital rights organizations can help India stay ahead in the fight against cybercrime and digital manipulation.

In addition to security measures, India must foster a culture of digital innovation while ensuring security and privacy. Encouraging the development of indigenous cybersecurity solutions, promoting ethical hacking initiatives, and incentivizing startups to focus on cybersecurity technology will contribute to a self-reliant and secure digital ecosystem. Government support for cybersecurity research and development will be crucial in building homegrown solutions tailored to India's unique cyber challenges.

As the digital battlefield continues to expand, India must remain adaptive, vigilant, and proactive in tackling cyber threats and information warfare. A resilient digital ecosystem requires the coordinated efforts of government agencies, private sector stakeholders, civil society organizations, and the general public. By integrating technological innovation, robust regulatory frameworks, international collaborations, and widespread digital literacy programs, India can fortify its cyber defenses, safeguard its democratic institutions, and maintain long-term national stability in an increasingly interconnected digital world.

Addressing India's vulnerabilities in digital and information warfare requires a comprehensive and forward-looking strategy that integrates cybersecurity advancements, regulatory measures, and public awareness initiatives. Strengthening cybersecurity infrastructure through investments in AI-driven threat detection, blockchain-based data protection, and quantum cryptography will enhance national cyber resilience. Legislative reforms, including enforcing the Personal Data Protection Bill, introducing strict cybersecurity policies, and implementing platform accountability laws, will help regulate the digital ecosystem more effectively.

Public awareness and media literacy must also be prioritized. Digital literacy campaigns should be launched to educate citizens on identifying fake news, verifying sources, and reporting misinformation. These initiatives should be integrated into educational curricula, community awareness programs, and corporate training modules to build a more informed and resilient population. Strengthening partnerships with global cybersecurity frameworks and intelligence-sharing networks will further enhance India's ability to counter foreign cyber threats.

As the digital battlefield expands, India must remain vigilant, adaptive, and proactive in tackling cyber threats and information warfare. By integrating technological innovation, strategic policymaking, and public engagement, India can safeguard its digital sovereignty, protect democratic institutions, and maintain social stability in the face of evolving digital challenges.

CHAPTER IX

India's Cyber Security Framework and Counter-Operations

As India's digital landscape continues to expand, the country faces an increasing array of cyber threats from hostile state actors, cybercriminal organizations, and non-state entities. These threats target critical infrastructure, government agencies, military operations, and private enterprises, making cybersecurity a national priority. The growing reliance on digital technologies in governance, banking, defense, and public services has increased India's attack surface, making it imperative to strengthen cyber defenses against a range of adversaries employing sophisticated tactics, techniques, and procedures.

To address these challenges, India has developed a multi-layered cybersecurity framework that includes dedicated agencies, policy frameworks, and technological advancements aimed at strengthening national cyber resilience. Government initiatives have focused on real-time threat intelligence sharing, development of indigenous cybersecurity solutions, and enhanced law enforcement capabilities to tackle emerging cyber threats. While India has made progress in strengthening its cyber infrastructure, challenges remain in terms of ensuring inter-agency coordination, preventing cyber espionage, and mitigating risks posed by evolving cyber warfare techniques.

India's cybersecurity strategy relies on a holistic approach that integrates government agencies, the private sector, and international cybersecurity alliances. Enhanced collaboration between stakeholders ensures that cyber threats are detected, prevented, and neutralized in real time. However, the increasing sophistication of cyber adversaries, including nation-state hackers and organized cybercriminal groups, requires India to continuously upgrade its cyber defense mechanisms. Strengthening incident response capabilities, improving cybersecurity awareness, and investing in next-generation cyber technologies will be crucial in ensuring long-term resilience against cyber threats.

Role of National Cyber Coordination Centre (NCCC)

The National Cyber Coordination Centre (NCCC) was established as a key component of India's cybersecurity infrastructure, tasked with real-time cyber threat monitoring, situational awareness, and information sharing among various government agencies. Operated under the Ministry of Electronics and Information Technology (MeitY), the NCCC plays a pivotal role in strengthening India's cyber defense mechanisms by analyzing network traffic across government and critical infrastructure systems. This real-time surveillance capability allows it to detect emerging threats, assess cyber incidents, and coordinate responses before they escalate into large-scale attacks.

The NCCC's primary function is to act as a central hub for collecting, analyzing, and disseminating cyber intelligence to relevant stakeholders, including law enforcement agencies, intelligence units, and national security bodies such as the National Security Council Secretariat (NSCS), the Defence Cyber Agency (DCA), and CERT-In. By leveraging artificial intelligence and big data analytics, the NCCC enhances India's ability to anticipate cyber threats, including ransomware attacks, state-sponsored cyber espionage, and critical infrastructure breaches. It continuously monitors cyber activities on both public and private networks, identifying vulnerabilities that could be exploited by malicious actors.

One of the critical roles of the NCCC is to act as an early warning system against cyber threats, providing government agencies with real-time intelligence on potential cyberattacks. This proactive approach ensures that cybersecurity teams can take preventive measures, mitigate risks, and strengthen their digital defenses before adversaries can exploit vulnerabilities. The NCCC also serves as a strategic center for coordinating national-level cyber exercises and simulated attack drills to test the resilience of India's cyber infrastructure.

The NCCC integrates cyber intelligence from multiple sources, including law enforcement databases, telecom service providers, and internet service providers, allowing for a multi-tiered approach to cyber defense. This extensive collaboration ensures that India's cybersecurity apparatus remains robust and adaptable to evolving threats. Furthermore, the NCCC works closely with international cybersecurity organizations, forging partnerships with agencies such as INTERPOL, the US Cyber Command, and Europol to share intelligence and counter cross-border cyber threats.

Another crucial function of the NCCC is monitoring and countering cyber threats emanating from hostile nations and state-sponsored cyber warfare units. Given the rise of cyber-enabled espionage and digital surveillance tactics employed by adversarial countries, the NCCC plays an instrumental role in detecting and neutralizing cyberattacks that target India's military infrastructure, nuclear assets, financial systems, and government databases. The center also assists in tracking and mitigating cyber threats linked to terrorist organizations, criminal syndicates, and hacktivist groups.

As cyber threats become more sophisticated, the NCCC continues to expand its capabilities by integrating next-generation cybersecurity technologies, including AI-driven threat intelligence, machine learning-based anomaly detection, and quantum-resistant cryptography. These advancements ensure that India remains resilient against the rapidly evolving landscape of cyber warfare. Additionally, the NCCC is exploring the use of blockchain technology for securing government transactions and communications, further fortifying India's digital ecosystem against cyber intrusions.

The NCCC's future roadmap includes expanding its operational scope to encompass broader aspects of cybersecurity, such as cloud security, IoT (Internet of Things) security, and critical infrastructure resilience. With the increasing digitization of key sectors such as banking, defense, healthcare, and telecommunications, the role of the NCCC in safeguarding India's cyber ecosystem is more critical than ever. Strengthening inter-agency coordination, enhancing threat response mechanisms, and fostering public-private partnerships will be essential in ensuring that the NCCC continues to serve as India's frontline defense against cyber threats and digital warfare.

The National Cyber Coordination Centre (NCCC) was established to enhance real-time cyber threat monitoring, situational awareness, and information sharing between various government agencies. Operated under the Ministry of Electronics and Information Technology (MeitY), the NCCC serves as India's premier cyber threat intelligence agency. Its primary objective is to provide early warnings about potential cyber threats by analyzing network traffic across government and critical infrastructure networks. By continuously scanning cyber activities, the NCCC identifies potential vulnerabilities, assesses cyber incidents, and shares actionable intelligence with security agencies such as the National Security Council Secretariat (NSCS), the Defence Cyber Agency (DCA), and CERT-In.

The NCCC plays a crucial role in coordinating responses to cyber incidents by integrating threat intelligence from various sources, including law enforcement agencies, telecom service providers, and internet service providers. Through its multi-tiered approach, it helps mitigate risks associated with ransomware attacks, state-sponsored cyber espionage, and critical infrastructure disruptions. By leveraging AI-based analytics and big data solutions, the NCCC enhances India's ability to anticipate and neutralize cyber threats before they escalate into large-scale attacks.

Indian Cyber Crime Coordination Centre (I4C)

Recognizing the increasing threat of cybercrime, the Indian government established the Indian Cyber Crime Coordination Centre (I4C) under the Ministry of Home Affairs as a dedicated national-level agency for cybercrime prevention, investigation, and response. The I4C plays a crucial role in enhancing India's law enforcement capabilities in cyberspace by providing a structured framework for tracking, analyzing, and mitigating digital crimes across the country. Given the rising number of cyber frauds, financial scams, identity theft cases, and cyberbullying incidents, the I4C acts as a critical enabler for law enforcement agencies to coordinate their efforts more effectively.

One of the key functions of I4C is the National Cybercrime Reporting Portal, which serves as a centralized platform for citizens to report cyber offenses, including online fraud, digital extortion, and crimes against women and children. This portal allows authorities to aggregate data on cybercrimes, identify trends, and track organized cybercriminal networks operating across multiple states. By integrating artificial intelligence and big data analytics, I4C is able to generate actionable insights that help in crime prevention, case resolution, and strategic policy-making.

To enhance law enforcement capabilities, I4C conducts specialized training programs for police officers, cybersecurity professionals, and forensic experts in digital forensics, ethical hacking, and cyber intelligence gathering. These capacity-building initiatives ensure that state and central law enforcement agencies remain equipped with the latest tools and techniques to combat emerging cyber threats. Additionally, I4C collaborates with international agencies such as INTERPOL, Europol, and foreign cybercrime units to facilitate intelligence sharing and joint operations against transnational cybercriminal networks.

With cybercrimes increasingly targeting India's digital economy, I4C has strengthened its partnerships with fintech companies, digital payment providers, and e-commerce platforms to monitor and counter financial cybercrimes. Through real-time coordination with banks and telecom regulators, I4C works to mitigate threats such as phishing scams, ATM frauds, and mobile payment vulnerabilities. The introduction of real-time fraud detection and prevention systems has significantly reduced financial losses due to cyber frauds, ensuring greater digital transaction security for Indian consumers and businesses.

The growing influence of social media platforms in cybercrimes has prompted I4C to focus on online radicalization, misinformation campaigns, and digital harassment cases. The agency works closely with social media platforms, messaging service providers, and content moderation teams to take down harmful content, identify perpetrators of cyber harassment, and counter misinformation that threatens national security and public order. By developing AI-based automated monitoring tools, I4C enhances its ability to detect and remove harmful digital content before it spreads widely.

Looking ahead, I4C aims to expand its operational scope by integrating blockchain analysis for tracking cryptocurrency-related cybercrimes, strengthening India's cybercrime laws to address emerging digital threats, and collaborating with private cybersecurity firms to build advanced threat intelligence platforms. As cybercriminals continue to evolve their tactics, I4C remains at the forefront of India's efforts to secure its digital landscape, protect citizens from cyber threats, and build a resilient cybercrime enforcement framework.

Recognizing the rising incidents of cybercrime, the Indian government established the Indian Cyber Crime Coordination Centre (I4C) under the Ministry of Home Affairs to serve as a national-level coordination body for law enforcement agencies. The I4C works towards preventing cybercrimes, improving investigation capabilities, and providing a framework for cybercrime reporting and analysis. It operates in collaboration with state cyber police departments, forensic laboratories, and cyber awareness programs to ensure a robust national response to cybercriminal activities.

A key feature of I4C is its National Cybercrime Reporting Portal, which allows citizens to report cyber frauds, identity theft, online financial crimes, and cyberstalking incidents. The data collected through this platform is analyzed to identify patterns, emerging threats, and criminal networks involved in cyber fraud. I4C also works on capacity-building initiatives, training law enforcement officers in digital forensics, cyber law enforcement, and ethical hacking techniques to improve cybercrime investigation and prosecution.

With the increasing number of financial frauds, social media-based scams, and data breaches, the role of I4C in ensuring citizen cybersecurity is critical. Its collaboration with fintech companies, digital payment service providers, and telecom regulators helps in tracking and neutralizing cyber threats targeting India's digital economy.

CERT-In and Its Role in Cyber Security

The Indian Computer Emergency Response Team (CERT-In) is a pivotal institution within India's cybersecurity framework, tasked with the responsibility of safeguarding the nation's digital assets from a wide range of cyber threats. Established under the Ministry of Electronics and Information Technology (MeitY), CERT-In functions as the primary incident response and threat intelligence agency, ensuring that government networks, corporate entities, and digital service providers remain secure against emerging cyber risks.

CERT-In's primary function is to detect, analyze, and respond to cyber threats targeting critical infrastructure, financial institutions, and sensitive government operations. The agency continuously monitors global cyber threats and issues security advisories to mitigate vulnerabilities before they can be exploited. One of its most critical roles is to function as a rapid-response unit during major cyber incidents, coordinating with various stakeholders, including law enforcement agencies, private cybersecurity firms, and international partners, to contain and neutralize threats efficiently.

In addition to responding to cyber threats, CERT-In is instrumental in developing and implementing national cybersecurity policies. It plays a key role in drafting cybersecurity guidelines for both public and private sector organizations, ensuring compliance with best security practices and regulatory frameworks. By issuing frequent advisories and vulnerability bulletins, CERT-In provides actionable recommendations on security patches, software updates, and countermeasures against evolving cyber threats such as ransomware, malware, and distributed denial-of-service (DDoS) attacks.

CERT-In also collaborates with international cybersecurity organizations to strengthen India's cyber defense mechanisms. Partnerships with global cybersecurity agencies such as the US-CERT, Europol's Cybercrime Centre, and ASEAN cybersecurity networks allow CERT-In to access real-time intelligence on global threat landscapes. This international collaboration facilitates information sharing, coordinated cyber threat responses, and the exchange of best practices in digital security.

A crucial aspect of CERT-In's mandate is its role in conducting cybersecurity drills and simulated cyberattack exercises. These drills help assess the preparedness of Indian institutions in handling cyber crises, enabling organizations to identify weaknesses in their security frameworks and improve their incident response capabilities. Participation in these exercises is encouraged across various sectors, including banking, telecommunications, e-commerce, and healthcare, ensuring that cybersecurity awareness and resilience extend beyond government agencies.

CERT-In has also taken significant steps toward securing India's growing digital economy by working closely with fintech companies, cloud service providers, and e-governance platforms to enhance security standards. The agency assists businesses in implementing strong encryption techniques, secure authentication mechanisms, and proactive threat monitoring solutions. With cybercriminals increasingly targeting India's financial infrastructure, CERT-In provides critical support in mitigating cyber fraud, phishing scams, and digital identity theft.

Recognizing the role of emerging technologies in cybersecurity, CERT-In has begun integrating artificial intelligence and machine learning into its threat detection and mitigation strategies. AI-driven security analytics allow the agency to detect anomalies in network behavior, flagging potential cyber intrusions before they escalate into full-scale attacks. Additionally, CERT-In is investing in blockchain-based security solutions for securing digital transactions and identity verification systems.

Looking ahead, CERT-In aims to expand its cybersecurity initiatives by strengthening threat intelligence-sharing networks, enhancing regulatory oversight of digital security compliance, and integrating cybersecurity education into mainstream curricula. As cyber threats continue to evolve, CERT-In remains at the forefront of India's efforts to build a robust, adaptive, and resilient cybersecurity ecosystem that can withstand future challenges in the digital age.

The Indian Computer Emergency Response Team (CERT-In) is one of the most crucial components of India's cybersecurity framework. Operating under MeitY, CERT-In is responsible for detecting, analyzing, and responding to cyber threats across government networks, corporate entities, and digital service providers. It plays a vital role in issuing security advisories, conducting cybersecurity audits, and ensuring compliance with national cybersecurity policies.

CERT-In works closely with global cybersecurity agencies, including the US-CERT, Europol's Cybercrime Centre, and various industry partners, to monitor cyber threats at an international level. It issues alerts about potential vulnerabilities in software and hardware systems, provides recommendations for security patch updates, and responds to large-scale cyber incidents such as Distributed Denial of Service (DDoS) attacks and malware infections.

CERT-In also plays a proactive role in conducting cybersecurity drills, including simulated cyberattack exercises that help assess the preparedness of Indian institutions in handling cyber crises. These exercises involve participation from banking institutions, telecommunications companies, and IT service providers to test resilience against evolving cyber threats. Through collaboration with private cybersecurity firms and academic institutions, CERT-In continues to enhance India's digital defense capabilities.

The Role of DRDO in Cyber and Electronic Warfare

The Defence Research and Development Organisation (DRDO) plays a crucial role in India's national security by spearheading research and development efforts in cyber and electronic warfare. With the increasing reliance on digital technologies in military operations, cyber warfare has become an integral part of modern defense strategies. DRDO is tasked with strengthening India's cyber resilience by developing advanced cybersecurity frameworks, artificial intelligence-driven threat detection systems, and next-generation electronic warfare solutions that can counter both cyber and electronic threats posed by adversarial nations.

One of DRDO's key contributions to cyber warfare is the development of network-centric warfare capabilities that allow India's armed forces to operate securely in highly contested digital environments. By integrating cybersecurity mechanisms into military communication systems, DRDO ensures the protection of classified data and secure transmission of battlefield intelligence. The organization has developed robust encryption technologies that safeguard military communications from cyber espionage, particularly against state-sponsored hacking groups that target command and control networks.

DRDO has also focused on intrusion detection and cyber deception techniques to mislead and deter adversaries attempting to infiltrate critical defense networks. Through artificial intelligence-powered anomaly detection systems, DRDO has enhanced the military's ability to identify and neutralize cyber threats in real time. Furthermore, cyber deception strategies, such as honeypots and misinformation channels, are deployed to misdirect enemy cyber units, minimizing their ability to compromise sensitive data.

Electronic warfare is another critical area where DRDO has made significant advancements. The organization has developed cutting-edge electronic countermeasure systems designed to jam enemy radar, disrupt electronic communications, and disable adversarial surveillance capabilities. These electronic warfare tools provide the Indian military with a strategic advantage in neutralizing threats before they escalate into full-scale conflicts. DRDO's electronic intelligence (ELINT) and signal intelligence (SIGINT) programs enable the armed forces to intercept and analyze enemy communication channels, providing valuable insights into potential threats and military strategies of adversarial forces.

Recognizing the increasing sophistication of cyber threats, DRDO has intensified its research into quantum cryptography and post-quantum encryption methods to secure military data against future cyber attacks. As quantum computing technologies evolve, traditional encryption methods may become vulnerable to decryption by adversarial states. To counter this threat, DRDO is working on quantum-resistant algorithms that will future-proof India's cybersecurity infrastructure and ensure long-term data security.

To further enhance India's cyber defense capabilities, DRDO collaborates with the Defence Cyber Agency (DCA) and the National Technical Research Organisation (NTRO) in conducting cyberwarfare simulations and penetration testing exercises. These joint initiatives help assess vulnerabilities in India's defense networks, improve cyber readiness, and develop counter-offensive cyber capabilities. By proactively testing and strengthening military cybersecurity protocols, DRDO ensures that the armed forces remain prepared to handle both conventional and asymmetric cyber threats.

Additionally, DRDO has established partnerships with academic institutions and private sector defense technology firms to accelerate innovation in cyber and electronic warfare. Through its collaboration with premier Indian research institutions, DRDO is investing in artificial intelligence-driven threat modeling, automated cyber threat response systems, and next-generation surveillance technologies. These initiatives not only enhance India's defense preparedness but also contribute to the development of indigenous cybersecurity solutions, reducing dependence on foreign technologies.

As India continues to modernize its defense capabilities, DRDO's role in cyber and electronic warfare will be instrumental in securing the nation against both known and emerging threats. The integration of cyber warfare strategies into national security planning, coupled with advancements in electronic countermeasures and cyber deception, ensures that India remains well-equipped to tackle the challenges of modern warfare. Strengthening DRDO's research and development in cyber resilience and artificial intelligence-driven defense mechanisms will be critical in maintaining India's strategic edge in an increasingly digitized and contested global security landscape.

The Defence Research and Development Organisation (DRDO) plays a significant role in strengthening India's cyber defense and electronic warfare capabilities. As cyber warfare increasingly becomes a strategic battlefield, DRDO focuses on developing cutting-edge solutions for military and national security applications. Its key areas of focus include network-centric warfare systems, encryption technologies, artificial intelligence-based threat detection, and electronic warfare capabilities that enhance India's ability to counter cyberattacks and electronic disruptions.

DRDO's contributions to cyber and electronic warfare include the development of secure communication networks for defense operations, intrusion detection systems for military installations, and cyber deception technologies that mislead adversaries attempting to breach security networks. DRDO also works on developing indigenous encryption systems that protect classified defense communications from cyber espionage by foreign adversaries. With cyber threats targeting military command and control structures, DRDO is actively engaged in creating offensive and defensive cyber capabilities to safeguard India's critical defense infrastructure.

As part of India's military modernization efforts, DRDO collaborates with the armed forces to integrate cyber warfare strategies into national defense planning. It also partners with academia and private defense technology firms to develop next-generation cyber tools that can counter emerging threats, including AI-driven cyberattacks and quantum computing-based decryption techniques. With the rapid evolution of cyber warfare tactics, DRDO's role in bolstering India's cyber resilience is more critical than ever.

The Need for a National Cyber Propaganda and Counter-Disinformation Unit

The rapid evolution of digital technologies has transformed the nature of modern warfare, where information manipulation and propaganda have become powerful tools for influencing public opinion and destabilizing adversaries. The proliferation of misinformation, deepfake technology, and AI-driven influence operations has amplified the risk of social discord, electoral interference, and national security threats. Recognizing this challenge, India must establish a dedicated National Cyber Propaganda and Counter-Disinformation Unit to monitor, analyze, and counteract these threats in real time.

This unit would serve as the primary agency responsible for detecting, mitigating, and neutralizing state-sponsored disinformation campaigns, extremist propaganda, and hostile influence operations that seek to undermine India's internal stability. By leveraging artificial intelligence, machine learning, and big data analytics, the unit would be able to track the origins of misinformation, identify coordinated bot activity, and map out the digital footprints of adversarial actors engaged in information warfare. Given the increasing use of social media platforms such as X (formerly Twitter), Facebook, WhatsApp, and YouTube for propaganda dissemination, this unit would focus on real-time surveillance of content trends, algorithmic manipulation, and misinformation amplification techniques.

In addition to monitoring, this unit would work closely with intelligence agencies, law enforcement authorities, and cybersecurity institutions such as CERT-In and NCCC to take swift countermeasures against digital disinformation. Collaboration with social media platforms and fact-checking organizations would enable quick identification and removal of misleading content, thereby preventing the spread of fake narratives. The unit would also be responsible for issuing public advisories, debunking falsehoods, and promoting accurate information to ensure that citizens receive verified and credible content.

A key component of this initiative would be its proactive engagement in strategic communication. Instead of merely reacting to misinformation, the unit should focus on strengthening India's digital resilience through awareness campaigns, digital literacy initiatives, and proactive information dissemination strategies. By educating citizens on how misinformation spreads and how to verify sources, the unit can build long-term resistance to psychological manipulation and influence operations.

The role of the proposed unit would not be limited to countering external threats alone. Domestically, it would also help mitigate internal challenges such as politically motivated fake news, communal propaganda, and misleading narratives that have the potential to trigger unrest. With AI-generated deepfake videos becoming increasingly sophisticated, this unit must develop advanced detection mechanisms to identify and expose manipulated content before it influences public discourse.

Furthermore, the unit should work on developing an early warning system to detect foreign influence in India's electoral processes. By analyzing social media activity, digital ad campaigns, and targeted disinformation, it can help ensure free and fair elections while preventing attempts to sway voter sentiments through covert influence operations. Advanced behavioral analytics can assist in recognizing sentiment shifts and assessing potential digital threats before they escalate into real-world consequences.

To ensure the effectiveness of the National Cyber Propaganda and Counter-Disinformation Unit, it should operate under a multi-agency framework, incorporating expertise from cybersecurity professionals, media analysts, behavioral scientists, and intelligence officers. Collaboration with international counterparts such as the European Union's East StratCom Task Force and the US State Department's Global Engagement Center would further bolster India's ability to counter emerging threats in the realm of information warfare.

As adversarial states and extremist organizations continue to exploit digital platforms to spread divisive narratives, India cannot afford to overlook the significance of cyber propaganda and disinformation warfare. Establishing a well-resourced, technologically advanced, and strategically positioned counter-disinformation unit is essential for safeguarding India's national security, democratic processes, and social harmony in the digital age. By integrating cutting-edge technologies, international cooperation, and a proactive communication strategy, India can ensure that its information space remains resilient against hostile influence operations.

The rise of information warfare and digital propaganda has made it imperative for India to establish a dedicated National Cyber Propaganda and Counter-Disinformation Unit. Information warfare tactics, including state-sponsored misinformation campaigns, deepfake technology, and AI-driven propaganda, have been used to manipulate public perception, influence elections, and create societal unrest. Adversarial nations and extremist groups exploit digital platforms to spread divisive narratives, posing a serious threat to national security and democratic stability.

A national-level counter-disinformation unit would focus on monitoring, analyzing, and neutralizing disinformation campaigns that threaten India's internal stability. This unit would work in collaboration with intelligence agencies, social media platforms, and fact-checking organizations to detect coordinated misinformation efforts and take swift action to counter them. The unit would leverage AI-driven content analysis, sentiment monitoring, and deepfake detection technologies to track and dismantle online influence operations.

Beyond reactive measures, this unit would also engage in strategic communication to promote accurate information and strengthen digital literacy among citizens. By enhancing public awareness on how misinformation spreads and equipping people with tools to identify false narratives, India can build a more informed and resilient digital society. The establishment of this unit would be a crucial step in protecting national interests in an era where information warfare is as critical as traditional military engagements.

Strategy for India's Information Warfare Preparedness

CHAPTER X

Building a Robust Cyber Defense System

As the digital landscape continues to evolve, cyber threats have become one of the most significant national security concerns. The increasing reliance on digital infrastructure for governance, commerce, military operations, and communication makes cybersecurity a critical component of national defense. Cyber warfare is no longer confined to traditional hacking and espionage; it has expanded into full-scale information warfare, ransomware attacks, and AI-driven cyber threats. To counter these emerging challenges, India must adopt a multi-layered cyber defense strategy, combining technological innovation, policy reforms, and international collaboration.

Need for a Dedicated Information Warfare Command

As cyber threats evolve into a primary battleground for national security, the establishment of a Dedicated Information Warfare Command (IWC) is imperative. Unlike traditional military engagements, cyber warfare operates on an unpredictable, continuous battlefield where threats emerge rapidly, requiring swift countermeasures. India must develop a structured command dedicated exclusively to cyber and information warfare, similar to the United States Cyber Command (USCYBERCOM) and China's Strategic Support Force (SSF). These entities integrate cyber operations with military intelligence, electronic warfare, and psychological operations, giving their respective nations a decisive advantage in digital conflicts.

An Indian Information Warfare Command would act as the nerve center for all cyber operations, consolidating expertise from defense, intelligence, and cybersecurity agencies. This command will oversee a broad spectrum of cyber activities, including cyber defense, cyber intelligence, offensive cyber capabilities, digital propaganda countermeasures, and real-time threat monitoring. It will also be responsible for conducting cyber drills, penetration testing of critical infrastructure, and simulations of adversarial cyberattacks to ensure national resilience.

A well-established Information Warfare Command would also play a crucial role in cyber deterrence by demonstrating India's ability to launch cyber counterstrikes against adversaries engaging in cyber espionage or digital warfare. It will enable rapid response to cyber intrusions, preventing hostile actors from infiltrating government and defense networks. The command will also lead efforts in cyber forensics, malware analysis, and tracking of Advanced Persistent Threats (APTs), particularly those originating from hostile state actors.

Additionally, the IWC would be responsible for developing coordinated cyber strategies with allied nations to combat transnational cyber threats, cyber terrorism, and digital misinformation campaigns. This includes bilateral and multilateral cooperation on cyber threat intelligence sharing and the creation of regional cybersecurity alliances.

To ensure the effectiveness of the Information Warfare Command, India must invest in skilled cybersecurity professionals, ethical hackers, AI-driven threat detection systems, and cyber-warfare training programs. The integration of Artificial Intelligence, Machine Learning, and Quantum Cryptography into cyber operations will provide a strategic advantage, enabling automated cyber threat detection and response. Additionally, fostering collaboration between government agencies, private tech firms, and research institutions will be essential for advancing India's cyber defense capabilities.

A dedicated Information Warfare Command is no longer an option—it is a necessity for safeguarding India's sovereignty in the digital domain. Its establishment will mark a transformative step in national security, positioning India as a formidable player in global cyber warfare and ensuring proactive defense mechanisms against emerging cyber threats.

Developing India's Cyber Offensive Capabilities

While defensive cybersecurity measures are essential, developing offensive cyber capabilities is equally critical to establishing deterrence and asserting cyber power. Offensive cyber operations enable a nation to conduct cyber espionage, disrupt adversarial networks, and launch counter-cyber operations to neutralize threats before they escalate. Leading global powers such as the United States, Russia, and China have heavily invested in these capabilities, allowing them to infiltrate enemy systems, disable critical infrastructure, and wage asymmetric warfare in the digital domain. India must recognize the strategic importance of offensive cyber capabilities and invest in a structured and well-equipped cyber warfare division to safeguard national interests.

Developing an advanced offensive cyber strategy requires India to enhance its cyber intelligence capabilities by integrating ethical hacking teams, advanced persistent threats (APTs), and cyber weapons that can penetrate adversarial networks. These capabilities will allow India to preemptively disable terrorist networks, track illicit cyber activities, and prevent adversaries from gaining an advantage in cyberspace. Cyber espionage and intelligence gathering will play a crucial role, enabling deep infiltration into hostile systems for extracting classified information. Monitoring enemy troop movements, digital communications, and vulnerabilities in foreign infrastructure will provide India with a significant strategic advantage.

One of the key offensive capabilities that India must develop is the use of zero-day exploits and APTs, which involve leveraging unknown security vulnerabilities to infiltrate adversary systems undetected. Zero-day vulnerabilities can be strategically used to disable enemy networks at critical moments, disrupting their operations. Additionally, custom-built malware and ransomware can be deployed to paralyze adversarial networks, degrade their technological infrastructure, and extract crucial intelligence. Ransomware, which has primarily been associated with cybercriminal organizations, is now being weaponized by nation-states to target financial institutions, defense systems, and communication networks.

Cyber sabotage and disruption are other critical aspects of offensive cyber strategies. Disabling an adversary's essential infrastructure—such as power grids, financial systems, and telecommunication networks—can significantly weaken their operational capabilities. By deploying logic bombs, Distributed Denial-of-Service (DDoS) attacks, and other advanced cyber intrusion techniques, India can disable hostile digital frameworks and exert control over adversarial cyber operations.

The role of artificial intelligence (AI) in cyber warfare is becoming increasingly significant. AI-powered offensive cyber tools can analyze vulnerabilities in real time, automate cyberattacks, and generate adaptive malware capable of bypassing traditional cybersecurity defenses. AI-driven cyber warfare is evolving rapidly, making it imperative for India to develop its AI-powered cyber offense infrastructure. Furthermore, quantum computing is emerging as a game-changer in cyber warfare. Countries investing in quantum research will have the ability to break existing encryption mechanisms, rendering conventional cybersecurity defenses ineffective. India must prioritize quantum computing research to remain competitive in cryptographic offense and counter emerging quantum threats posed by adversaries.

Another crucial factor in India's offensive cyber strategy is integrating cyber command with traditional military operations. Synchronizing cyber offensives with kinetic military actions can provide a decisive edge in conflicts, allowing India to neutralize adversaries through both digital and physical domains. Coordinated cyber operations alongside ground, naval, and air campaigns can disrupt enemy logistics, disable digital communications, and provide real-time intelligence on battlefield conditions.

International collaboration is also vital in enhancing India's offensive cyber capabilities. Establishing cyber alliances with technologically advanced nations such as the United States, Israel, and Japan can bolster India's cyber warfare readiness. Engaging in intelligence-sharing networks and joint cyber warfare exercises will further enable India to preemptively counter transnational cyber threats and cyber terrorism. Additionally, mutual cyber defense treaties with allied nations can act as a deterrent against potential large-scale digital attacks from adversaries.

By proactively enhancing its offensive cyber capabilities, India can transition from a reactive cybersecurity stance to a forward-looking cyber warfare strategy. A robust offensive cyber program will not only deter adversaries from launching digital attacks but will also position India as a dominant player in the global cyber landscape, capable of launching preemptive strikes to safeguard national sovereignty and security interests in an increasingly digitized world.

AI and Machine Learning in Cyber Defense

Artificial Intelligence (AI) and Machine Learning (ML) are transforming the cybersecurity landscape, providing sophisticated tools to detect, mitigate, and neutralize cyber threats in real time. The increasing complexity of cyberattacks, particularly those involving state-sponsored actors, necessitates advanced AI-driven security measures. AI-powered systems can process vast amounts of data, identifying attack patterns and predicting cyber threats before they manifest. This proactive approach significantly enhances national cyber resilience, allowing defense mechanisms to adapt dynamically to evolving threats.

One of the most significant applications of AI in cyber defense is threat intelligence and predictive analytics. Machine learning algorithms can analyze historical attack data to recognize anomalies, detect malicious activity, and flag potential cyber threats before they materialize. Advanced AI-driven threat detection systems utilize behavioral analytics to identify deviations from normal network activity, enabling security teams to take immediate action. This is particularly useful in combating zero-day vulnerabilities, where conventional signature-based defenses fail to detect new, unrecognized threats.

AI is also playing a crucial role in real-time cybersecurity monitoring and automated response mechanisms. Traditional cybersecurity approaches often involve manual monitoring and response, which can be slow and ineffective against highly automated cyberattacks. AI-driven security solutions, such as Security Orchestration, Automation, and Response (SOAR) platforms, enable automated threat detection, incident response, and containment. These systems can isolate compromised networks, shut down malicious processes, and deploy countermeasures within milliseconds, preventing widespread damage.

Another emerging threat in cyber warfare is adversarial AI and AI-powered cyberattacks. Malicious actors are increasingly leveraging AI to create sophisticated malware that can evade traditional security measures. AI-enhanced cyber threats include deepfake-driven social engineering attacks, AI-powered phishing campaigns, and self-mutating malware capable of adapting to security defenses. To counter this, India must invest in adversarial AI defense strategies, where AI-driven cybersecurity systems are trained to anticipate and neutralize AI-based threats in real time.

Machine learning is also being integrated into cyber deception techniques. AI-powered honeypots and deception technology can mislead attackers by creating false data environments, making it difficult for adversaries to distinguish between real and simulated systems. This approach not only disrupts cyberattacks but also allows intelligence agencies to track adversaries, analyze their attack methodologies, and develop counter-strategies.

Another critical aspect of AI in cyber defense is automated malware analysis and forensic investigations. AI-driven tools can analyze malware behavior, reverse-engineer malicious code, and trace cybercriminal activities back to their source. These forensic capabilities are crucial in attributing cyberattacks to specific threat actors, enabling targeted countermeasures against state-sponsored cyber espionage.

To fully harness AI and ML in cybersecurity, India must focus on building an AI-driven cyber defense ecosystem. This involves developing indigenous AI-powered cybersecurity solutions, fostering collaboration between government agencies and AI research institutions, and investing in quantum-safe cryptographic technologies. Additionally, public-private partnerships with cybersecurity firms can help accelerate AI innovations in threat intelligence and automated response mechanisms.

As AI continues to evolve, its role in cyber defense will only become more critical. By integrating AI and ML into cybersecurity frameworks, India can enhance its ability to detect, prevent, and neutralize cyber threats in an increasingly hostile digital environment. The future of cybersecurity will be defined by AI-driven automation, intelligent threat prediction, and adaptive cyber defense strategies, making it essential for India to stay at the forefront of AI innovation in cybersecurity.

Strengthening National Cybersecurity Policies

A robust national cybersecurity policy is essential for safeguarding a nation's digital infrastructure, protecting sensitive government and private sector data, and countering cyber threats from both domestic and foreign adversaries. With India's rapid digital expansion, the need for comprehensive and dynamic cybersecurity policies has never been more pressing. Strengthening national cybersecurity policies involves a multi-faceted approach that includes regulatory frameworks, institutional coordination, public-private partnerships, and international cooperation.

One of the foundational elements of cybersecurity policy reform is the establishment of a centralized cybersecurity governance framework. India must enhance coordination between different governmental entities, including the National Cyber Coordination Centre (NCCC), Computer Emergency Response Team (CERT-In), Ministry of Home Affairs, Ministry of Defense, and private cybersecurity firms. This will enable faster response times to cyber incidents and ensure a more structured approach to tackling cyber threats. A national Cybersecurity Operations Center (CSOC) should be established to provide real-time monitoring of cyber threats and coordinate rapid responses to large-scale cyberattacks.

In addition to governance, legal and regulatory frameworks must be continuously updated to address evolving cyber threats. India's existing cybersecurity laws, such as the Information Technology Act, 2000, need amendments to include provisions for emerging threats like ransomware, AI-powered cyberattacks, quantum computing threats, and cross-border cyber espionage.

Another critical component of cybersecurity policy is the mandatory cybersecurity standards for critical infrastructure. Sectors such as banking, energy, healthcare, transportation, and defense must be required to implement high-level cybersecurity measures, including multi-factor authentication, end-to-end encryption, AI-driven threat detection, and zero-trust security models. The Bureau of Indian Standards (BIS) should work closely with cybersecurity agencies to develop sector-specific cybersecurity compliance frameworks.

Cyber awareness and capacity building must also be a major focus of national cybersecurity policies. A large portion of cyber threats stem from phishing attacks, social engineering, and human errors. National cybersecurity policies should mandate cyber hygiene awareness programs, training for government employees, and public awareness campaigns to educate citizens about cybersecurity best practices. Furthermore, cybersecurity education should be integrated into the national academic curriculum, equipping future generations with the necessary skills to navigate an increasingly digital world securely.

To ensure financial security, cybersecurity policies must also address cyber fraud, financial data protection, and digital payment security. As India continues its transition towards a cashless economy with UPI (Unified Payments Interface), e-wallets, and digital banking services, policies should focus on securing digital transactions, preventing financial fraud, and establishing compensation mechanisms for victims of cyber fraud.

By strengthening national cybersecurity policies through legislative reforms, institutional coordination, technological advancements, and international collaboration, India can fortify its digital ecosystem against emerging cyber threats and ensure national security, economic stability, and digital sovereignty in an increasingly interconnected world.

Countering the Digital Influence of Adversaries Through Cyber-Enabled Diplomacy

In the modern digital landscape, adversarial nations and non-state actors are increasingly leveraging cyber tools to influence political narratives, manipulate public opinion, and disrupt national security frameworks. Cyber-enabled diplomacy has emerged as a crucial strategy in countering the digital influence of adversaries, combining traditional diplomatic tactics with cybersecurity measures to safeguard national interests in the cyber domain. Nations must proactively engage in digital diplomacy, leveraging cyber capabilities to shape global discourse, counter misinformation, and neutralize adversarial influence campaigns.

One of the primary threats posed by adversarial nations is the use of covert cyber operations to spread disinformation and influence public perception. State-sponsored cyber campaigns use social media platforms, fake news portals, and AI-generated content to manipulate narratives and deepen societal divisions. Misinformation campaigns orchestrated by foreign actors have been known to interfere in elections, fuel civil unrest, and create geopolitical instability. India, like many other nations, has been a target of such campaigns, with adversarial nations attempting to exploit communal and political sensitivities to destabilize internal harmony. Countering these influence operations requires a strategic approach that integrates cybersecurity, intelligence gathering, and diplomatic engagement.

One of the key elements of cyber-enabled diplomacy is developing strategic alliances with other nations to combat cyber threats collectively. India must strengthen its cybersecurity partnerships with like-minded democracies, participating in intelligence-sharing networks, joint cyber exercises, and coordinated diplomatic responses to cyber threats. Engaging in multilateral platforms such as the United Nations Group of Governmental Experts (UNGGE), the Quad Cybersecurity Partnership, and INTERPOL's Cybercrime Directorate will help in formulating international norms and policies for responsible state behavior in cyberspace. Establishing bilateral cyber cooperation agreements with nations like the United States, Japan, Israel, and European allies can enhance India's cybersecurity posture through joint research, technology sharing, and real-time threat intelligence exchange.

Another critical aspect of cyber-enabled diplomacy is neutralizing adversarial influence campaigns through coordinated counter-messaging strategies. Governments must actively debunk misinformation propagated by foreign actors through official fact-checking mechanisms, strategic communication initiatives, and engagement with social media platforms to remove misleading content. The use of AI-powered misinformation detection tools can help identify and flag false narratives in real time, allowing authorities to implement preemptive countermeasures. Collaborating with media organizations and digital platforms to implement transparency measures, such as verifying sources and promoting digital literacy, will also play a crucial role in reducing the impact of cyber propaganda.

India must also invest in cyber deterrence capabilities to prevent adversarial nations from exploiting digital platforms for subversive activities. Establishing a clear cyber deterrence doctrine that outlines the consequences of cyber intrusions and influence operations will serve as a warning to potential adversaries. Implementing active cyber defense strategies, such as offensive cyber countermeasures and real-time tracking of digital propaganda networks, will ensure that adversaries face substantial risks when attempting to manipulate Indian digital spaces. In extreme cases, targeted sanctions and diplomatic actions against nations engaging in cyber manipulation can be leveraged to exert pressure and deter further activities.

In addition to governmental efforts, public-private partnerships play a crucial role in countering the digital influence of adversaries. Collaborating with social media platforms, cybersecurity firms, and AI researchers can lead to the development of more effective digital threat mitigation strategies. Encouraging tech companies to implement robust misinformation detection algorithms, enforcing transparency in political advertising, and promoting platform accountability are essential steps in preventing digital manipulation by foreign entities.

Finally, India must prioritize capacity-building initiatives to strengthen its diplomatic and cybersecurity workforce. Training diplomats in cyber diplomacy, fostering expertise in cyber conflict resolution, and equipping intelligence agencies with advanced cyber threat monitoring capabilities will enable India to navigate the complexities of cyber-enabled influence operations. Investing in AI-driven cybersecurity solutions, deepfake detection technologies, and real-time cyber intelligence gathering will further bolster India's ability to counter digital threats effectively.

Cyber-enabled diplomacy is a critical tool in securing national interests in an era where digital influence operations have become a major geopolitical weapon. By strengthening international alliances, implementing proactive counter-messaging strategies, enhancing cyber deterrence measures, fostering public-private collaboration, and building cybersecurity expertise, India can effectively counter the digital influence of adversaries and maintain its strategic autonomy in the digital age.

CHAPTER XI

Role of Media and Civil Society in Information Warfare

In the modern digital age, information warfare has become an essential tool for both state and non-state actors, influencing public perception, shaping political narratives, and even destabilizing societies. The role of media and civil society in countering this growing threat is paramount, as responsible journalism, strategic research communities, digital literacy programs, and proactive fact-checking mechanisms serve as critical defenses against disinformation campaigns. In a country as diverse and complex as India, these elements play a crucial role in national security, ensuring that adversarial influence operations do not erode democratic values and social harmony.

Importance of Responsible Journalism in National Security

In an era where information is weaponized, responsible journalism plays a critical role in safeguarding national security by ensuring factual reporting, countering misinformation, and preventing the spread of propaganda. The media serves as a vital conduit between the government and the public, influencing perceptions, shaping discourse, and maintaining societal cohesion. However, the digital age has introduced new complexities where fake news, sensationalism, and politically motivated narratives can be exploited by adversarial actors to destabilize nations. Responsible journalism is no longer just about ethical reporting—it is a frontline defense mechanism against information warfare.

Journalists must be trained to identify and counter disinformation campaigns, particularly those orchestrated by foreign entities seeking to manipulate public sentiment. Governments and media institutions must collaborate to ensure that reporting remains transparent, unbiased, and rooted in verifiable facts. The rise of social media has amplified the challenge, as unverified content can go viral within minutes, creating a distorted reality that can mislead the public. Media organizations should adopt robust fact-checking protocols, AI-driven content verification tools, and editorial oversight mechanisms to ensure that only credible information is disseminated.

Moreover, the role of investigative journalism is crucial in exposing covert influence operations, cyber-enabled propaganda efforts, and state-sponsored disinformation networks. Journalists working in national security reporting must have access to credible intelligence sources and cybersecurity experts to verify claims before publishing. Additionally, governments should engage in strategic communication efforts to counter false narratives without infringing on press freedom.

One of the biggest threats to responsible journalism is the weaponization of fake news by both internal and external actors. In politically charged environments, media houses must ensure that their reporting does not unintentionally amplify propaganda. The use of misleading headlines, manipulated statistics, and sensationalist reporting often serves as a catalyst for public unrest. News agencies must adhere to strict journalistic ethics, ensuring that their content does not serve as a tool for information warfare.

State-sponsored media outlets and propaganda networks also pose a significant challenge, as adversarial nations utilize controlled news agencies to push narratives that align with their strategic interests. Governments must invest in counter-disinformation programs, support independent journalism, and create digital literacy initiatives to help citizens critically analyze news sources. Collaborations between media watchdog organizations, academic institutions, and cybersecurity agencies can further help in tracking and exposing misinformation campaigns before they gain traction.

In addition, media organizations must recognize the importance of digital security to protect journalists from cyber threats, harassment, and online manipulation. Cyber espionage, hacking attempts, and targeted online harassment campaigns against investigative journalists are growing concerns. To ensure press freedom while maintaining security, governments should implement legal safeguards for journalists while equipping them with tools to defend against digital threats.

Responsible journalism is an essential pillar of national security, acting as both a gatekeeper of credible information and a barrier against the spread of disinformation. Media institutions must prioritize integrity over virality, accuracy over speed, and national security over partisan interests. By fostering transparency, accountability, and resilience against propaganda, the media can effectively safeguard democratic values while countering the ever-growing threats posed by information warfare.

Media is often referred to as the fourth pillar of democracy, but in the realm of information warfare, it also serves as a double-edged sword. On one hand, credible journalism acts as a bulwark against propaganda, exposing false narratives and providing factual reporting. On the other hand, irresponsible journalism, sensationalism, and politically motivated reporting can amplify misinformation, creating unnecessary panic and social discord. It is imperative that media organizations uphold journalistic integrity, ethical reporting standards, and fact-checking mechanisms to prevent their platforms from being exploited as conduits of disinformation.

In times of geopolitical crises, war, or political unrest, adversarial nations often engage in media manipulation, leveraging local and international news networks to push specific narratives. State-sponsored news agencies, propaganda outlets, and biased digital platforms attempt to influence public discourse by injecting false or misleading information into mainstream conversations. To counter this, journalists and media houses must be trained in recognizing misinformation tactics, ensuring source verification, and maintaining editorial independence. Additionally, government agencies can collaborate with media organizations to establish transparent communication channels that provide fact-based information in real time, reducing the space for fake news to proliferate.

Role of Think Tanks and Strategic Communities

Think tanks and strategic communities play a pivotal role in understanding, analyzing, and countering information warfare threats. These research institutions provide valuable insights into global disinformation trends, state-sponsored influence operations, cyber warfare tactics, and digital propaganda mechanisms. By conducting in-depth research, they help policymakers develop counterstrategies that mitigate the impact of information warfare on national security. In an era where information manipulation has become a key tool in geopolitical conflicts, the work of think tanks is more critical than ever.

India has a growing network of think tanks specializing in cybersecurity, media studies, and geopolitical analysis. Institutions such as the Observer Research Foundation (ORF), Centre for Land Warfare Studies (CLAWS), and Institute for Defence Studies and Analyses (IDSA) have contributed significantly to understanding the evolving nature of information warfare. However, greater investments are needed in research and development to strengthen India's information warfare capabilities. Cross-collaboration between think tanks, government agencies, intelligence bodies, and media organizations can ensure a more coordinated approach to countering disinformation campaigns.

Think tanks also play a crucial role in forecasting future threats and identifying emerging trends in digital warfare. By analyzing data from social media platforms, online forums, and encrypted communication channels, they can detect early warning signs of coordinated disinformation efforts. Research institutions must work closely with government agencies to develop AI-driven threat detection systems that can map and track online influence operations. This intelligence can then be used to inform national security strategies and policy responses.

Additionally, think tanks serve as forums for debate and policy advocacy, ensuring that national cybersecurity policies evolve in response to new challenges. By bringing together experts from diverse fields—including cybersecurity, political science, psychology, and international relations—these institutions can generate holistic solutions that address both technological and human factors in information warfare. Moreover, they must engage with global think tanks to exchange knowledge, strategies, and best practices in countering disinformation campaigns.

Strategic communities, including academic researchers, retired military personnel, and cybersecurity professionals, contribute by offering independent perspectives on national security threats. Their work helps bridge the gap between government policy and technological innovation, ensuring that India's cyber defenses remain adaptive and resilient. Furthermore, their insights into psychological manipulation techniques, media influence strategies, and digital propaganda frameworks help shape effective counter-narratives to neutralize misinformation at its source.

Public engagement is another crucial aspect of the role of think tanks. Organizing seminars, policy discussions, and awareness workshops on topics related to information warfare fosters a well-informed citizenry that can critically evaluate news and media content. Educating journalists, government officials, and civil society actors on the tactics employed by adversarial states in information warfare is essential to strengthening India's national resilience.

Moreover, think tanks should actively participate in track-two diplomacy initiatives, collaborating with their counterparts in allied nations to counteract global disinformation threats. This includes sharing intelligence on cyber threats, coordinating international responses to state-sponsored propaganda campaigns, and contributing to multilateral efforts aimed at regulating digital misinformation.

To further enhance their effectiveness, think tanks must embrace emerging technologies such as big data analytics, machine learning, and network analysis to study the dynamics of online information warfare. Developing indigenous software tools to track and analyze digital influence operations will provide India with a strategic advantage in the cyber domain. Funding and institutional support for such initiatives must be prioritized to ensure that think tanks remain at the forefront of digital security research.

Ultimately, think tanks and strategic communities are indispensable in shaping national security policies, advising governments on counter-disinformation measures, and educating the public on media literacy. Their work must be integrated into a broader, multi-sectoral approach to countering information warfare, ensuring that India remains well-prepared to tackle the evolving challenges of the digital battlefield.

Public Awareness and Digital Literacy Programs

Public awareness and digital literacy programs play a critical role in strengthening societal resilience against information warfare. With the rapid proliferation of social media and instant messaging platforms, misinformation and propaganda campaigns have gained unprecedented reach, often influencing public opinion, election outcomes, and even national security. To combat this growing threat, governments, educational institutions, media organizations, and civil society must work together to develop comprehensive digital literacy programs that educate citizens on identifying, analyzing, and countering disinformation.

One of the most effective ways to foster public resilience is by integrating digital literacy education into school and university curricula. Students should be taught the fundamentals of media literacy, critical thinking, and source verification to ensure they can differentiate between credible news sources and manipulated content. Hands-on workshops that simulate real-world misinformation scenarios can provide practical training on spotting deepfake videos, misleading headlines, and bot-driven disinformation campaigns. Additionally, cybersecurity awareness should be included as part of digital education to help individuals recognize phishing attempts, social engineering tactics, and personal data vulnerabilities.

Governments and civil society organizations should also launch nationwide public awareness campaigns that educate citizens on the dangers of misinformation and the role they play in preventing its spread.

These campaigns should leverage television, radio, digital platforms, and local community centers to reach diverse demographics, particularly rural populations that may be more susceptible to digital misinformation due to lower media literacy levels. Fact-checking organizations should be supported to debunk viral misinformation in real time, ensuring that false narratives do not gain widespread traction. Governments can collaborate with media watchdogs, cybersecurity experts, and tech companies to promote fact-checking services and create accessible tools for verifying news stories.

Corporate entities and private organizations also have a role to play in promoting digital literacy among employees. Training programs focused on recognizing online manipulation, preventing cyber threats, and verifying information sources should be standard practice in both government and private sector workplaces. Additionally, digital platforms such as Facebook, Twitter, and YouTube must be encouraged to implement proactive misinformation detection mechanisms, including AI-driven content moderation, flagging systems, and user education pop-ups that provide context about misleading content.

Another crucial element of digital literacy efforts is countering cognitive biases that make people vulnerable to misinformation. Psychological studies show that individuals are more likely to believe and share information that aligns with their pre-existing beliefs, even if the content is false. Digital literacy programs should therefore incorporate behavioral science approaches to teach users how to critically assess emotionally charged content, avoid confirmation bias, and seek out multiple credible sources before accepting information as fact.

Governments must also work closely with social media companies to regulate and minimize the spread of misinformation without infringing on freedom of speech. Transparency measures, such as labeling manipulated content and providing visibility into algorithmic decision-making, can help users make more informed judgments about the information they consume. Additionally, AI-driven bot-detection systems should be enhanced to identify and shut down networks of fake accounts that amplify disinformation campaigns.

To ensure lasting impact, digital literacy programs must be continuously updated to address emerging threats in the information warfare landscape, including AI-generated fake content, cyber espionage tactics, and the use of deepfake technology to manipulate public perception. By fostering a well-informed and digitally literate society, nations can effectively build resilience against the weaponization of information and safeguard democratic institutions from adversarial influence.

Digital literacy is one of the most effective tools in countering information warfare. In an era where social media has become a primary source of news for millions, educating citizens on how to identify fake news, misinformation, and propaganda is critical to safeguarding democratic institutions. Digital literacy programs must be implemented at the grassroots level, focusing on schools, universities, corporate organizations, and community centers.

Governments and civil society organizations should work together to design curriculum-based programs that teach media literacy, critical thinking, and responsible online behavior. These programs should include practical training on recognizing deepfake videos, identifying misleading headlines, and verifying news sources. Additionally, platforms like Facebook, Twitter, and YouTube must be encouraged to integrate fact-checking tools and misinformation warnings into their algorithms to prevent the spread of false information.

Governments must also invest in public awareness campaigns that debunk viral misinformation in real-time, ensuring that the general population is not misled by false narratives. Collaborations between the media, government fact-checking bodies, and independent digital literacy organizations can ensure a well-informed public that is resilient to manipulation.

Combating Fake News and Deepfake Propaganda

Fake news and deepfake propaganda represent a major battlefield in the ongoing war for truth. While digital platforms have allowed for the rapid exchange of information, they have also enabled the mass manipulation of facts. The fight against disinformation must be relentless, combining AI-driven solutions, legal enforcement, and widespread public education. Without proactive countermeasures, the future of democratic societies will remain at risk, as adversaries continue to exploit these digital tools to reshape reality for their own interests.

One of the most potent threats in information warfare is the rise of deepfake technology and the increasing prevalence of fake news. Deepfakes—AI-generated synthetic media that manipulates videos, images, or audio—have become powerful tools for propaganda, defamation, and misinformation. These technologies can be used to create fabricated videos of political leaders, celebrities, or government officials making statements they never actually made, leading to potential diplomatic crises or political unrest.

India has already witnessed instances where deepfake technology has been used to spread election-related misinformation, defame public figures, and influence voter perceptions. As this technology becomes more sophisticated, governments, media organizations, and civil society must work together to develop AI-based detection systems that can identify and debunk deepfake content before it spreads.

Additionally, independent fact-checking organizations such as Alt News, Boom Live, and Factly have played a critical role in exposing fake news and deepfake content. However, their efforts need to be amplified through greater funding, increased collaboration with social media platforms, and government-backed initiatives that promote fact-checking at scale. Building AI-powered misinformation detection algorithms and integrating them into mainstream social media channels can help combat the growing influence of fabricated content.

To further strengthen efforts against fake news, stringent regulations should be introduced to hold content creators, digital platforms, and media organizations accountable for spreading misinformation. Governments should also explore the possibility of establishing a central digital regulatory body that monitors online content and works with international agencies to track and shut down disinformation networks operating across borders.

CHAPTER XII

The Future of Information Warfare and India's Preparedness

The evolution of technology has significantly altered the landscape of warfare, with information warfare emerging as a dominant force in geopolitical conflicts. As cyber capabilities continue to advance, nations must prepare for a future where misinformation, cyber espionage, and digital influence campaigns play a crucial role in shaping global power dynamics. India, as a rising digital powerhouse, must anticipate and address these challenges by strengthening its cyber defenses, investing in cutting-edge technologies, and fostering international alliances to safeguard its national security and sovereignty in the digital realm.

Quantum Computing and Next-Generation Cyber Threats

Quantum computing is poised to be one of the most revolutionary technological advancements of the coming decades, fundamentally altering the landscape of cybersecurity and information warfare. Unlike classical computing, which relies on binary bits, quantum computing operates using qubits, enabling the execution of highly complex calculations at speeds that are currently unimaginable. This capability has far-reaching implications across multiple domains, from artificial intelligence and big data analytics to cryptography and national security. While quantum computing offers significant benefits for scientific research and problem-solving, it also presents a severe cybersecurity threat. Traditional encryption methods that secure global communications, financial transactions, and classified government data could become obsolete, as quantum computers will have the capability to break cryptographic keys within seconds. This unprecedented decryption ability raises serious concerns about the security of sensitive information, military communications, and global financial networks, making quantum computing one of the foremost challenges in modern cyber defense.

India must take proactive steps to safeguard its digital infrastructure against the threats posed by quantum computing. One of the most critical areas of focus should be the development of post-quantum cryptographic solutions designed to withstand quantum-powered decryption attempts.

Research institutions, defense organizations, and private technology firms must collaborate to create quantum-resistant encryption algorithms that will provide long-term security for government, military, and financial sectors. In addition to developing indigenous quantum-secure cryptographic frameworks, India must also invest in quantum key distribution technology, which leverages the principles of quantum mechanics to ensure unbreakable communication channels. Ensuring secure quantum communications will be crucial for protecting military strategies, diplomatic correspondences, and classified intelligence exchanges from foreign adversaries that may exploit quantum computing for cyber espionage.

To remain at the forefront of quantum cybersecurity, India must actively participate in global quantum security initiatives. Leading technological powers such as the United States, China, and the European Union are already making significant strides in quantum research, and India must engage in international collaborations to stay ahead of emerging threats. Participation in joint quantum research projects, multilateral cybersecurity agreements, and information-sharing alliances will be instrumental in enhancing India's quantum resilience. In addition to international cooperation, India must strengthen its domestic quantum computing ecosystem by fostering research and innovation in the field. Government-backed programs should encourage investment in quantum technology, the establishment of quantum research hubs, and the creation of a skilled workforce capable of addressing the challenges posed by next-generation cyber threats.

Beyond cryptographic concerns, quantum computing could also revolutionize offensive cyber capabilities, allowing state and non-state actors to develop advanced cyberattack methods that bypass conventional security measures. Cybercriminal groups and hostile nation-states may leverage quantum computing to carry out large-scale cyber espionage campaigns, disrupt critical infrastructure, and undermine national security through quantum-enhanced hacking techniques. Given these risks, India must enhance its quantum cybersecurity defenses by integrating quantum-safe security protocols, deploying AI-driven quantum threat detection systems, and continuously monitoring global developments in quantum technology.

The strategic adoption of quantum computing is not just about countering threats; it also presents an opportunity for India to establish itself as a leader in next-generation computing and cybersecurity. By developing indigenous quantum technologies, securing intellectual property rights for quantum innovations, and training a new generation of quantum computing experts, India can position itself as a key player in the global quantum race. The intersection of quantum computing and cybersecurity will define the future of information warfare, and India's preparedness in this domain will determine its ability to safeguard its digital sovereignty, maintain national security, and counter emerging cyber threats in an increasingly interconnected world.

Future Trends in Cyber and Information Warfare

As cyber and information warfare continue to evolve, several key trends are expected to shape the future battlefield. The rise of autonomous cyber warfare powered by artificial intelligence will allow cyber adversaries to launch self-learning and adaptive cyberattacks that evolve in real time. AI-driven disinformation campaigns will become more sophisticated, leveraging machine learning algorithms to tailor propaganda and misinformation to specific demographic groups, making countermeasures increasingly challenging. Cybercriminal organizations and state-sponsored actors will increasingly use AI-generated content to manipulate public opinion, influence elections, and undermine trust in democratic institutions. The ability to generate highly convincing synthetic media, including deepfakes, will complicate efforts to discern reality from fabrication, heightening the risks of geopolitical instability and misinformation-fueled social unrest.

The proliferation of Internet of Things devices will further expand the attack surface for cyber adversaries. With billions of interconnected devices controlling essential services such as power grids, transportation systems, and healthcare networks, cyber vulnerabilities in IoT infrastructure could be exploited for large-scale cyber sabotage. Attackers may target smart city infrastructure, industrial control systems, and autonomous vehicles to disrupt critical operations and create widespread chaos. The increasing reliance on cloud computing and remote work environments further intensifies the risk, making robust encryption protocols, zero-trust security models, and AI-driven anomaly detection crucial in mitigating cyber threats. The security of IoT ecosystems must become a national priority, requiring strict regulatory frameworks, industry-wide security standards, and proactive threat monitoring to prevent catastrophic breaches.

Another significant trend is the weaponization of deepfake technology for political and military deception. AI-generated deepfakes will be used to impersonate political leaders, manipulate diplomatic negotiations, and incite civil unrest. Fabricated videos, audio recordings, and fake social media personas could be deployed to spread false narratives, influence public sentiment, and distort the outcomes of key events. With deepfake creation tools becoming more accessible, bad actors will exploit this technology to conduct blackmail, defamation, and information warfare at an unprecedented scale. The implications of deepfake technology extend beyond individual manipulation; entire populations could be swayed by highly realistic fabricated media, undermining the credibility of legitimate sources and fueling societal divisions. Developing advanced forensic AI tools for deepfake detection and authentication will be essential in countering this growing threat.

The rise of offensive cyber capabilities will see an increase in state-sponsored cyber sabotage, election interference, and digital blackmail tactics, requiring nations to bolster their defensive and retaliatory cyber strategies. Governments and intelligence agencies will need to develop cyber resilience programs that emphasize rapid threat detection, coordinated response mechanisms, and robust counteroffensive measures. Cyber defense strategies must integrate AI-driven security analytics, real-time intelligence sharing, and simulation-based training to prepare for evolving cyber threats. Additionally, cross-sector collaboration between governments, private enterprises, and academia will be vital in addressing the complexities of modern cyber warfare. Nations that fail to adapt to these trends risk falling victim to sophisticated cyberattacks that could cripple economies, compromise national security, and erode public trust in institutions. As cyber warfare becomes an increasingly integral component of global conflicts, preemptive defense measures and strategic deterrence will play a critical role in maintaining stability and securing the digital landscape.

India's Role in Global Cyber Governance

As one of the world's fastest-growing digital economies, India has a significant role to play in shaping the global cyber governance framework. The absence of universally accepted cyber laws and regulations has created a fragmented digital landscape where cyber warfare, misinformation campaigns, and state-sponsored cyber operations operate with little accountability. India must advocate for the establishment of international norms and legal frameworks to define acceptable state behavior in cyberspace and prevent the misuse of cyber technologies for malicious purposes. As a country with vast digital aspirations, India must lead initiatives that focus on responsible cyber conduct, cyber sovereignty, and ensuring an open, safe, and resilient digital space for all.

India's participation in global cyber governance forums such as the United Nations Group of Governmental Experts, the Global Forum on Cyber Expertise, and the International Telecommunication Union provides a platform to shape cybersecurity policies, data privacy regulations, and mechanisms for cyber conflict resolution. Through active diplomatic engagements, India must work towards establishing a more structured cyber governance framework, ensuring that cyber norms align with democratic principles and digital human rights. Additionally, India should reinforce its role in multilateral organizations like the Indo-Pacific region's cybersecurity partnerships, the Quad Cybersecurity Partnership, and BRICS digital security initiatives to develop collective strategies for countering cyber threats.

Domestically, India must focus on enhancing legal frameworks for cybercrime, data protection, and online privacy by updating laws such as the Personal Data Protection Bill and implementing the National Cyber Security Strategy. The rapid digitization of public and private infrastructure makes it necessary to have strong policies addressing cyber espionage, data sovereignty, and cross-border cybercrime. Cyber law enforcement agencies must be equipped with state-of-the-art forensic capabilities, while the judicial system should integrate specialized cyber courts to expedite legal proceedings related to cyber threats. India's digital economy must be safeguarded through stringent regulatory measures that ensure data localization, mandatory cybersecurity compliance for corporations, and periodic cybersecurity audits of critical infrastructure.

To enhance its cybersecurity posture, India must engage in technological collaborations with global cybersecurity leaders and invest in developing indigenous cybersecurity solutions. Government agencies should collaborate with private sector leaders and academic institutions to drive innovation in cybersecurity technologies, including AI-powered threat intelligence, cyber deception techniques, and real-time intrusion detection systems. Additionally, India's participation in global cyber alliances must include the sharing of intelligence related to emerging cyber threats, facilitating joint cyber drills, and contributing to international efforts to combat digital terrorism, ransomware attacks, and financial fraud.

As information warfare increasingly becomes a tool for geopolitical maneuvering, India must ensure that its cyber governance policies not only defend national security interests but also contribute to global stability. By strengthening regional cybersecurity cooperation through SAARC, ASEAN, and BIMSTEC, India can help its neighbors build cyber resilience while jointly addressing the threat of cross-border cyber warfare. Establishing a South Asian Cyber Defense Cooperation Framework could be instrumental in mitigating regional cyber threats, securing digital infrastructures, and countering misinformation campaigns that threaten national sovereignty. With strategic cyber alliances, legislative advancements, and a proactive diplomatic approach, India can emerge as a global leader in cyber governance, ensuring a secure digital future in an increasingly complex and volatile cyber landscape.

Need for International Alliances Against Information Warfare

The evolving nature of information warfare makes international alliances an essential aspect of cybersecurity and digital defense. Cyber threats transcend national borders, making no country immune to cyber espionage, misinformation campaigns, and state-sponsored attacks. The interconnected digital landscape allows adversaries to exploit vulnerabilities in global networks, impacting national security, critical infrastructure, and democratic processes. To combat these threats, India must build strong international alliances that foster collaboration in cybersecurity, intelligence sharing, and coordinated defense mechanisms.

Forging bilateral and multilateral cybersecurity partnerships with technologically advanced nations is crucial for India's defense strategy. Strategic cooperation with countries like the United States, Israel, Japan, and key European nations will provide India access to cutting-edge cybersecurity technologies, advanced threat intelligence frameworks, and expertise in countering cyber warfare. These alliances will enable India to adopt best practices in cyber defense, cyber hygiene, and proactive risk mitigation. Cyber intelligence-sharing agreements between allied nations will facilitate real-time exchange of threat intelligence, allowing countries to preemptively address cyber risks before they escalate into large-scale attacks. India's participation in global cybersecurity initiatives such as the Budapest Convention on Cybercrime and the Paris Call for Trust and Security in Cyberspace will further strengthen its role in shaping international cyber norms and promoting responsible state behavior in cyberspace.

Regional collaboration is equally vital in countering cyber threats that originate from neighboring adversaries. India must enhance cyber cooperation within SAARC, ASEAN, and BIMSTEC to bolster regional cyber resilience. Establishing a South Asian Cyber Defense Cooperation Framework could facilitate knowledge sharing, joint cyber drills, and coordinated responses to cyber incidents affecting multiple nations in the region. By fostering cybersecurity capacity-building programs and assisting smaller nations in developing robust cyber defense mechanisms, India can position itself as a cybersecurity leader in South Asia. Cross-border cooperation in combating misinformation, election interference, and digital sabotage will be key to maintaining regional stability and security.

India must also engage in technology-sharing agreements that focus on quantum-safe encryption, AI-driven cybersecurity solutions, and advanced threat detection systems. Strengthening diplomatic ties with cybersecurity research institutions in allied nations will help India remain at the forefront of emerging technologies and cyber defense innovations. Collaborative research on cyber threat intelligence, cyber forensics, and security analytics can provide deeper insights into evolving attack vectors and new-age cyber threats. Additionally, participation in global cyber defense exercises with NATO and Indo-Pacific security frameworks will help India refine its cyber warfare strategies and build expertise in cyber conflict management.

Another critical aspect of international cyber alliances is countering transnational cybercrime. Organized cybercriminal networks operate across jurisdictions, making law enforcement cooperation imperative. India must establish stronger channels for cross-border cybercrime investigations, extradition agreements for cyber offenders, and joint operations to dismantle cybercriminal infrastructures. Agreements with INTERPOL, Europol, and regional cybercrime task forces will help India crack down on cyber fraud, ransomware networks, and illicit financial transactions in the digital realm. Strengthening legal cooperation on cybercrime prosecution will also be essential in ensuring cybercriminals do not exploit jurisdictional loopholes to evade justice.

As cyber warfare becomes a dominant tool of modern conflicts, the importance of cyber diplomacy will continue to grow. India must leverage diplomatic channels to advocate for the establishment of international norms that regulate state behavior in cyberspace and prevent cyberattacks on civilian infrastructure, electoral processes, and financial systems. By taking a leadership role in cyber governance discussions at the United Nations and G20, India can help define a rules-based digital order that promotes cybersecurity, privacy, and digital rights.

The need for international alliances in information warfare cannot be overstated. India must proactively engage in cybersecurity coalitions, intelligence-sharing agreements, and regional defense partnerships to ensure a secure digital future. Strengthening international collaborations will not only enhance India's cybersecurity resilience but also contribute to global efforts in maintaining a stable, rules-based cyberspace that upholds democratic values and technological sovereignty.

Case Studies & Lessons for India

CHAPTER XIII

Case Studies on Information Warfare Targeting India

2019 Balakot Airstrike: Social Media Narratives and Information Manipulation

The 2019 Balakot airstrike was a defining moment in India-Pakistan relations, not just in terms of military engagement but also in the realm of information warfare. Following the Indian Air Force's precision strikes on a Jaish-e-Mohammed training camp in Balakot, Pakistan, in response to the Pulwama terror attack, social media became a battleground for competing narratives. The digital domain played a critical role in shaping public perception, influencing international discourse, and spreading both verified information and disinformation at an unprecedented scale.

On February 14, 2019, a suicide bombing attack in Pulwama, Jammu and Kashmir, killed 40 personnel of India's Central Reserve Police Force (CRPF). The attack was claimed by the Pakistan-based terror group Jaish-e-Mohammed, intensifying hostilities between the two nuclear-armed neighbors. In retaliation, on February 26, 2019, the Indian Air Force conducted a pre-dawn airstrike targeting a JeM facility in Balakot, Khyber Pakhtunkhwa province of Pakistan. India maintained that the strikes inflicted heavy damage on terrorist infrastructure, neutralizing a significant number of JeM operatives, sending a strong message against terrorism emanating from Pakistani soil.

Both Indian and Pakistani governments engaged in digital narrative-building to establish their respective versions of the event. The Indian government framed the airstrike as a decisive counterterrorism measure, emphasizing its success in striking a terror stronghold and demonstrating India's capability to respond effectively to cross-border terrorism. Key officials, including the Prime Minister and the Ministry of External Affairs, utilized social media platforms to project the operation as a strategic victory. Meanwhile, the Pakistani government, particularly through the Inter-Services Public Relations (ISPR), attempted to counter these claims by asserting that Indian jets had only struck an empty hillside, with no casualties or structural damage, despite independent reports indicating otherwise.

Hashtags became powerful tools in the information war, with Indian social media users promoting tags like #BalakotAirstrike, #IndiaStrikesBack, and #SurgicalStrike2 to celebrate the mission and reinforce India's national security stance. Meanwhile, Pakistan-based accounts countered with #BalakotDrama, #PakistanStrikesBack, and #FalseFlag to discredit India's claims. These digital campaigns were amplified by thousands of users, including journalists, politicians, and influencers, who engaged in a fierce online debate. While India's side largely relied on official reports and evidence provided by military sources, Pakistan's counter-narrative often relied on deflection and misinformation to create confusion regarding the impact of the strikes.

The Balakot airstrike was also accompanied by an influx of misinformation, including fake images and videos purporting to show the aftermath of the strike. Some widely shared visuals turned out to be unrelated, originating from past conflicts or being digitally altered to fit the respective narratives. Pro-Pakistan social media accounts circulated manipulated satellite images and staged video footage to suggest minimal damage, while pro-India accounts emphasized the operational success of the strike, relying on intelligence inputs. Despite attempts at misinformation from the Pakistani side, Indian agencies released radar images and other evidence that corroborated the success of the operation.

Mainstream media outlets in both India and Pakistan played a crucial role in amplifying their respective governments' narratives. Indian media largely echoed the government's stance, citing intelligence sources and satellite imagery analysis to support the claim of high terrorist casualties. In contrast, Pakistani media focused on downplaying the impact of the strike, featuring testimonies from local villagers and controlled state narratives that were not independently verified. The divergence in media coverage underscored the role of state-aligned journalism in information warfare.

Pakistan's ISPR demonstrated a high level of coordination in digital warfare, leveraging social media, video releases, and misinformation campaigns to contest India's claims. By releasing selectively edited images, manipulated statements, and controlled interviews with local villagers, ISPR aimed to inject doubt into India's version of events. However, several independent investigations, including reports by Reuters and international satellite imaging firms, indicated visible structural damage at the targeted site, confirming India's assertion that the strike had successfully hit its intended target.

India's digital response was more structured, relying primarily on official briefings, military statements, and intelligence-based counterclaims rather than aggressive propaganda. Unlike Pakistan's extensive use of social media-driven misinformation, India chose a factual approach, with limited but strategic releases of verifiable evidence. This method, while restrained, proved more effective in maintaining credibility in international discourse.

The Balakot airstrike illustrated several key lessons about modern information warfare. The rapid spread of real-time updates, coupled with misinformation, highlighted the need for fact-checking mechanisms and media literacy to counter propaganda. It also showcased the power of social media as both an asset and a liability in national security operations. Governments must develop agile digital strategies that balance official communication with proactive counter-disinformation efforts to prevent adversaries from controlling the narrative. The role of artificial intelligence in detecting deepfake content, analyzing bot activity, and identifying coordinated misinformation campaigns will be crucial in future conflicts.

This case study reinforces the importance of integrating information warfare into military strategy. Future engagements will not only be determined by battlefield successes but also by how effectively a nation controls the narrative in the digital sphere. As cyber and information warfare continue to evolve, countries must invest in sophisticated digital defense mechanisms, real-time intelligence analysis, and strategic communication frameworks to ensure that truth prevails over manipulation in the age of digital conflict.

Case Study: Terrorist Recruitment in Kashmir – The Burhan Wani Phenomenon

The Kashmir Valley has long been a focal point of cross-border terrorism and insurgency, with Pakistan-backed terror groups exploiting local grievances to radicalize and recruit youth into their ranks. Among the many cases of terrorist recruitment, the rise and subsequent death of Hizbul Mujahideen commander Burhan Wani in 2016 marked a significant shift in the way terrorism was marketed and propagated in Kashmir. Wani's transformation into a poster boy for militancy in the region was largely facilitated by social media, where his persona was carefully curated to appeal to disenchanted youth. His influence signified a new era of digital radicalization, blurring the lines between insurgency and social media-driven propaganda.

Burhan Wani, a young militant from Tral in South Kashmir, gained prominence for his extensive use of social media to promote terrorism. Unlike previous generations of militants who operated in secrecy, Wani became the face of a new-age insurgency, using platforms like Facebook and YouTube to spread his ideology, recruit youth, and challenge the Indian state. His video messages, featuring him and his associates in military fatigues and armed with sophisticated weapons, were designed to glorify terrorism and attract impressionable young minds. By leveraging social media, Wani transformed Hizbul Mujahideen's recruitment strategies, making militancy appear aspirational rather than clandestine. His digital outreach created a sense of heroism around terrorism, fueling a wave of radicalization across the region.

Pakistan's Inter-Services Intelligence (ISI) and its affiliated propaganda arms played a critical role in amplifying Wani's image as a martyr for the Kashmiri cause. The Pakistani media, both mainstream and social, consistently portrayed him as a revolutionary, fueling unrest and anti-India sentiment in Kashmir. Hashtags like #BurhanWani and #KashmirMartyr flooded digital spaces, generating sympathy for Wani's cause. His death in an encounter with Indian security forces on July 8, 2016, triggered massive unrest, leading to violent protests and clashes across the Valley. The reaction to his killing demonstrated the extent to which digital propaganda had influenced the minds of young Kashmiris, transforming Wani from a militant into a larger-than-life figure.

The narrative surrounding Wani's recruitment and radicalization was carefully crafted through the use of misinformation and selective storytelling. While his supporters projected him as a symbol of Kashmiri resistance, they conveniently ignored his involvement in armed militancy and terrorist activities. Pakistan-sponsored media outlets and social media accounts created an emotional narrative that downplayed the dangers of terrorism and instead painted Wani as a freedom fighter. The widespread misinformation campaign not only misled local youth but also shaped international perceptions, with foreign media often echoing biased narratives that overlooked Pakistan's role in fueling terrorism in the region.

Following Wani's death, Pakistan's cyber propaganda machinery intensified efforts to radicalize Kashmiri youth. Social media accounts linked to Pakistan-based terror outfits such as Lashkar-e-Taiba (LeT) and Jaish-e-Mohammed (JeM) circulated highly emotive content, including edited videos, eulogies, and fabricated accounts of Indian security forces' actions. Encrypted messaging platforms such as Telegram and WhatsApp were also used extensively to recruit and communicate with potential militants. The shift from traditional recruitment methods to digital indoctrination made it harder for Indian intelligence agencies to track and counter radicalization efforts.

In response to this growing challenge, the Indian government and security agencies implemented counter-radicalization initiatives aimed at deconstructing the propaganda surrounding Wani and other terrorist figures. Digital monitoring cells were set up to identify and take down extremist content, while counter-narratives emphasizing peace, development, and the dangers of militancy were promoted. The government also ramped up its efforts to engage with Kashmiri youth through employment programs, educational scholarships, and de-radicalization initiatives. Additionally, social media companies were urged to cooperate in identifying and removing extremist content to prevent further radicalization.

The case of Burhan Wani highlights the evolving nature of terrorist recruitment, where the battlefield is no longer just the streets of Kashmir but also the virtual world of social media. The use of digital platforms to spread extremist ideology, recruit operatives, and incite violence presents a formidable challenge for counter-terrorism agencies. It underscores the need for a multi-pronged approach that includes stringent cyber-monitoring, grassroots engagement, and international cooperation to dismantle terror networks operating in the digital space. As terrorism continues to adapt to the digital age, India must remain vigilant in countering not just the physical threats posed by militant groups but also the psychological and ideological battles being waged online.

India's Strategic Response to Pakistan's Information Warfare During Article 370 Revocation

The revocation of Article 370 on August 5, 2019, by the Indian government marked a historic and bold step toward integrating Jammu and Kashmir into the national framework, bringing it at par with other Indian states. Anticipating Pakistan's hostile reaction, India proactively fortified its communication and security apparatus to counter the anticipated information warfare and ensure stability in the region.

Pakistan immediately launched a coordinated misinformation campaign to discredit India's decision, attempting to portray the move as a human rights crisis. This narrative was artificially amplified through bot networks, fake accounts, and propaganda channels, primarily leveraging Twitter, Facebook, and YouTube. Hashtags like #KashmirUnderSiege and #FreeKashmir were artificially trended, aiming to mislead global audiences. AI-generated deepfake videos and doctored images were deliberately disseminated to create a false sense of unrest, despite the region remaining largely peaceful due to India's proactive security measures.

State-backed media outlets in Pakistan, along with unofficial propaganda channels, churned out misleading reports about mass detentions, curfews, and alleged civilian oppression. In reality, the Indian government ensured the availability of essential services, economic continuity, and law and order to prevent Pakistan's false narratives from gaining traction. Pakistan also resorted to cyber warfare tactics, targeting Indian government websites in an attempt to spread panic, but India's robust cybersecurity infrastructure effectively neutralized such threats.

On the diplomatic front, Pakistan sought to internationalize the issue by lobbying organizations like the United Nations and the Organisation of Islamic Cooperation (OIC). However, India successfully countered these efforts through strategic diplomatic outreach, presenting facts and highlighting the progressive initiatives introduced post-Article 370 abrogation. Indian diplomats effectively communicated the region's improved governance and economic opportunities, contrasting Pakistan's outdated and divisive rhetoric.

Another key tactic in Pakistan's psychological warfare was the use of radicalization through religious institutions in Pakistan-occupied Kashmir and certain Gulf nations. Mosques and extremist elements propagated misinformation, attempting to incite Kashmiri youth. However, India's stringent security measures, combined with community engagement programs, significantly curtailed their ability to provoke unrest.

Pakistan also attempted to escalate cross-border terrorism under the guise of resistance. Terror outfits like Lashkar-e-Taiba (LeT) and Jaish-e-Mohammed (JeM) sought to exploit the situation, but India's intelligence and counterterrorism forces preemptively thwarted infiltration attempts. Through increased surveillance, security operations, and intelligence-sharing, India ensured that Pakistan's hybrid warfare strategy did not escalate into significant ground unrest.

India's comprehensive response involved a multi-pronged strategy to counter disinformation and maintain stability. The government proactively debunked fake news through official channels, strengthening its digital presence to neutralize propaganda. Collaboration with social media platforms allowed for the identification and removal of misinformation campaigns originating from Pakistan. Cyber defenses were reinforced to counter digital threats, ensuring the safety of sensitive governmental and civilian communication channels.

Additionally, India's focus on development in Jammu and Kashmir post-revocation further discredited Pakistan's negative propaganda. Infrastructure projects, educational reforms, and economic investments underscored the benefits of integration, contrasting starkly with Pakistan's destructive agenda. These initiatives reinforced India's commitment to the region's prosperity and highlighted the hollowness of Pakistan's disinformation campaign.

Pakistan's information warfare during the revocation of Article 370 underscores the evolving nature of modern conflicts, where digital propaganda, cyber attacks, and psychological manipulation play a crucial role. However, India's strategic resilience, effective countermeasures, and developmental initiatives not only neutralized these threats but also positioned the nation as a leader in countering hybrid warfare. This case serves as a testament to India's ability to navigate complex geopolitical challenges while ensuring national security and regional progress.

Case Study: Misinformation Campaigns During COVID-19 in India

The COVID-19 pandemic was not only a global health crisis but also an information warfare battleground where misinformation, disinformation, and conspiracy theories spread rapidly across digital platforms. In India, where social media penetration is high, misinformation campaigns played a significant role in shaping public perception, influencing health behaviors, and even impacting governmental response strategies. The pandemic saw the deliberate spread of false narratives concerning the virus's origins, treatment options, vaccination efforts, and government policies. These misinformation campaigns created widespread panic, mistrust, and in some cases, fueled resistance against life-saving interventions.

The proliferation of false information during COVID-19 in India was driven by multiple factors, including fear, uncertainty, lack of verified information, and the strategic use of misinformation by adversarial forces. The rapid digitalization and increased dependence on social media as a primary news source exacerbated the problem. Platforms like WhatsApp, Twitter, Facebook, and YouTube became major channels for spreading both organic and organized disinformation. Many of these narratives had direct implications for public health and government policy, creating challenges in managing the pandemic response effectively.

One of the most widespread misinformation campaigns involved promoting unscientific and unverified treatments as cures for COVID-19. Rumors about herbal concoctions, homeopathy, and traditional remedies gained traction, often overshadowing evidence-based medical treatments. Social media posts falsely claimed that ginger, turmeric, cow urine, and steam inhalation could prevent or cure COVID-19, leading to a diversion of public attention from scientifically approved treatments. During the second wave of COVID-19 in India, when hospitals were overwhelmed with patients and oxygen shortages were rampant, a wave of misinformation suggested that consuming neem leaves or using alternative therapies like pranayama (breathing exercises) could boost immunity and prevent severe illness. While some traditional remedies may have had general health benefits, their misleading promotion as primary COVID-19 treatments delayed critical medical interventions and led to avoidable fatalities.

The development and rollout of vaccines were accompanied by widespread misinformation campaigns aimed at fueling vaccine hesitancy. Rumors circulating on WhatsApp and Telegram groups falsely claimed that vaccines caused infertility, genetic mutations, or were part of a global conspiracy to implant microchips. Some narratives targeted religious and minority communities, falsely alleging that vaccines were a tool to control or harm specific populations. This disinformation was not just organic but often strategically deployed by anti-vaccine groups and foreign influence operations, seeking to disrupt India's vaccine drive. Videos falsely portraying people collapsing after receiving vaccines were widely circulated, creating fear among the masses. Even political leaders and celebrities were targeted with deepfake videos that purportedly showed them speaking against vaccination. The Indian government and health authorities faced a major challenge in countering these narratives, launching extensive public awareness campaigns, involving doctors, influencers, and religious leaders to dispel myths and build public confidence in vaccines. Social media platforms also played a role by flagging misleading content, though these efforts often lagged behind the spread of misinformation.

Several misinformation campaigns targeted India's government response, including lockdown measures, economic relief programs, and public health guidelines. Fake news articles and deepfake videos falsely attributed controversial statements to government officials, spreading panic about food shortages, forced vaccinations, and exaggerated lockdown extensions. Misinformation about the CoWIN vaccine registration portal also circulated, with fraudulent links being shared, leading to cybersecurity concerns as scammers attempted to steal personal data. Similarly, fraudulent charity campaigns claimed to be collecting funds for COVID-19 relief but turned out to be scams, exploiting the generosity of people during the crisis.

Cyber intelligence agencies also detected state-sponsored disinformation campaigns from adversarial countries like Pakistan and China that sought to exploit India's pandemic crisis. These campaigns amplified vaccine hesitancy, criticized India's medical infrastructure, and promoted divisive narratives on social media platforms. Automated bot networks were found circulating fake news articles portraying India's COVID-19 response as a failure, while promoting exaggerated success stories of other countries. In some cases, these operations used AI-generated deepfake videos and fake accounts to spread false information.

The objective was clear—to erode trust in the Indian government, create panic, and weaken India's global image during an already difficult time.

The Indian government, in collaboration with social media platforms and fact-checking organizations, took multiple steps to counter misinformation. The Press Information Bureau (PIB) Fact Check Unit, along with platforms like Alt News and Boom Live, actively debunked fake news and viral false claims. The government also worked with social media giants to take down misleading posts, flag false information, and promote verified content from health authorities. Public awareness campaigns were intensified, featuring health professionals, celebrities, and religious leaders who played a crucial role in building vaccine confidence and discouraging misinformation. State governments and local authorities also deployed grassroots campaigns, particularly in rural areas where word-of-mouth misinformation was more prevalent than digital propaganda.

Cybersecurity agencies stepped up efforts to detect and neutralize state-sponsored disinformation campaigns, leading to the identification of fake social media accounts and bot-driven narratives targeting India. The government also imposed stricter regulations on fake news, warning individuals and groups against spreading misinformation that could create panic or harm public health initiatives.

The COVID-19 misinformation campaigns in India highlighted the urgent need for digital literacy, stronger regulations, and real-time fact-checking mechanisms. It became evident that combating misinformation required a multi-stakeholder approach involving governments, tech companies, media organizations, and civil society. Key takeaways from India's battle against COVID-19 misinformation include strengthening real-time fact-checking mechanisms through dedicated government agencies and independent watchdogs, enhancing AI-driven misinformation detection tools to identify and curb the spread of false narratives, implementing stricter penalties for spreading false information, particularly during national emergencies, encouraging responsible journalism and media ethics to prevent the amplification of unverified claims, and increasing public awareness campaigns to educate citizens on identifying misinformation and relying on credible sources.

The COVID-19 pandemic in India was as much an information crisis as it was a public health emergency. The widespread misinformation campaigns exposed vulnerabilities in digital information ecosystems, public health communication, and national security. While government efforts, fact-checking organizations, and public awareness initiatives helped mitigate some of the damage, the impact of misinformation on public perception, vaccine hesitancy, and communal harmony was deeply concerning. Moving forward, building a more resilient information ecosystem, investing in cybersecurity defenses, and fostering digital literacy will be essential to prevent future misinformation crises. As India continues to embrace digital transformation, strengthening cyber resilience and countering disinformation will be crucial for safeguarding public health and national security.

CHAPTER XIV

The Way Forward for India

As the world enters an era of rapidly evolving digital threats, India must adopt a forward-thinking and comprehensive approach to safeguard its national security, economic stability, and democratic institutions from the growing menace of information warfare. The increasing reliance on digital platforms for communication, governance, and public discourse has opened new battlefronts where state and non-state actors engage in cyber espionage, disinformation campaigns, and digital subversion. To effectively counter these threats, India must develop a multi-faceted strategy that encompasses cyber resilience, digital sovereignty, private-sector collaboration, and robust policy interventions. A national approach to information warfare should integrate military, intelligence, diplomatic, and technological capabilities to establish a proactive and defensive framework that protects the country's digital frontiers.

A Comprehensive Information Warfare Strategy

A strong information warfare strategy for India should be built on three primary pillars: defense, deterrence, and counter-offensive capabilities. Defensive mechanisms involve strengthening cybersecurity infrastructure, training government agencies in counter-disinformation measures, and enhancing public awareness through digital literacy campaigns. India must establish a centralized national information warfare command that coordinates efforts across defense, intelligence, and law enforcement agencies to counter disinformation and cyber threats in real-time. The integration of artificial intelligence, big data analytics, and machine learning into intelligence gathering and threat analysis will enable proactive detection of adversarial information warfare campaigns before they can cause significant damage.

Deterrence should be based on a combination of diplomatic pressure, economic countermeasures, and legal frameworks that hold foreign and domestic actors accountable for engaging in information warfare against India. The creation of international partnerships with allied nations for intelligence-sharing and joint cyber operations will further strengthen India's ability to deter adversarial attacks. Legal provisions must be updated to classify digital misinformation campaigns as acts of hybrid warfare,

185

allowing for stronger penalties against perpetrators, whether domestic or foreign. Strengthening cooperation between the government and social media platforms is also crucial, ensuring that digital spaces do not become tools for misinformation, incitement, or subversion.

Counter-offensive capabilities involve developing India's own cyber and information warfare arsenal, including the ability to expose and neutralize adversarial disinformation campaigns, engage in strategic narrative control, and conduct digital countermeasures against state-sponsored propaganda networks. By leveraging its technological expertise, India can actively monitor and counter foreign influence operations, particularly from adversarial states that seek to destabilize the country through cyber attacks and information warfare. Establishing dedicated cyber warfare units within the armed forces and intelligence agencies will enable the country to respond to digital threats in real time while maintaining plausible deniability in the global geopolitical landscape.

Strengthening India's Digital Sovereignty

The concept of digital sovereignty is essential for India to maintain control over its cyberspace, protect critical digital infrastructure, and ensure data security for its citizens. Digital sovereignty means that India must reduce its dependence on foreign technology providers, cloud services, and software ecosystems that could potentially compromise national security. Developing indigenous alternatives to global technology giants, particularly in sectors like cloud computing, artificial intelligence, and cybersecurity, will enhance India's ability to secure its digital domain.

Data localization is a key component of digital sovereignty. India must implement stringent regulations that ensure sensitive government and corporate data is stored within the country's borders, reducing vulnerabilities associated with foreign-hosted servers and cloud platforms. Initiatives such as India's Personal Data Protection Bill and policies promoting indigenous cloud services are steps in the right direction. Expanding these efforts by incentivizing domestic companies to develop secure and scalable digital solutions will further strengthen India's technological independence.

The protection of critical national infrastructure from cyber threats is another major priority. Power grids, financial institutions, defense networks, and government databases must be secured through advanced encryption, AI-driven threat detection, and regular cybersecurity audits. Ensuring that government agencies and businesses adhere to stringent cybersecurity protocols will mitigate risks associated with cyber espionage, ransomware attacks, and state-sponsored hacking attempts. Encouraging the use of open-source and homegrown digital technologies will further reduce reliance on foreign software with potential security vulnerabilities.

Additionally, India must play an active role in shaping global internet governance policies to prevent foreign entities from exerting undue influence over its digital space. Actively participating in international forums on cybersecurity, digital privacy, and internet regulations will enable India to advocate for policies that align with its national interests. A strong diplomatic push for greater accountability from multinational technology corporations regarding data privacy, misinformation, and cybersecurity threats will ensure that India's digital ecosystem remains resilient and secure.

Role of Private Sector, Startups, and Ethical Hackers

A robust public-private partnership is crucial in strengthening India's information warfare capabilities. The private sector, particularly technology firms, cybersecurity companies, and social media platforms, plays a vital role in protecting digital infrastructure, countering misinformation, and ensuring data security. Startups specializing in artificial intelligence, blockchain security, and deepfake detection can contribute significantly to building resilient digital ecosystems. India's thriving tech industry should be incentivized to invest in cybersecurity research and development, creating indigenous solutions that address national security concerns.

Cybersecurity startups can be integrated into national security frameworks through strategic partnerships, funding opportunities, and collaboration with defense and intelligence agencies. Hackathons, innovation challenges, and government-backed initiatives can be utilized to harness the potential of young innovators and entrepreneurs in developing advanced cybersecurity tools. Strengthening collaboration between the defense sector and private technology firms will enhance India's ability to develop cutting-edge cyber defense mechanisms.

Ethical hackers, or white-hat hackers, are an invaluable asset in identifying and mitigating cyber vulnerabilities. Establishing structured programs where ethical hackers can collaborate with government agencies will help in securing digital platforms and critical infrastructure from cyber threats. Bug bounty programs, cybersecurity training initiatives, and national competitions can encourage ethical hacking practices while equipping the next generation of cybersecurity professionals with the necessary skills to safeguard India's digital frontiers.

Social media platforms and digital content providers must also be held accountable for their role in information warfare. Regulations mandating transparency in content moderation, algorithmic accountability, and misinformation detection should be enforced to prevent digital platforms from being exploited for malicious activities. Encouraging self-regulation by social media companies while also establishing legal frameworks for government oversight will ensure that online platforms do not become conduits for cyber subversion.

Policy Recommendations for Government and Military

To counter the rising threats of cyber warfare and information manipulation, the Indian government and military must implement a comprehensive set of policy measures. Strengthening cyber laws to classify state-sponsored misinformation and cyber espionage as acts of aggression will enable India to take appropriate countermeasures. The creation of a dedicated cyber and information warfare command within the armed forces will ensure that national security agencies have the necessary resources and capabilities to combat digital threats effectively.

The military must integrate cyber capabilities into its strategic defense planning, ensuring that cyber resilience is a fundamental component of national security. Training programs for defense personnel in cyber operations, digital intelligence gathering, and counter-disinformation tactics will enhance India's ability to respond to hybrid warfare threats. Establishing military-grade cybersecurity protocols across defense communication networks, satellite systems, and operational infrastructure will reduce vulnerabilities to cyber sabotage and espionage.

Government policies should also focus on strengthening public awareness regarding digital misinformation and cyber threats. Educational institutions must incorporate digital literacy programs into their curricula, teaching students how to critically evaluate online information, recognize fake news, and safeguard their personal data. Public awareness campaigns must be launched to educate citizens on cybersecurity best practices, responsible social media usage, and the dangers of misinformation campaigns.

Inference

As India navigates the complexities of modern information warfare, a holistic approach that integrates technological advancements, strategic policy interventions, and international cooperation is imperative.

Strengthening digital sovereignty, fostering innovation in cybersecurity, engaging the private sector, and developing advanced counter-disinformation strategies will be key to safeguarding India's national security in the digital age. By implementing a comprehensive information warfare strategy, investing in homegrown technology solutions, and fostering cyber resilience, India can establish itself as a formidable force in the evolving landscape of global digital conflicts. The way forward demands a proactive, collaborative, and technologically driven approach that ensures India's digital infrastructure remains secure, its citizens remain informed, and its national interests remain protected against emerging cyber and information warfare threats.

Glossary Of Terms

Active Measures – A psychological and information warfare strategy used by state actors to influence public opinion, manipulate narratives, and destabilize adversaries through propaganda, misinformation, and covert operations.

Advanced Persistent Threat (APT) – A long-term, stealthy cyberattack conducted by nation-states or organized cybercriminals to infiltrate sensitive networks for espionage, data theft, or cyber warfare.

AI-Powered Deepfake Technology – The use of artificial intelligence to create highly realistic but fake videos, images, and audio to manipulate public perception, discredit opponents, and influence elections or political events.

Algorithmic Manipulation – The strategic exploitation of social media algorithms to amplify certain narratives, discredit adversaries, and influence public perception through artificially boosted content.

Anonymous Networks – Encrypted and decentralized digital communication channels, such as the dark web and VPNs, used for covert operations, cyber warfare, and misinformation campaigns.

Article 370 Revocation – The Indian government's move to revoke Jammu and Kashmir's special status on August 5, 2019, leading to extensive information warfare efforts, psychological operations, and misinformation campaigns from adversaries like Pakistan.

Artificial Intelligence (AI): The simulation of human intelligence by machines, particularly computer systems, to perform tasks such as learning, reasoning, and problem-solving.

Artificial Intelligence (AI) in Information Warfare – The use of AI-driven tools for cyber operations, automated disinformation campaigns, deepfake generation, and digital propaganda to manipulate geopolitical narratives.

Asymmetric Warfare – A form of conflict where weaker actors use unconventional strategies, such as cyberattacks, propaganda, and digital misinformation, to counter stronger adversaries.

Attack Surface in Cyber Warfare – The total number of vulnerabilities and entry points in a nation's digital infrastructure that adversaries can exploit for cyberattacks or psychological operations.

Automated Disinformation Campaigns – The deployment of AI, bots, and fake personas to spread false or misleading narratives on social media and news platforms, often used by adversaries to destabilize nations.

Backdoor – A hidden or unauthorized access point in a computer system or network that allows attackers or state-sponsored cyber units to bypass security controls and gain remote access for espionage or sabotage.

Big Data in Cyber Warfare – The use of massive datasets in intelligence gathering, cyber threat analysis, and disinformation campaigns to manipulate public opinion and predict geopolitical trends.

Black Hat Operations – Cyber espionage or hacking activities carried out by state-sponsored actors or criminal groups to infiltrate, sabotage, or manipulate networks of adversary nations.

Black Propaganda – A form of covert information warfare where false or misleading content is presented as originating from a credible source to deceive and manipulate public perception.

Bot-Assisted Psychological Warfare – The deployment of automated social media bots to create an illusion of widespread dissent, influence political discourse, or incite unrest through coordinated disinformation campaigns.

Botnet Manipulation in Information Warfare – The use of large networks of automated bots to spread disinformation, amplify political propaganda, and disrupt the digital information space.

Broadcast Manipulation in Psychological Warfare – The deliberate use of radio, television, and digital media to spread misleading narratives, amplify propaganda, and sway public opinion during geopolitical conflicts.

Buffer Overflow Attack – A type of cyber exploit where an attacker sends excessive data to a program's buffer, causing it to overwrite memory and execute malicious code.

Camouflaged Disinformation – A deceptive tactic in information warfare where false narratives are blended with selective truths to make propaganda appear credible and manipulate public perception.

Cognitive Warfare – The strategic targeting of human perception through misinformation, deepfake technology, and AI-generated content to alter decision-making and destabilize adversaries.

Content Moderation: The practice of monitoring and managing user-generated content to ensure compliance with community guidelines and reduce harmful content.

Counter-Disinformation Strategies – Measures taken by governments and intelligence agencies to detect, expose, and neutralize foreign disinformation campaigns through cybersecurity, fact-checking, and media literacy initiatives.

Covert Influence Operations – Hidden or deceptive efforts by state actors to manipulate narratives, infiltrate media platforms, and shape opinions in foreign nations without direct attribution.

Cyber Diplomacy: The use of diplomatic channels and negotiations to address cyber threats and establish international norms for behavior in cyberspace.

Cyber Espionage: The act of using cyber tools to gather intelligence from governments, organizations, or individuals without permission.

Cyber Forensics: The application of investigative techniques to analyze digital devices and data for evidence of cybercrimes.

Cyber Influence Operations – The use of digital platforms, bot networks, and AI-driven content to spread false narratives, manipulate election outcomes, and influence public discourse in adversary nations.

Cyber Propaganda: The use of digital platforms to spread false or misleading information to influence public opinion or political outcomes.

Cyber Resilience: The ability of an organization to prepare for, respond to, and recover from cyberattacks or disruptions effectively.

Cyber Sabotage: Deliberate attacks on systems, networks, or infrastructures to disrupt or destroy their functionality.

Cyber Troops and State-Sponsored Online Manipulation – Organized groups, often controlled by governments, that engage in digital propaganda, fake news dissemination, and cyber espionage to achieve geopolitical objectives.

Cybersecurity: The practice of protecting systems, networks, and programs from digital attacks, unauthorized access, and data breaches.

Dark Web and Anonymous Channels in Misinformation – The use of encrypted platforms, underground forums, and anonymous networks to spread false narratives, recruit operatives, and coordinate cyber warfare tactics against adversary nations.

Dark Web: A part of the internet not indexed by standard search engines, often associated with anonymity and illicit activities.

Data Breach: The unauthorized access and retrieval of sensitive or confidential information, often leading to significant repercussions.

Deception Operations in Cyber Warfare – A technique in which adversaries use fake cyber infrastructure, misinformation, and fabricated threats to mislead intelligence agencies and security forces.

Deep Fakes: Synthetic media, often video or audio, created using AI technologies to impersonate individuals or fabricate events, making them appear authentic.

Deepfake Technology in Disinformation Campaigns – The use of AI-generated synthetic videos and audio to fabricate political speeches, manipulate public perception, and create false narratives in psychological warfare.

Defensive Cyber Warfare Strategies – National security policies and technical measures designed to protect a country's digital infrastructure from cyber threats, foreign disinformation, and psychological warfare tactics.

Deniable Cyber Attacks – A strategy used by nation-states where cyberattacks are conducted through proxy groups or anonymous channels, allowing the attacker to avoid direct attribution and diplomatic consequences.

Digital Espionage in Information Warfare – The covert collection of intelligence through hacking, cyber infiltration, and electronic surveillance to gain a strategic advantage in military and geopolitical conflicts.

Digital Literacy: The ability to find, evaluate, and use information effectively and responsibly in the digital environment.

Digital Media Manipulation in Conflict Zones – The deliberate exploitation of social media, video-sharing platforms, and news websites to control narratives, spread propaganda, and incite hostility in politically sensitive regions.

Digital Radicalization – The process by which individuals are indoctrinated into extremist ideologies through social media, encrypted messaging apps, and propaganda-laced digital content.

Diplomatic Cyber Influence – The use of cyber tools and digital narratives to shape international opinion, influence diplomatic negotiations, and project soft power.

Disinformation Warfare Against India – Coordinated campaigns by Pakistan, China, and other adversaries using digital platforms to spread falsehoods, incite unrest, and weaken India's global standing.

Disinformation: False or misleading information deliberately spread to deceive or manipulate public opinion.

DNS Spoofing: A cyberattack technique that redirects traffic from a legitimate website to a malicious one by corrupting domain name system (DNS) data.

Doxxing: The act of publicly revealing private information about an individual, often to harass or intimidate them.

Echo Chambers in Information Warfare – The phenomenon where social media algorithms and targeted disinformation create insulated digital environments, reinforcing pre-existing beliefs and preventing exposure to alternative viewpoints.

Economic Information Warfare – The use of financial misinformation, trade-related cyberattacks, and economic manipulation to weaken adversary nations through digital propaganda and cyber sabotage.

Election Misinformation and Influence Campaigns – The systematic dissemination of fake news, propaganda, and AI-generated content to manipulate voters, discredit political opponents, and sway democratic processes.

Electronic Warfare in Cyber Conflict – The use of electromagnetic spectrum operations, including jamming, interception, and electronic surveillance, to disrupt enemy communication, radar, and digital networks.

Emerging Threats in AI-Driven Disinformation – The evolving use of artificial intelligence for generating fake content, deepfakes, and automated propaganda to influence public perception and political outcomes.

Encryption: The process of converting information into a code to prevent unauthorized access, ensuring data security and privacy.

Encryption and Secure Communication in Cyber Warfare – The use of cryptographic techniques to protect sensitive data and communications from interception by adversaries in geopolitical conflicts.

Espionage Through Cyber Operations – The use of hacking, spyware, and cyber intelligence techniques by state actors to steal classified information, monitor adversaries, and disrupt critical infrastructure.

Ethnic and Religious Disinformation in Conflict Zones – The strategic use of fake news and divisive narratives to inflame ethnic and religious tensions, particularly in sensitive regions.

Exfiltration of Sensitive Data – The unauthorized extraction of classified government or military data through hacking, cyber espionage, and insider threats in information warfare.

Exploitation of Social Media Platforms – The manipulation of platforms like Twitter, Facebook, and YouTube for spreading propaganda, executing disinformation campaigns, and influencing political and social discourse.

Fabricated Atrocities for Propaganda – The deliberate use of fake images, edited videos, and misleading reports to falsely portray human rights violations and war crimes, often to incite international pressure against a target nation.

Fake News Ecosystem in Information Warfare – A coordinated network of fake news websites, propaganda portals, and social media influencers used to manipulate public opinion, spread misinformation, and distort narratives.

Fake News: Fabricated news stories created to mislead, provoke emotions, or serve specific agendas.

Fake Social Media Influencers in Disinformation – The creation of AI-generated or human-controlled social media personas that spread propaganda and manipulate discourse.

False Flag Cyber Operations – Covert cyberattacks designed to appear as if they were conducted by a third party, misleading adversaries and creating diplomatic tensions.

False Narratives in Geopolitical Conflicts – Deliberately misleading stories spread by adversarial states to frame events in a way that aligns with their strategic objectives.

Fear, Uncertainty, and Doubt (FUD) in Psychological Warfare – A psychological tactic used in disinformation campaigns to create panic, distrust, and confusion among the target population.

Foreign Cyber Troops in Information Warfare – State-sponsored online armies and bot farms that conduct cyber propaganda, spread misinformation, and engage in digital espionage.

Foreign Influence Operations Against India – State-backed propaganda and cyber campaigns aimed at destabilizing India by exploiting sensitive issues such as Kashmir, religious tensions, and political divisions.

Forensic Analysis of Cyber Attacks – The process of investigating and tracing the origins of cyberattacks to identify perpetrators and understand their tactics.

Framing and Agenda Setting in Propaganda – The psychological method of shaping public perception by emphasizing certain issues while omitting others to control the narrative.

General Intelligence Operations in Cyber Espionage – The collection and analysis of digital intelligence by state agencies to monitor adversaries, predict threats, and conduct cyber warfare.

Geopolitical Cyber Warfare – The use of digital attacks, cyber espionage, and information manipulation to achieve strategic geopolitical goals.

Ghost Accounts in Disinformation Campaigns – Fake social media accounts used to spread propaganda, create the illusion of mass support, and manipulate online debates.

Global Disinformation Networks – Internationally coordinated efforts by adversarial states and organizations to spread false information and influence global events.

Government Censorship in Information Warfare – The deliberate suppression of information by governments to control narratives, limit dissent, and manipulate public opinion.

Government-Controlled Troll Farms – Large-scale digital operations, often run by intelligence agencies, designed to spread misinformation, attack critics, and manipulate political discourse.

Gray Zone Warfare – A strategy that falls between conventional warfare and peacetime diplomacy, involving cyberattacks, psychological operations, and economic coercion to weaken an adversary without direct military confrontation.

Guerrilla Cyber Tactics – Small-scale, unconventional digital attacks conducted by hacktivists, cyber militias, or state-backed cyber cells to disrupt adversary operations.

Hacked Social Media Accounts in Disinformation – The practice of hijacking verified social media accounts to spread fake news, incite communal violence, or push misleading narratives.

Hacktivism in Geopolitical Conflicts – The use of hacking by politically motivated groups to expose government secrets, disrupt adversarial systems, or spread ideological messages.

Hacktivism: The use of hacking techniques to promote a political agenda or social cause, often involving the unauthorized access of computer systems.

Hashtag Campaigns in Psychological Warfare – The use of coordinated social media hashtags to spread propaganda, shape narratives, and amplify disinformation campaigns.

Historical Revisionism in Propaganda – The deliberate alteration or distortion of historical facts to serve political or ideological objectives.

Honeypots in Cyber Espionage – Decoy digital systems set up by intelligence agencies to lure hackers, cybercriminals, or state-backed cyber attackers into revealing their tactics.

Human Intelligence (HUMINT) in Cyber Operations – The collection of intelligence through human sources, such as informants or undercover operatives, to supplement cyber espionage efforts.

Hybrid Warfare – A military strategy that blends conventional warfare, cyber operations, misinformation campaigns, and economic coercion to weaken an adversary without direct military engagement.

Hybrid Warfare: A strategy that combines conventional warfare, cyber operations, disinformation, and other non-traditional methods to achieve strategic objectives.

India's Digital Counter-Propaganda Efforts – The initiatives by Indian intelligence and cybersecurity agencies to expose, debunk, and neutralize adversarial misinformation campaigns.

Indian Cybersecurity Infrastructure – The network of national agencies, policies, and frameworks designed to defend India's digital sovereignty against cyber threats and disinformation campaigns.

Influence Operations: Coordinated campaigns aimed at shaping public perception, influencing opinions, or altering behavior, often conducted by state or non-state actors.

Influencer-Based Disinformation – The strategic use of social media influencers to subtly push propaganda, spread falsehoods, and manipulate public perception on political or geopolitical matters.

Information Warfare: The use and management of information to gain a competitive advantage over adversaries through tactics such as propaganda, disinformation, and cyberattacks.

Intelligence-Gathering Through Social Media – The use of open-source intelligence (OSINT) methods to collect and analyze social media data for monitoring threats and countering cyber warfare.

Internet Censorship in Cyber Warfare – The strategic control of online content by governments to restrict adversary propaganda while ensuring national security and cyber sovereignty.

IoT Vulnerabilities: Security weaknesses in Internet of Things (IoT) devices, which can be exploited to launch cyberattacks or gather unauthorized data.

Jihadi Cyber Networks – Online extremist groups that use encrypted messaging services, dark web forums, and social media to promote radical ideologies and coordinate terrorist activities.

Joint Cyber Defense Strategies – Collaborative efforts between India and allied nations to strengthen cybersecurity, share intelligence, and counter state-sponsored cyber threats.

Journalistic Ethics in the Age of Disinformation – The challenges faced by media organizations in verifying sources, combating fake news, and resisting state-sponsored propaganda in modern information warfare.

Judicial Challenges in Countering Cyber Terrorism – The legal and policy hurdles in prosecuting cybercriminals, online propagandists, and misinformation agents who operate across international borders.

Keyloggers in Cyber Espionage – Malicious software tools used in cyber warfare to track and record keystrokes on a victim's device, often employed in cyber espionage and hacking operations.

Kill Chain in Cyber Warfare – A structured sequence of steps used by cyber attackers to infiltrate, exploit, and maintain access to a target system, often used in advanced persistent threats (APTs) against government or defense institutions.

Kinetic and Non-Kinetic Warfare – The combination of traditional military operations (kinetic) with cyberattacks, psychological warfare, and digital influence campaigns (non-kinetic) to destabilize an adversary without direct military conflict.

Kinetic Cyber Retaliation – The use of digital tools to cause real-world effects, such as shutting down power grids, disabling infrastructure, or targeting military assets through cyberattacks.

Lateral Movement in Cyber Attacks – The process by which hackers, after gaining initial access, move through a system's network undetected to extract intelligence, escalate privileges, or deploy further exploits.

Lawfare in Cyber and Information Conflicts – The use of legal frameworks, international regulations, and judicial manipulation as a tool for information warfare, including lawsuits, trade restrictions, and diplomatic pressure campaigns.

Leaks and Classified Information Manipulation – The deliberate leaking of sensitive or classified information to create political instability, discredit governments, or alter the strategic balance in conflicts.

Lethal Autonomous Weapons and AI in Warfare – The integration of artificial intelligence in autonomous military systems capable of selecting and engaging targets without direct human intervention, raising ethical and security concerns.

Linguistic Manipulation in Psychological Warfare – The strategic use of language and terminology in media and online content to frame conflicts in a particular way, influencing perception and international discourse.

Local Media Exploitation in Information Warfare – The tactic of infiltrating and manipulating regional media outlets to push propaganda, influence local populations, and amplify fake narratives in politically sensitive areas.

Logical Bombs in Cyber Warfare – A type of malware that remains dormant until triggered by a specific event, often used by state-sponsored cyber operatives for sabotage against critical infrastructure.

Lone-Wolf Terrorist Radicalization Online – The process by which individuals are self-radicalized through extremist propaganda, digital forums, and misinformation, without direct recruitment by terror organizations.

Low-Cost Cyber Warfare Strategies – The adoption of inexpensive yet highly effective cyber tools, such as misinformation campaigns, bot networks, and social media manipulation, to destabilize stronger adversaries.

Machine Learning in Cybersecurity Defense – The application of artificial intelligence in detecting cyber threats, analyzing patterns in misinformation campaigns, and countering digital propaganda with automated tools.

Malware in Cyber Espionage – Malicious software programs used in cyberattacks, such as Trojans, spyware, and ransomware, to steal data, disrupt networks, and conduct cyber espionage operations.

Manipulation of Digital Platforms in Geopolitical Conflicts – The strategic exploitation of social media algorithms, SEO techniques, and content moderation loopholes to amplify state-sponsored propaganda and suppress dissenting voices.

Media Manipulation in Information Warfare – The use of digital media, fake news portals, and propaganda-driven content to shape public opinion and international narratives in favor of a specific geopolitical agenda.

Mediated Conflict Narratives – The role of global media in framing geopolitical conflicts, influencing public perception, and shaping diplomatic responses through selective reporting and agenda-driven storytelling.

Meme-Based Radicalization in Online Extremism – The use of viral internet content to indoctrinate individuals, glorify militant ideologies, and subtly push extremist narratives through engaging visual content.

Memetic Warfare – The use of internet memes as psychological warfare tools to spread propaganda, discredit adversaries, and shape public discourse through humor, satire, and visual storytelling.

Military Deception in Cyber Conflicts – The practice of using digital camouflage, fake cyber footprints, and artificial intelligence to mislead adversaries about military capabilities and strategies.

Misinformation Warfare – The deliberate spread of false or misleading information by state and non-state actors to manipulate public perception, influence elections, or create social unrest.

Misinformation: False or inaccurate information spread without the intent to deceive, often due to misunderstanding or lack of verification.

Mobile Device Exploitation in Cyber Warfare – The targeting of smartphones and mobile networks by intelligence agencies and hackers to extract sensitive data, conduct surveillance, and spread disinformation.

Monetization of Propaganda Networks – The financial incentives behind fake news websites, clickbait content, and digital advertising schemes that sustain misinformation ecosystems.

Multi-Domain Operations in Hybrid Warfare – The integration of cyber warfare, electronic warfare, space operations, and traditional military tactics to conduct coordinated attacks across multiple strategic domains.

Narrative Warfare – The battle over controlling public perception through strategic storytelling, misinformation campaigns, and media framing to align geopolitical events with national interests.

National Cybersecurity Policies in India – The set of regulations, frameworks, and strategic initiatives implemented by the Indian government to defend against cyber threats and information warfare.

National Sovereignty in Cyber Space – The debate over a country's right to regulate digital content, control its cyberspace, and implement internet governance policies against foreign interference.

Nation-State Cyber Espionage – The practice of governments using cyber tools to spy on other countries, steal classified information, and disrupt critical infrastructure through digital means.

NATO's Response to Digital Warfare – The strategies employed by the North Atlantic Treaty Organization (NATO) to counter cyber threats, combat disinformation, and enhance digital resilience among member states.

Network Intrusion in Cyber Warfare – Unauthorized access to government, military, or corporate networks by hackers and state-backed cyber units for intelligence gathering, sabotage, or disruption.

Network-Centric Psychological Operations – The application of cyber-enabled tools to conduct psychological operations, influence target audiences, and shape international narratives through coordinated digital campaigns.

Neural Networks in Misinformation Detection – The use of artificial intelligence and deep learning models to analyze digital content, identify deepfake videos, and detect disinformation patterns.

News Portals as Propaganda Tools – The establishment of fake news websites or state-backed media channels to spread government-aligned narratives and mislead global audiences.

Non-Kinetic Warfare – A form of conflict that does not involve direct military action but relies on cyberattacks, economic coercion, disinformation campaigns, and diplomatic pressure to weaken adversaries.

Obfuscation Techniques in Cyber Attacks – The use of encryption, VPNs, and proxy networks by hackers to mask their digital footprint and evade detection.

Offensive Cyber Capabilities in National Security – The development and deployment of cyber tools by nations to conduct preemptive strikes, disrupt enemy infrastructure, and gather intelligence.

Offshore Cyber Espionage Operations – The practice of establishing cyber units outside a country's borders to conduct hacking, surveillance, and digital infiltration while maintaining plausible deniability.

Online Influence Campaigns in Geopolitical Conflicts – The strategic use of social media, blogs, and digital platforms by governments to sway public opinion, discredit adversaries, and promote national interests.

Online Radicalization in Terrorist Recruitment – The use of digital platforms, encrypted messaging apps, and extremist propaganda to recruit individuals into terrorist organizations, particularly in conflict regions like Kashmir.

Online Troll Armies in Digital Propaganda – The use of organized groups to spread misinformation, attack critics, and amplify state-sponsored narratives on social media platforms.

Open-Source Intelligence (OSINT) in Information Warfare – The collection and analysis of publicly available information from news reports, social media, and digital platforms to monitor adversary activities and counter disinformation.

Operational Security (OPSEC) in Cyber Warfare – The strategic measures taken to protect sensitive military and intelligence data from cyber threats and adversarial espionage.

Orchestrated Cyber Attacks on Indian Infrastructure – The targeted cyber operations conducted by adversarial states to compromise India's critical infrastructure, banking systems, and government networks.

Overlapping Disinformation Networks – The interconnected nature of fake news websites, bot accounts, and state-backed media outlets working together to push a unified false narrative.

Pakistan's Digital Proxy Warfare in Kashmir – The use of fake social media influencers, cyber cells, and radicalized digital content to manipulate Kashmiri youth and promote anti-India sentiments.

Pakistan's Information Warfare Against India – The systematic disinformation campaigns run by Pakistan's intelligence agencies and ISPR to destabilize India through cyber propaganda, false narratives on Kashmir, and digital radicalization.

Patriotic Hacking and National Cyber Defense – The rise of non-state actors, often known as ethical hackers, who conduct cyber operations to protect national interests or retaliate against adversarial threats.

Penetration Testing in National Cybersecurity – The simulated cyberattacks conducted by cybersecurity agencies to identify vulnerabilities in critical national infrastructure and improve digital defense mechanisms.

Phishing Attacks in Cyber Espionage – Cyber tactics used to deceive individuals into revealing sensitive information through fraudulent emails, fake websites, or social engineering techniques.

Phishing: A cyberattack technique that involves deceiving individuals into providing sensitive information, such as passwords or credit card numbers, through fake communications.

Polarization Through Fake News – The deliberate creation and spread of misleading or false news to deepen societal divisions, incite communal tensions, and influence political discourse.

Political Bot Networks in Elections – The deployment of automated social media accounts to amplify political messaging, discredit opponents, and manipulate voter opinions during elections.

Predictive Analytics in Cyber Threat Detection – The use of AI and big data analytics to forecast potential cyber threats, detect patterns in misinformation campaigns, and preemptively counter disinformation.

Pre-Emptive Cyber Strikes in National Security – The use of offensive cyber operations to neutralize adversarial threats before they can cause harm to a nation's digital or physical infrastructure.

Propaganda Models in Cyber Warfare – The different frameworks used by states to disseminate propaganda, including black propaganda (false information disguised as truth), white propaganda (openly acknowledged messaging), and gray propaganda (partially misleading information).

Propaganda: Information, often biased or misleading, disseminated to promote a particular political cause or point of view.

Psychological Warfare in Digital Age – The use of misinformation, propaganda, and psychological manipulation techniques to weaken an adversary's morale and influence public perception.

Public Awareness Programs Against Disinformation – Initiatives by governments and civil society to educate citizens on digital literacy, misinformation detection, and responsible media consumption.

QAnon-Style Conspiracies in Psychological Operations – The use of fabricated conspiracy theories to manipulate public perception, radicalize individuals, and promote state-backed agendas through digital platforms.

Quantum Computing and Its Impact on Cyber Warfare – The emerging field of quantum computing, which has the potential to break current encryption standards and revolutionize cybersecurity, posing both threats and opportunities in information warfare.

Quantum Cryptography in National Security – The development of ultra-secure communication networks using quantum mechanics to safeguard military and intelligence transmissions from cyber espionage.

Quasi-State Cyber Actors in Information Warfare – Non-governmental organizations, ideological groups, and independent cyber militias that engage in digital propaganda, hacking, and misinformation campaigns to support state or political agendas.

Questionable Attribution in Cyber Attacks – The difficulty in identifying the true source of cyberattacks, as adversaries use false flags, VPNs, and obfuscation techniques to mislead investigators.

Quick Reaction Cyber Defense Teams – Specialized units within national cybersecurity agencies tasked with responding to real-time cyber threats, disinformation campaigns, and digital warfare incidents.

Radicalization Through Digital Platforms – The process of indoctrinating individuals into extremist ideologies using social media, encrypted messaging apps, and AI-driven personalized content.

Ransomware Attacks as Geopolitical Weapons – The use of ransomware by state-backed cybercriminal groups to paralyze critical infrastructure, disrupt government operations, and extract intelligence from adversaries.

Ransomware: Malicious software that encrypts a victim's data, demanding payment for its decryption.

Reactive vs. Proactive Cyber Defense Strategies – The debate between waiting for cyberattacks to occur before responding (reactive) versus actively preempting cyber threats through intelligence gathering and preemptive action (proactive).

Red Teaming in Cyber Warfare Simulations – The practice of employing ethical hackers and cybersecurity experts to simulate cyberattacks on national infrastructure to identify vulnerabilities and improve defense strategies.

Regional Cyber Influence Campaigns – The practice of using digital tools to manipulate public opinion in specific regions, such as targeting ethnic minorities, separatist movements, or politically unstable areas.

Reinforcement of Echo Chambers in Information Warfare – The deliberate feeding of biased or polarized content to individuals through digital algorithms to strengthen existing beliefs and prevent exposure to counter-narratives.

Reputation Sabotage in Cyber Conflicts – The use of digital tools, fake news, and deepfakes to discredit politicians, military leaders, or national institutions as part of an adversary's psychological warfare tactics.

Reverse Engineering in Cyber Espionage – The process of deconstructing malware, hacking tools, or foreign cyber capabilities to understand their functionality and develop countermeasures.

Rumor-Based Warfare in Social Media – The strategic use of false rumors, fake news, and misleading narratives to sow confusion, panic, or political unrest in adversarial nations.

Russia's Hybrid Warfare Model – The combination of cyberattacks, digital propaganda, disinformation campaigns, and military strategies employed by Russia to destabilize adversaries and manipulate global narratives.

Satellite Hacking in Cyber Warfare – The potential cyber threats to communication, surveillance, and military satellites, which could be hijacked or disabled to disrupt critical infrastructure.

Smartphone-Based Cyber Surveillance – The use of spyware and malware to monitor individuals' mobile activities, track locations, and collect intelligence in cyber-espionage operations.

Social Bots: Automated social media accounts programmed to mimic human users and disseminate information, often used in disinformation campaigns.

Social Engineering Attacks in Cyber Warfare – The psychological manipulation of individuals into revealing confidential information, often through phishing, impersonation, or misinformation tactics.

Social Engineering: Psychological manipulation tactics used to trick individuals into divulging confidential information or performing specific actions.

Social Media Warfare and Narrative Control – The use of digital platforms like Twitter, YouTube, and Facebook to spread propaganda, manipulate public opinion, and shape national and international narratives.

Soft Power in Digital Influence Operations – The use of media, cultural diplomacy, and digital engagement to influence international perceptions and strengthen a nation's geopolitical standing.

State-Sponsored Cyber Propaganda – The systematic dissemination of misleading information by governments through social media campaigns, fake news websites, and digital influencers to manipulate domestic and foreign audiences.

Steganography in Covert Cyber Operations – The practice of embedding hidden messages within images, videos, or files to secretly transmit sensitive information without detection.

Strategic Cyber Alliances in Global Security – The formation of cybersecurity partnerships between nations to share intelligence, collaborate on digital defense strategies, and counter emerging cyber threats.

Strategic Deepfake Deployment in Information Warfare – The use of AI-generated videos and synthetic media to create realistic but fake content, influencing elections, discrediting political figures, and altering historical records.

Surgical Information Strikes in Cyber Conflicts – Targeted disinformation or cyberattacks aimed at disrupting specific institutions, electoral processes, or military operations.

Surveillance Capitalism and Information Warfare – The intersection of corporate data collection and government intelligence operations, where private sector digital surveillance is leveraged for national security or influence campaigns.

Swarm Attacks in AI-Driven Cyber Warfare – The use of AI-coordinated cyberattacks that involve multiple attack vectors simultaneously targeting an adversary's digital infrastructure.

Synthetic Media: AI-generated content, including images, videos, and audio, designed to mimic real-world media.

Tactical Disinformation in Geopolitical Conflicts – The selective spread of misinformation to mislead adversaries, disrupt diplomatic negotiations, and shape international public opinion.

Targeted Cyber Attacks on Indian Institutions – The cyber threats directed at India's government agencies, defense infrastructure, and financial sectors by adversarial states and non-state actors.

Technological Propaganda in Psychological Warfare – The use of AI-generated content, deepfake videos, and algorithmic amplification to spread state-sponsored propaganda and disinformation.

Terrorist Recruitment Through Digital Platforms – The use of social media, encrypted messaging apps, and propaganda websites by extremist groups to radicalize and recruit individuals, particularly in conflict zones like Kashmir.

Threat Actors in Cyber Warfare – The various individuals, groups, or state-sponsored entities responsible for conducting cyberattacks, espionage, and misinformation campaigns.

Threat Intelligence in Cyber Defense – The collection and analysis of data related to cyber threats to anticipate, mitigate, and prevent cyberattacks on national security assets.

Threat Intelligence: The process of gathering and analyzing information about potential cyber threats to identify and mitigate risks.

Trade Wars and Economic Cyber Sabotage – The strategic use of cyber operations to disrupt adversaries' economies, including attacks on financial institutions, intellectual property theft, and market manipulation.

Trojan Horses in Cyber Espionage – Malicious software disguised as legitimate programs that enable adversaries to infiltrate networks, steal sensitive information, or disrupt operations.

Troll Armies in Information Warfare – State-backed or ideological groups that use fake accounts, coordinated online harassment, and mass reporting tactics to manipulate public discourse and suppress opposing viewpoints.

Trolling: The act of posting inflammatory or provocative content online to disrupt conversations or provoke emotional reactions.

Twitter Diplomacy and Digital Influence – The use of social media platforms like Twitter by world leaders, governments, and intelligence agencies to communicate policy stances, influence narratives, and engage in digital diplomacy.

U.S. Cybersecurity Policies and Their Global Impact – The influence of U.S. cyber policies on global cyber norms, international digital regulations, and joint intelligence-sharing agreements.

UAVs (Unmanned Aerial Vehicles) and Cybersecurity Risks – The potential for cyberattacks on drones used for surveillance, military operations, and intelligence gathering.

Unauthorized Data Mining in Information Warfare – The covert collection of personal, financial, and strategic data through cyber espionage, often used for blackmail, political manipulation, or economic advantage.

Unconventional Warfare in Cyberspace – The use of asymmetric and non-traditional methods, including misinformation, cyberattacks, and economic sabotage, to undermine adversaries without direct military confrontation.

Underground Dark Web Networks in Propaganda Operations – The role of hidden internet platforms in spreading radical ideologies, coordinating cybercrime, and facilitating illegal cyber warfare activities.

Underground Hacktivist Groups in Geopolitical Conflicts – Non-state hacker collectives that engage in cyber activism, exposing government secrets, launching digital protests, or disrupting adversarial cyber operations.

United Front Strategy in Digital Influence Operations – The coordinated use of state and non-state actors to push a unified disinformation campaign, often seen in adversarial information warfare against India.

Untraceable Cyber Attacks and False Flag Operations – The practice of masking the origin of cyberattacks using proxies, VPNs, and obfuscation techniques to mislead forensic investigations.

User-Generated Content as a Weapon in Information Warfare – The exploitation of organic social media posts, viral trends, and community-driven narratives to amplify misinformation campaigns.

Vaccine Misinformation and Biowarfare Disinformation – The spread of fake news and conspiracy theories regarding public health crises, often used by adversarial states to undermine trust in governance and global institutions.

Vector-Based Cyber Attacks on National Infrastructure – The different pathways through which cyberattacks are delivered, including phishing, malware, zero-day exploits, and insider threats.

Viral Disinformation Campaigns – The deliberate use of social media, bots, and AI to rapidly spread false narratives, influencing elections, policy decisions, and public perception.

Viral Hashtag Manipulation in Social Media Warfare – The coordinated hijacking of trending hashtags to push disinformation, disrupt narratives, or sway online political discussions.

Virtual Private Networks (VPNs) in Cyber Warfare – The use of encrypted tunnels to protect anonymity online, often leveraged by cybercriminals, intelligence agencies, and hacktivists.

Virtual Societies and Psychological Warfare – The impact of digital communities, online gaming platforms, and metaverse-like spaces in shaping ideologies and recruiting for cyber militias.

Visual Propaganda in Digital Conflicts – The use of AI-generated images, manipulated videos, and deceptive infographics to influence public opinion in geopolitical disputes.

Voice Cloning in Deepfake Propaganda – The use of AI-generated synthetic voices to manipulate public figures' statements, spread fake audio recordings, and create fabricated confessions or endorsements.

Vulnerability Exploitation in National Security Systems – The identification and exploitation of weaknesses in government and defense networks by adversarial cyber operatives.

War Gaming in Cyber Defense Strategy – The simulation of cyberattacks and information warfare scenarios by intelligence agencies to prepare for potential digital conflicts.

Watering Hole Attacks in Cyber Espionage – A cyberattack method where hackers compromise commonly visited websites to infect targeted users, often employed in geopolitical cyber operations.

Weaponization of Artificial Intelligence in Information Warfare – The use of AI-powered deepfakes, automated disinformation campaigns, and intelligent cyberattacks to manipulate public perception and conduct psychological operations.

Weaponization of Social Media in Information Warfare – The deliberate use of social media platforms to spread misinformation, manipulate public opinion, and destabilize adversaries through coordinated propaganda campaigns.

Whistleblower Leaks in Cyber Espionage – The unauthorized release of classified or sensitive information by insiders or whistleblowers, often impacting national security and diplomatic relations.

White, Gray, and Black Propaganda in Digital Conflicts – Different forms of propaganda classified based on transparency and deception: white propaganda (openly acknowledged sources), gray propaganda (partially disguised sources), and black propaganda (completely false attribution).

Widespread Fake News Networks in Misinformation Warfare – The systematic creation of fake news websites, bot-generated articles, and AI-written reports to mislead global audiences.

WikiLeaks and Its Role in Digital Transparency and Cyber Conflicts – The impact of leaked classified government documents on international politics, national security, and cyber intelligence.

X (Formerly Twitter) as a Battlefield for Digital Influence – The strategic use of X (formerly Twitter) by intelligence agencies, political groups, and cyber operatives to amplify narratives, engage in hashtag warfare, and conduct influence operations.

X Factor in Psychological Warfare – The unpredictable element in information warfare where public reactions, viral content, or unforeseen events influence the effectiveness of disinformation campaigns.

Xenophobia-Based Cyber Radicalization – The exploitation of nationalistic and xenophobic sentiments in online forums to recruit and mobilize individuals for extremist or state-sponsored agendas.

Xenophobic Narratives in Digital Propaganda – The deliberate spread of anti-immigrant, racist, or nationalist rhetoric through online disinformation campaigns to fuel social divisions and political unrest.

X-Mode Data Tracking in Cyber Surveillance – The practice of gathering geolocation and personal data through apps and online behavior to monitor individuals, often used by intelligence agencies and cybercriminals.

XSS (Cross-Site Scripting) Attacks in Cyber Warfare – A cyberattack technique where malicious scripts are injected into trusted websites to compromise users' data and online activities.

Yellow Journalism in Misinformation Warfare – The use of sensationalized, exaggerated, and often false reporting to manipulate public sentiment and push political agendas.

Yielding Influence Through Fake Accounts and Bots – The use of automated accounts and digital personas to artificially inflate engagement, sway public opinion, and disrupt online discussions.

Youth Radicalization Through Digital Platforms – The recruitment of young individuals into extremist ideologies through online propaganda, gaming forums, and encrypted communication channels.

Youth-Led Digital Movements in Information Warfare – The mobilization of younger generations through social media activism, often exploited for disinformation, political manipulation, or ideological recruitment.

YouTube Algorithm Manipulation in Disinformation Warfare – The strategic use of AI-driven content recommendations to push specific narratives, amplify extremist views, and suppress counter-narratives.

YouTube as a Digital Propaganda Platform – The exploitation of YouTube for spreading fake news, deepfake videos, and state-sponsored narratives, influencing public perception on global conflicts.

Zero Trust Security Model in National Cyber Defense – A cybersecurity framework that assumes no digital entity is trustworthy by default, requiring continuous authentication to protect against cyber threats.

Zero-Day Exploits in Cyber Warfare – The use of unknown software vulnerabilities to launch cyberattacks before the vendor has a chance to develop a security patch.

Zero-Day Vulnerability: A software flaw that is exploited by attackers before the vendor has released a patch to fix it.

Zersetzung Techniques in Modern Psychological Warfare – A Cold War-era psychological manipulation technique used in digital warfare to demoralize adversaries through targeted harassment, disinformation, and social disruption.

Zodiac-Based Cyber Influence Tactics – The use of astrological and cultural superstitions in targeted psychological operations, particularly in countries where such beliefs hold significant influence.

Zombie Botnets in State-Sponsored Cyber Attacks – Large networks of compromised computers controlled by cybercriminals or state actors to launch massive disinformation campaigns and Distributed Denial-of-Service (DDoS) attacks.

Zonal Targeting in Misinformation Campaigns – The strategic dissemination of disinformation targeting specific regions or ethnic groups to deepen political and social divisions.